INSIGHT GUIDES

PERTH
& SURROUNDINGS

WITHDRAWN

APA PUBLICATIONS L

Part of the Langenscheidt Publishing Group

How to Use This Book

This book is carefully structured both to convey an understanding of the city and its culture and to guide readers through its attractions and activities:

◆ The Best Of section at the front of the book helps you to prioritize. The first spread contains all the Top Sights, while the Editor's Choice details unique experiences, the best buys or other recommendations.

◆ To understand Perth, you need to know something of its past. The city's history and culture are described in authoritative essays written by specialists in their

fields who have lived in and documented the city for many years.

◆ The Places section details all the attractions worth seeing. The main places of interest are coordinated by number with the maps.

◆ Each chapter includes lists of recommended shops, restaurants, bars and cafés.

◆ Photographs throughout the book are chosen not only to illustrate geography and buildings, but also to convey the moods of the city and the life of its people.

◆ The Travel Tips section includes all the practical information you will need, divided into four key sections: transport, accommodation, activities (including nightlife, events, tours and sports), and an A–Z of practical tips. Information may be located quickly by using the index on the back cover flap of the book.

◆ A detailed street atlas is included at the back of the book, with all restaurants, bars, cafés and hotels plotted for your convenience.

Places and Sights

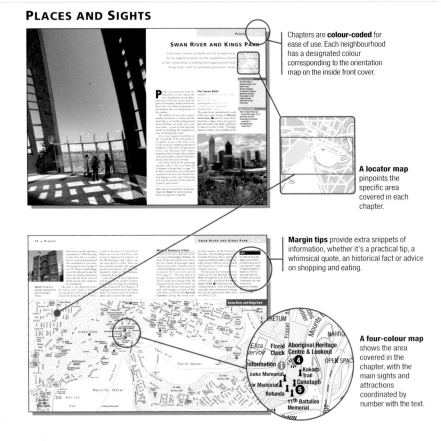

Chapters are **colour-coded** for ease of use. Each neighbourhood has a designated colour corresponding to the orientation map on the inside front cover.

A locator map pinpoints the specific area covered in each chapter.

Margin tips provide extra snippets of information, whether it's a practical tip, a whimsical quote, an historical fact or advice on shopping and eating.

A four-colour map shows the area covered in the chapter, with the main sights and attractions coordinated by number with the text.

PHOTO FEATURES

Photo features offer visual coverage of major sights or unusual attractions. Where relevant, there is a map showing the location and essential information on opening times, entrance charges, transport and contact details.

SHOPPING AND RESTAURANT LISTINGS

Shopping listings provide details of the best shops in each area. **Restaurant listings** give the establishment's contact details, opening times and price category, followed by a useful review. Bars and cafés are also covered here. The coloured dot and grid reference refers to the atlas section at the back of the book.

Jo Jo's

End of the jetty off Broadway, Nedlands. www.jojos restaurant.com. Tel: 08-9386 8757 Open: Tue–Sat 11.30am–late, Sun 11.30am–4pm $$$ ❸ p256, A4

TRAVEL TIPS

...e in between. Equ... ...n sun hat, dark glasses, su... ...lock and a bottle of water, you'r... fit for anything.

Buses

Transperth (InfoLine; tel: 13 62 13) runs city buses, trains and the ferry.

Central city bus travel is free in the inner zone, which includes ...st parts visitors will want to ...affic jams are few, an...

Travel Tips provide all the practical knowledge you'll need before and during your trip: how to get there, getting around, where to stay and what to do. The A–Z section is a handy summary of practical information, arranged alphabetically.

LEFT: celebrating at a surf
carnival on Cottesloe Beach.

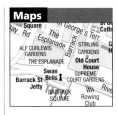

Maps

Travel Tips

THE BEST OF PERTH: TOP SIGHTS

At a glance, these are the Perth attractions you can't afford to miss, from the city's inner-city park and very own Rottnest Island to an award-winning wine region and iconic city sites

◁ **Kings Park and Botanic Garden**, which overlooks the Swan River and is in the heart of the city, is visited by more than six million people each year. With its remarkable expanses of unique bushland, tranquil parkland and botanic garden, the park is the most popular visitor destination in Western Australia. The total are of the park is 400 hectares (988 acres). *See page 73*

▽ **Rottnest Island**, just 19km (12 miles) off Perth's coast is this idyllic gem, known as "Rotto", where coral reefs, hidden bays and deserted cycle paths wait to be explored. Stay a few nights or just go for the day and meet the small marsupial quokka (a bit like a small kangaroo), and in some parts they have become very tame. *See page 163*

◁ Located 45 minutes from Perth is **Yanchep National Park**, home to many different water and bush birds, grey kangaroos, koalas and native plants. Take a guided tour of Crystal Cave, or a leisurely bush walk through one of its many trails. *See page 190*

▽ Grassy parkland lines most of the **Swan River**, which sweeps by the city centre. Hire a bike or a yacht to explore its quiet reaches or have a picnic and watch the sunset while the city comes alive with light. *See page 73*

◁ With more than 150 stalls from fresh crêpes, nuts and coffee to antiques, children's toys and local fashion, the **Fremantle Markets** have souvenirs that are as unique and local as the markets themselves. *See page 139*

▷ Just 25km (15 miles) from Perth, the **Swan Valley** is WA's oldest wine region and seduces visitors with its rich fusion of wine, art, food, scenery and nature. Take a trip along the Swan Valley Food and Wine Trail – 32km (20-mile) loop taking in more than 150 attractions. *See page 169*

▽ The **Bell Tower** is one of Perth's most unique attractions. Filled with historic content and a unique design it has become an icon for Perth and Western Australia. *See page 73*

▽ Perched on the Indian Ocean's shore, the **Maritime Museum** is symbolic of Fremantle's past, present and future as a coastal city and port. The museum houses several unique galleries that explore WA's relationship with the sea from leisure boats and handcrafted sailing boats to commercial pearl luggers. *See page 146*

△ **Fremantle Prison** was built as a convict barracks in the 19th century and remained in use until 1991. The prison was a place of hangings, floggings, dramatic convict escapes and prisoner riots. *See page 136*

▷ Shop till you drop in **King Street**, located in the heart of the CBD, and revel in its distinct European feel with its early 20th-century architecture. Names such as Gucci, Louis Vuitton and Cartier line the cobbled stone street as well as some home-grown designers and stores such as Ruth Tarvydas. *See page 94*

△ Perth's **Cottesloe Beach** is one of the city's most popular places for swimming, snorkelling and surfing. Here, towering Norfolk Pines line a boulevard of cafés and pubs evoking a buzzing yet super-relaxed atmosphere – the perfect place to have a drink and watch the sun go down. *See page 151*

THE BEST OF PERTH: EDITOR'S CHOICE

Setting priorities, saving money, unique attractions... here, at a glance, are our recommendations, plus some tips and tricks even the locals won't always know

BEST MUSEUMS AND GALLERIES

- **WA Museum** Has six locations but the grand building in Perth Cultural Centre is tops, with special activities for children. *See page 95.*
- **Maritime Museum** Spectacular museum on Victoria Quay, Fremantle. The Shipwreck Gallery displays historic vessels. *See pages 146–7.*
- **Kalamunda History Village** Buildings and artefacts in a real village depict life in WA, c.1895. *See page 178.*
- **No. 1 Pump Station** C.Y. O'Connor's monumental achievement was to deliver water to the Perth Goldfields from here at Mundaring Weir. *See page 178.*
- **Motor Museum of WA, Whiteman Park** The best display of classic vehicles in WA. There is another branch on Victoria Quay in Fremantle. *See pages 175 and 196.*
- **WACA Museum** Cricketing memorabilia, trophies, etc. *See page 107.*
- **New Norcia Museum & Art Gallery** Fascinating coverage of pioneer settlement and early missionary work by Dom Salvado, who founded a Benedictine community. *See page 194.*
- **The Art Gallery of Western Australia** Founded in 1895, the gallery houses the State Art Collection, which includes one of the world's finest collections of indigenous art. *See page 93.*

BEST VIEWS

- **Kings Park** Offers panoramic views of the city, river and hills from the middle of the metropolis. From the War Memorial Cenotaph at dusk, the setting sun reflected in the Swan River and glass towers of the CBD is stunning. *See page 73.*
- **St Martin's Tower** C Restaurant Lounge, the revolving restaurant and bar on the 33rd and 34th floor of St Martin's Tower, high above the CBD, provides a 360-degree view across the city and suburbs from hills to ocean. Arrive late afternoon and see the City of Lights by night, too. *See page 97.*
- **Sunset on the Indian Ocean** Take a picnic and watch the sunset from any metropolitan beach, or from the Indiana Teahouse at Cottesloe. *See page 60.*
- **South Perth** For lovely evening views of the illuminated CBD twinkling over the Swan, drive to Mends Street in South Perth. *See page 81.*

ABOVE: the Perth city skyline towers over the Swan River.

BEST BEACHES

WA has many fabulous beaches. Some of the best are:

- **Two People's Bay**, east of Albany. Flat, white sand curves in a 5km (3-mile) horseshoe facing Mount Manypeaks in the Stirling Ranges. Access is easy on a sealed road with parking, barbecues and toilets. *See page 210.*

- **Little Beach** Just along from Two People's *(see above)* – this is WA's most beautiful beach, with clear blue water from the Antarctic and pristine white sand, ringed with bush-clad slopes. At one end of the beach a gap in the rocks leads to Waterfall Beach. *See page 210.*

- **Cottesloe** This is the only WA beach with a "European feel" – with pubs, cafés, hotels etc along Marine Parade. It is also the place for festivals, concerts, art shows and volleyball championships. *See page 152.*

- **Scarborough** and **Trigg** These are two of the best beaches for surfing. *See page 154.*

- **Hillary's Boat Harbour** This sheltered cove is ideal for children, with lots of entertainment close at hand, including a water park. *See page 155.*

ABOVE: celebrating cultural differences in a street parade.

BEST FESTIVALS AND EVENTS

- **Perth Cup, New Year's Day** This extravagant day out at the races greets the New Year with big hats, daring frocks and wild cavorting at the elegant Ascot race track. *See page 237.*

- **Test cricket matches** at WACA – especially if it's England versus Australia. *See page 105.*

- **Australia Day Skyshow** Perth's most spectacular firework display brings thousands of people to the riverside. After a day of picnics and games, fireworks rain down on the Swan from skyscrapers and barges. *See page 237.*

- **Festival of Perth** A month-long arts celebration held in many city venues – Perth Concert Hall, theatres, parks and riverside. Includes an extended open-air cinema at the University of Western Australia and Edith Cowan's Joondalup campus. *See page 237.*

- **Fremantle Festival** A carnival atmosphere prevails at this long-standing annual festival. *See pages 137 and 237.*

- **Bridgetown Blues** The best in blues and roots music in this pretty southern town. *See page 207.*

- **Outdoor cinemas** Perth has a number of outdoor cinemas that run during the warmer months. It's a great way to spend a summer evening with a picnic hamper. *See page 236.*

BELOW: Australia is a country of beaches, which means it's also a country of surfers. **RIGHT:** a local band member plays on.

● **Beaches** In addition to the Indian Ocean beaches (Hillary's, Hammersley Pool), the river has several lovely beaches. Go to Mosman Bay and paddle in front of the AUS$55 million mansion that's the most expensive house in Australia. *See page 151.*

● **AQWA**, the walk-through aquarium at Hillary's Boat Harbour, containing sharks, loggerhead turtles and rays, is entrancing. There are also saltwater crocodiles and a touch pool. *See page 156.*

● **Western Power Playground**, Kings Park. Most of Perth's parks and beaches have play areas, but this one, with a lake and an island dedicated to a dinosaur theme, is considered the best. *See page 78.*

● **Scitech and Planetarium** Fascinating hands-on science centre. More rewarding for older kids

(and parents love it too). Admission includes a visit to the Planetarium. *See page 241.*

● **Spare Parts Puppet Theatre** in Short Street, Fremantle, puts on a changing programme of creative productions. It's a far cry from Punch and Judy. *See page 236.*

● **Whiteman Park** Trains, trams, vintage cars, swimming pool, and Caversham Wildlife Park. Prepare to spend the day here, because children never want to leave. *See page 174.*

● **Chocolate Factory** How to lure them out of Whiteman Park? Visit the Chocolate Factory, also in Swan Valley. *See page 174.*

● **Fremantle Prison Ghost Tour** This is a quirky and fun way to see a part of WA's history in an hour-long walking tour of the old Fremantle Asylum. *See page 136.*

ABOVE: the Pinnacles Desert, Nambung National Park.
LEFT: shark in the dark, AQWA, Hillary's Boat Harbour.
BELOW: a joey pauses in Caversham Wildlife Park.

BEST EXCURSIONS

● **Swan Valley** For fine wine, food, historic Guildford and children's attractions galore, head for the Swan Valley, 30 minutes from the city centre. *See page 169.*

● **Rottnest Island** Car-free holiday island just 19km (12 miles) from Fremantle, where you can cycle, swim and dive. *See page 163.*

● **Pinnacles, Kalbarri and Monkey Mia** These natural highlights north of Perth can be combined in a three-day itinerary. *See pages 190–92.*

● **Margaret River** Come here for superb wineries, spectacular limestone caves and idyllic beaches. *See page 204.*

● **The Great Southern** Cross the Valley of the Giants Treetop Walk in Walpole, explore the whaling past of Albany and sample the state's loveliest beaches. *See page 208.*

● **Kalgoorlie** If you want to understand what fuels Perth, fly to the mining town of Kalgoorlie to see the Super Pit. *See page 199.*

GREAT WINERIES

- **Leeuwin Estate** Margaret River is among the world's top wine regions and Leeuwin is one of the best estates, with the style and quality of a fine château. *See page 61.*
- **Vasse Felix** Another great Margaret River vineyard. *See page 61.*
- **Sandalford** A stone's throw from Perth, Sandalford in the

Swan Valley is one of the region's oldest wineries. Its Cabernets are especially recommended. Also offers a restaurant, concerts and more. *See page 172.*
- **Millbrook** in the Jarrahdale area has a delightful lakeside location. Excellent food as well as great wines make for a rewarding day out. *See page 179.*

BEST BUYS

- **Argyle diamonds** Unique, coloured stones mined near Lake Argyle in the north of Western Australia; available for purchase. *See page 89.*
- **Broome Pearls** From the early 1870s Japanese, Chinese and indigenous divers braved the ocean deep to make Broome, in northern WA, the pearling capital of the world. *See page 141.*
- **Opals** These are a South Australian speciality and sold in good Perth jewellery stores alongside WA's diamonds and pearls. *See page 89.*
- **Leather shoes** Australian leather boots and shoes are excellent value in all shoe stores, but especially in outback emporia. *See page 139.*

- **Aboriginal artefacts** Replicas of boomerangs are everywhere, but look for the genuine articles, as well as other items in galleries in Central Perth and Fremantle. *See page 76.*

ABOVE LEFT: a painted wine barrel. **ABOVE:** seek out galleries in Central Perth and Fremantle for genuine Aboriginal artefacts.

MONEY-SAVING TIPS

Concessions are offered to senior people (over-60s) and students, allowing big savings on all kinds of shows and events as well as cinema and theatre tickets and admission fees. If you qualify, carry any relevant identifying card, though at many places they'll take your word.

Transport Day Rider tickets give unlimited all-day travel on Transperth buses, trains and ferries, after 9am weekdays, all day at weekends and on public holidays. The standard cost is AUS$8.10; concession price only AUS$3.20. Don't forget that buses in central Perth are free. These Central Area Transport (CAT) buses link the main tourist sights.

Cinemas The small chains such as Luna and Ace are cheaper than the large ones, and offer all-day midweek specials for around AUS$7.

BYO Lots of restaurants let you bring your own wine: just ask. Combine this with cleanskin (minimum labelling) wines, which are great value. You will find wines for AUS$6 that are far superior to European cheapies. Restaurants will charge as little as AUS$2–3 corkage.

Food markets Markets such as Subiaco's Station Street are far better and cheaper for food than supermarkets.

Food Halls In some city arcades multiple food vendors set up around shared central seating. Their lower overheads are reflected in bargain prices.

SPLENDID ISOLATION

A booming economy, an equitable climate and an outstanding natural setting; what's not to like in this seemingly effortless paradise on earth?

Closer to Singapore and Jakarta than the nearest large Australian city, Adelaide, and separated from Melbourne and Sydney by some 4,000km (2,500 miles), Perth is famously remote. What's more, it is the capital of the largest but least densely populated state, where 2 million people inhabit a third of the continent.

Founded some 60 years later than Sydney, the Swan River Colony, as Perth was first called, was relatively slow to develop, remaining for many years a community of embattled pioneers. It was the gold rush of the 1890s that put the city on the map, attracting fortune-seekers from all over the world.

Perth's citizens are both envied and ridiculed by their eastern peers. Though tempted by Perth's laid-back lifestyle, many would say they could never live somewhere so terminally unsophisticated. Perth's media is parochial, nightlife is low-key and an obstinate resistance to change means

Sunday trading is minimal. The city's lack of conspicuous effort is relished by Perthites. After a decent day's work, they prefer to head off to the beach or to their boats (one in three families is said to have one) rather than put in extra hours at work.

But this relaxed, no-worries image is deceptive. As the economic hub of a resources-rich state, and mindful of the boom-and-bust lessons of the 1980s, Perth has a responsibility to manage its good fortune well. Its business leaders are shrewd and hard-headed with a keen eye on the future. Western Australia is forging ever stronger ties with Asia, especially China, where much of its nickel, coal, zinc and aluminium are traded. The latest resources boom has enabled major city improvements, just as the gold rush did in the 19th century. Railways are being sunk underground and major highways built to create a sleek, integrated city where tourism can prosper.   ❏

PRECEDING PAGES: marina at Matilda Bay; Cottesloe Life Saving Club in training. **LEFT:** Fremantle Festival. **ABOVE LEFT:** Scarborough beach. **ABOVE RIGHT:** Perth skyline from Kings Park.

THE PEOPLE OF PERTH

This wealthy, attractive city has long sought skilled and hard-working inhabitants. The result is that nearly a third of its population was born outside Australia, with more than 200 different nationalities contributing to Perth's dynamic multicultural mix

In many ways, Perth is the forgotten capital of Australia – and that's just how the locals like it. Affectionately referred to as Sandgropers (named, oddly enough, after a grub-like subterranean insect), Perth dwellers are a mightily friendly bunch, though reluctant to shout the praises of their home town. While proud of their own pocket, as far as the average Sandgroper is concerned the clean, quiet and peaceful paradise they call home is perfect as it is. The fact that many visitors overlook Perth in favour of Sydney and Melbourne is fine by them – it means the best-kept secret in Australia is likely to stay that way.

The good life

Make no mistake, any visitor who does arrive in the world's most isolated mainland city will be welcomed with a warm chorus of "G'days". Sandgropers are renowned for being extremely hospitable and, once you've discovered their secret land, will revel in sharing its hidden jewels with you. Surrounded by fresh air, blue skies, endless sunshine and clean beaches, Western Australians are a relaxed and friendly breed who love nothing more than good food, good wine and good company in the great outdoors.

Delighted to be dull

Home to 1.55 million people, Perth was stung when a local newspaper tagged the city "Dullsville" in 2003, largely due to a few commentators who disapproved of its limited

LEFT: entertainment in Subiaco market.
RIGHT: captivating the crowds outside London Court.

trading hours and facilities. Most Sandgropers felt these critics were missing Perth's point. The city has never claimed to be as fast as Sydney or as culturally rich as Melbourne; what makes it unique is that it is unhurried and relatively uncommercial (a fact recognised when Perth was voted the world's 21st most liveable city in the 2010 Mercer Quality of Living Survey, a global survey based on 39 criteria, including political, socio-economic, environmental, health, education and transport). As of 2010 Perth's retail trading hours were extended to 9pm weekdays. Not all stores have been taking advantage of this opportunity though, so be prepared for variation among the shops.

Green city

While Perth may not be a buzzing, open-all-hours epicentre, it is blessed with breathtaking natural beauty. Blue skies turn into clear, star-filled nights; fiery sunsets melt into coppery seas at dusk; the Swan River's still waters are almost always bathed in sunlight, and dolphins can often be spotted off the metropolitan beaches. With such an idyllic playground at their dis-

posal, most Sandgropers ensure this backdrop plays a big part in their laid-back lifestyles.

Demographics

According to statistics, the average Perthite is a 34-year-old, Roman Catholic, married female (ladies outnumber the men by over 5,000 in this state). The average weekly pay packet in Perth contains AUS$1,124.50. The highest income earners tend to live in the Western Suburbs, a 30km (18-mile) strip between the CBD and the Indian Ocean that contains many of Perth's wealthiest

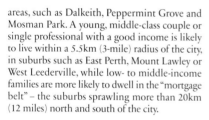

areas, such as Dalkeith, Peppermint Grove and Mosman Park. A young, middle-class couple or single professional with a good income is likely to live within a 5.5km (3-mile) radius of the city, in suburbs such as East Perth, Mount Lawley or West Leederville, while low- to middle-income families are more likely to dwell in the "mortgage belt" – the suburbs sprawling more than 20km (12 miles) north and south of the city.

Thanks to the success of the local mining industry, Perth has the highest per capita number of self-made millionaires of any city in the world.

Boom town

Western Australia is one of the most productive mineral and petroleum regions in the entire world. With 58 oilfields, 1,222 mining sites and 171 processing plants, WA is considered the

powerhouse of the resources industry in the Asia-Pacific region – and Perth reaped the benefits of this in its 2007–2008 resources boom. House prices rose more than 30 percent during the past decade, the biggest rise of any Australian city except Darwin; Perth now has Australia's fourth-highest median house price in Australia after Sydney, Melbourne and Canberra.

Multiculturalism

Perth has the highest number of migrants in Australia, with more than one half of its population born elsewhere. The state has experienced a massive 60 percent jump in immigration over the past 10 years, with Perth now home to at least 217 different nationalities. The vast majority of citizens embrace the ethos of multiculturalism, and racial tension is rare.

Historically, Perth's overseas-born population has been overwhelmingly Anglo. In 1901, of the 54,431 overseas-born people living in WA, 87 percent hailed from Europe, over half of whom came from England, Ireland and Scotland. In the 1950s and 60s, Perth experienced an influx of Italian, Croatian and Greek migrants. Many settled here simply because Fremantle was the first landfall in Australia for migrant ships.

LEFT: stopping off for coffee at No. 44 King Street café.
ABOVE: catching up while shopping, and over a drink.

By 1981, the number of overseas-born people living in WA had risen to 362,658, and the variety of their origins had dramatically widened (hello Tonga and Kampuchea). But the Anglo intake was still much higher than any other, accounting for nearly half of the migrant population. Italy (8.05 percent), Scotland (5.63 percent), New Zealand (5.09 percent), the Netherlands (3.11 percent), Yugoslavia (3.03 percent) and India (2.78 percent) followed. Chinese and Japanese migrants accounted for 0.25 and 0.20

percent of the population respectively, while South Africa accounted for 1.17 percent and the US 1.12 percent.

In recent years, there's also been substantial immigration from Eastern Europe and Southeast Asia. Many migrants from Malaysia, Hong Kong, Indonesia, China, India and Sri Lanka emigrate to Perth to attend one of four public universities – the University of WA, Curtin University, Murdoch University and the University of Notre Dame.

WA led the nation for population growth in the 2008–2009 financial year, which was due to overseas immigration, followed by natural increase, then interstate migration. ❏

LEAGUE OF IMMIGRANTS

Australia is considered a very appealing destination for immigrants, and WA, with its surging economy and labour shortages, is particularly attractive. Immigration figures from 2005 indicate that the birthplace of over one-quarter of permanent arrivals in WA is still the United Kingdom. Rounding out the top five birthplaces of WA's newest permanent residents are:

1. UK (5,172 people)
2. South Africa (1,511 people)
3. New Zealand (1,483 people)
4. Malaysia (951 people)
5. Singapore (817 people)

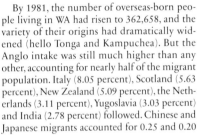

TOP LEFT AND RIGHT: working in the food industry.
ABOVE: a performer from the popular television show *So You Think You Can Dance*.

Noongar People

The Aboriginal people of the Perth area are referred to by various names. The best known are Nyoongar, Nyungar, Noongar, Wajuk and Wdjari

Collectively known as the Noongar people, Perth's indigenous tribes belong to the southwest corner of WA. Before the Europeans arrived in 1829, they were divided into 13 separate tribes, which lived in large, extended family groups on lands that stretched from Geraldton in the north to Esperance in the south. The tribes shared a common culture and religious or mythical belief in the Dreaming, a philosophy that closely connected the Noongar people to the land.

When European settlers arrived, tribal numbers were decimated by disease and violence. Measles, smallpox and influenza all took their toll, as did bloody confrontations with the Europeans, including the 1834 "Battle of Pinjarra", in which many Aboriginals were killed (see page 34). Although the Europeans initially traded amicably with Noongar people, rifts developed when local tribes were suddenly declared British subjects and sacred land was seized for the Crown.

In 1839, Rottnest Island became a penal establishment for indigenous people. More than 3,700 men and boys, most of them Noongar, were imprisoned for offences such as burning bush or digging up vegetables on their own land. There are believed to be at least 369 indigenous people buried there.

As more land in the region was turned over to farming, most Aboriginal people were forced into towns or camps.

From 1890 to 1958, the Native Welfare Act wreaked further havoc on the lives of Noongar people. A Chief Protector was appointed, with the power to remove indigenous children from their biological parents, especially children of mixed European and Aboriginal descent. Many Noongar children became part of this "stolen generation" after being forcibly removed from their homes and placed in camps at Carrolup and Moore River. About 25 percent of Noongar children were sent to these concentration camps.

In the latter decades of the 20th century these past wrongs began to be recognised. Pressure to recognise Aboriginal land rights mounted, culminating, in 1992, with the High Court Mabo ruling, acknowledging Aboriginal rights to some traditional lands. This was ratified a year

later with the Native Title Act, which has resulted in many long and tortuous claims passing through the courts.

To find out more about Aboriginal history and culture in Western Australia, visit the Katta Djinoong Gallery in the Western Australian Museum (see page 95) or the Aboriginal Galleries in the Art Gallery of WA (see page 93).   ❑

RIGHT: an Aborigine of the Guildford tribe.

DECISIVE DATES

50,000 BC
Aborigines populate all of Australia.

1606
First authenticated voyage to Australia, by the Dutch ship, the *Duyfken*.

1616
Dutch explorer Dirk Hartog in the *Eendracht* makes first authenticated landing in Western Australia, at Shark Bay.

1696–7
Discovery of Swan River by Willem de Vlamingh.

1791
Discovery of King George Sound by Captain George Vancouver.

1826
King George Sound is occupied by convicts from Sydney under Major Lockyer.

1827
Examination of Swan River by Captain Stirling in HMS *Success*.

1828
British government approves founding of Swan River Colony; appoints Captain Stirling lieutenant-governor.

1829
Formal possession of the colony is taken by Captain Fremantle; in June Stirling arrives to found the colony.

1831
Stirling made governor; King George Sound convict settlement is withdrawn; Agricultural Society set up; first newspaper issued.

1834
Battle of Pinjarra.

1837
Bank of Western Australia opened.

1840
Western Australian Company formed to settle the west.

1846
New Norcia Mission established; discovery of coal.

1848
Arrival of Governor Fitzgerald; discovery of lead and copper.

1843
Petitions for the introduction of convicts.

1850
Convicts sent from Britain to meet labour shortage and help build Perth.

1856
Queen Victoria grants Perth city status.

1868
Convict transportation ends.

1869
First telegraph line erected. John Forrest's expedition in search of explorer Leichhardt.

1870
Colony gains representative government.

1871
Compulsory school for children aged six to 14 years.

1871
Municipalities Act and Elementary Education Act passed; first private railway.

1876
Escape of Fenian convicts.

1877
Telegraph links Perth and London via Adelaide.

1881
Eastern railway links Perth, Fremantle and Guildford.

1885
Gold found at Halls Creek.

1886
Kimberley goldfield discovered.

1887
Local telephone service begins.

1888
Yilgarn and Pilbara goldfields discovered.

1889
Great Southern Railway opened.

FAR TOP LEFT: 16th-century Dutch map of New Holland (Australia). LEFT: wood engraving of the town hall in Howick Street, now known as Hay Street, in 1886. ABOVE: trams mingle with horses and carts on William Street in the 1900s.

1890
WA gains responsible government. Sir John Forrest forms first government.

1891
Murchison goldfield discovered.

1892
Coolgardie goldfield discovered; construction of Fremantle Harbour begins.

1893
Paddy Hannan's Kalgoorlie find becomes "The Golden Mile", and the gold rush transforms Perth.

1894
Menzies goldfield discovered; Midland Railway opened.

1896
Great Southern Railway purchased by government.

1898
Free education introduced.

1899
Women get the vote, ahead of Britain, Canada and the US.

1899
Perth Electric Tramway begins to supersede horse transport.

1899
Boer War. 1,231 WA men go to South Africa; 126 die, one wins the Victoria Cross.

1899
The building of the Goldfields Water Supply commences (completed January 1903).

1900
WA votes "yes" in federal referendum.

1901
Commonwealth of Australia inaugurated 1 January, and WA becomes a state of federal Australia.

1901
WA joins the British Empire. Duke of York visits Perth and names Kings Park.

1902
First "kinema" opens.

1911
University of Western Australia opens.

1911
WA adopts compulsory military training.

1914–18
6,000 Western Australians die and thousands more are wounded in World War I.

1915
Anzac fleet assembles in King George Sound for the assault on Gallipoli, Turkey. WA's 10th Light Horse Regiment prominent in Gallipoli campaign.

1917
Trans-Australian Railway links WA to eastern states.

1919
First music broadcast heard in Perth, transmitted from Sydney.

1924
City's own radio service begins with broadcasts by 6WF.

1920s
Fremantle is busiest oil-fuelling port in Australia; world's first long-distance air service operates from Perth centre.

1929
Amid centenary celebrations of the 1829 founding, George V declares Perth a "Lord Mayoralty", and Fremantle becomes a city.

1931
One in four Perth men is jobless; a 5,000-strong protest march ends in violence and arrests.

1930s
Depression-fighting project creates Langley Park and Riverside Drive by river reclamation.

1933
State of WA votes to opt out of federation, but the UK government rules the move "unconstitutional".

1939–45
Perth men and women serve in World War II; city prepares for air raids.

Fremantle is essential to the war effort, the secret base for 170 allied submarines. Sunderland and Catalina flying boats are based on the Swan. Victory in the Pacific – VP Day – celebrated in Perth on 15 August 1945.

1950s
The Causeway and Narrows Bridge span the Swan; parking meters introduced and buses replace trams. Kwinana is founded with building of BP refinery.

1952
Britain's first atomic bomb explosion, on the Monte Bello islands, can be viewed from Onslow on the WA coast. Two more bombs are exploded in 1956.

1954
Visit of Queen Elizabeth II.

1954–8
More of the Swan River reclaimed for building of the Narrows Bridge and Freeway.

1959
First television service begins.

1962
Perth hosts Empire Games.

1963
New airport opens.

TOP LEFT: Flying Doctor Service in WA in 1939. LEFT: a train on the east–west Trans-Australian railway crossing the mighty Nullarbor Plain in 1973. ABOVE: earthquake fissures in 1968. RIGHT: the Labor Party's Kevin Rudd served as prime minister for four years.

1968
Worst tremors in memory rock Perth as Meckering, 130km (80 miles) east of the city, is destroyed by earthquake.

1971
Concert Hall opens.

1978
HMAS *Stirling* is naval base for Australia's submarine fleet.

1979
WA celebrates first 150 years.

1983
Australia II wins America's Cup off Rhode Island. It is the first non-American entrant to win. Labor begins 10-year period of government in WA.

1987
America's Cup held in Fremantle.

1993
WA Liberal/National coalition ousts Labor.

1999
World's earliest-known lifeform, 3.5 billion-year-old stromatolites, are found in the outback.

2001
Labor regains state power after eight years in opposition.

2004
Perth Convention Centre opens.

2005
Labor wins state election.

2006
WA experiences resources boom driving property prices up 33.3 percent in one year.

2007
Labor Party, under Kevin Rudd, wins landslide national election victory in November, ending more than 11 years in power for Liberal Party leader John Howard.

2008
WA actor Heath Ledger dies from a cocktail of pre-scription painkillers in his New York apartment.

2009
Black Saturday bushfires resulting in Australia's highest ever loss of life with 173 deaths and 414 injured.

2010
Kevin Rudd steps down as Labor Party leader and Australia swears in its 27th and first female prime minister, Julia Gillard.

THE STORY OF PERTH

Early colonists struggled to carve out a life in the inhospitable bush around the Swan River, but eventually the nub of a community took hold, and within 60 years Perth was booming, fuelled by the gold rush

Perth is the capital of a sparsely populated, resource-rich state that occupies one-third of the massive Australian continent. In 1829 Britain established the Swan River Colony as a useful outpost to thwart likely French ambitions in what Europeans considered *terra nullius* – an empty land owned by nobody.

The British were, of course, wrong in holding this position. Aboriginal Australians flourished across the whole continent thousands of years before Europeans touched the land. Early Aborigines used no written records, but anthropologists have identified tools, weapons and paintings of theirs dating back at least 50,000 years.

Australia's native people are of Asiatic stock, and it is most likely they travelled south from Asia, first crossing into Western Australia's north between 60,000 and 150,000 years ago, when sea passages were narrower and easier to navigate. Nomadic hunter-gatherers, they comprised around 250 tribes and numbered about 300,000 in total, with each group having its own territory, traditions, beliefs and language. But from the time of European encroachment, Aboriginal culture – traditionally sustained in harmony with nature – was doomed. Settlers moved in and occupied the fertile lands, forcing the Aborigines into the arid interior.

Killed and exploited until well into the 20th century, the Aboriginal population has

dwindled to about 60,000 today. Long considered second-class citizens, Aborigines were not given the vote until 1967. Progressive enlightenment since then culminated in the 1992 High Court of Australia (Supreme Court) ruling that the Aborigines were indeed the first human occupants of Australia with ownership and traditional rights over some lands, a landmark ruling that has led to numerous claims in the courts, by and large long and tortuous proceedings made infinitely more complex by the lack of written documents. Though many Aboriginal groups have attempted to rebuild their culture, they remain the most disadvantaged people in Australia.

LEFT: Aborigines study settlers in John William Huggins' 1827 painting of the Swan River in Western Australia.
RIGHT: Sir John Forrest, an early explorer of WA, as well as the state's first premier.

European discovery

Aristotle, Strabo and other ancient writers theorised about the existence of a Great South Land. In the 13th century the adventurer Marco Polo suggested that Chinese merchants had discovered it. A little later, Portuguese and other navigators found a way round the Cape of Good Hope to the East Indies, and probably sighted the Western Australian coast.

In 1606 the Dutch sailor Willem Jansz made the first verifiable landing on the western side of Cape York Peninsula, in the *Duyfken*. Ten years later his countryman Dirk Hartog sailed the *Eendracht* into Shark Bay and was the first European to land on the shores of Western Australia. He nailed a tin plate to a post marking the spot. The inscription read: "On the 25th of October, 1616, arrived here the ship *Eendracht*, of Amsterdam: the first merchant, Gilles Milbais van Luyck: captain, Dirk Hartog, of Amsterdam; the 27th ditto set sail for Bantam; under merchant, Jan Stins; upper steersman, Pieter Dockes, of Bil; A.D. 1616."

First settlers

British colonisation of Australia was sparked by Captain James Cook's famous voyage of discovery to the eastern side of the continent. In 1770 he landed in Botany Bay and sailed on to chart 4,000km (2,500 miles) of coast, name it New South Wales and claim the land for Britain. The first European settlers, mostly convicts, arrived in 1778 aboard the ships of the First Fleet led by Captain Arthur Phillip.

In 1829 WA would become Britain's third colony in Australia, after NSW and Tasmania, and ahead of South Australia, Victoria and Queensland. But the first official British outpost in the west came as a spoiling action to keep out the French, who by 1826 were sailing

---

WE WERE HERE

Etching plates caught on among visiting sea captains. When Dutch captain Willem de Vlamingh arrived in 1697, Dirk Hartog's plate of 1616 was still nailed to a post. He took the original to Batavia, but replaced it with a new one on which the old inscription was copied, along with his own details. A century on, Captain Hamelin, of the *Naturaliste*, fixed Vlamingh's plate to a new post and left one of his own, and in 1818 another Frenchman, Freycinet, took Hamelin's one "for safekeeping" to Paris.

Hartog's original was rediscovered in 1902 in the State Museum at Amsterdam. Willem de Vlamingh's 1697 version can be seen at Fremantle Museum.

ABOVE: St George's Terrace in 1850.

around the western and southern coasts. Major Edmund Lockyer was dispatched from Sydney, leading an expedition of soldiers and convicts to build a fortress in the southwest corner of the continent, near today's Albany. They were to guard the strategically valuable King George Sound, claimed for Britain in 1791 by Captain George Vancouver. He discovered magnificent waterways, which he named King George III Sound and Princess Royal Harbour.

Ten years after Vancouver, Matthew Flinders charted the waterways during a momentous voyage aboard the *Investigator*. Instructed to explore the remaining unknown coastline of Australia for Britain, he proved that Australia was not divided into two large islands as some had imagined. He coined the name Australia to define the continent, which had been variously known as New Holland, Terra Australis or the Great South Land.

Swan River mania

The soldiers left Albany and returned to Sydney in 1831, but Captain James Stirling had more permanent ambitions for the west. In 1826 he sailed from New South Wales to explore the west coast. Backed by NSW governor Ralph Darling and some parliamentarians – especially his Scots friend Sir George Murray, the Secretary for the Colonies – Stirling fired up Britain with dreams of a Swan River colony. He made it sound wonderful: Perth was close to likely agricultural land, the Swan was a good commercial route to the ocean, and the city would be safe from naval shelling.

> *Britain was convinced that the settlements in Western Australia would thrive on commercialism rather than on government handouts.*

British government permission to found the settlement was based on Stirling's arguments in favour, plus fears of imminent French intrusion. He was given power to make laws in "His Majesty's Settlements in Western Australia" (the first official use of the term Australia).

Britain didn't want to spend too much money on the venture. There were to be no convicts, and little money: this would be an empire built on private enterprise. From the start the colony

was planned as a money-maker, and the British government encouraged investors (including Stirling himself) with generous land grants.

The newspapers called it a "get-rich-quick scheme", but the public was inspired by stories of an idyllic land where just £3 would buy 16 hectares (40 acres) of land. Settlers bringing labourers gained another 80 hectares (200 acres) for every worker who landed with his master.

Investors pooled their resources to take advantage of the offer. The well-connected Thomas Peel headed one ambitious group. The cousin of the British Home Secretary Robert Peel (famous for setting up the British police force), he planned to ship 10,000 people to the colony and claim 1.6 million hectares (4 million acres) along the Swan River.

That scheme failed to get off the ground, and a smaller venture that did go ahead was a dismal failure. Most of his would-be farmers were short of experience and unable to cope with the harsh bush conditions. Peel ended his days in Mandurah *(see page 180)*, which is still known as the Peel region.

The foundation of Perth

The territory was formally claimed on 2 May 1829, when Captain Charles Howe Fremantle landed in the Swan estuary to plant the Union flag. In June Stirling and 68 settlers made an unimpressive arrival. Taking the wheel, Stirling ran his ship *Parmelia* aground in the mouth of the Swan, and it took heroic work led by Captain Fremantle to save the day. The port city was named Fremantle in his honour.

The city was founded on 12 August 1829 (the king's birthday), but it was hardly practicable to lay a foundation stone. There were no buildings, nor any kind of stone available. Instead, it was decided that the felling of a tree on Mount Eliza (now occupied by Kings Park)

SCOTTISH FAVOURITISM

Naming the colony's capital city Perth – to thank Stirling's Scots friend and supporter Sir George Murray, who was born in Perthshire – was a controversial decision. Some investors accused Stirling of "Scotch prejudice" because he'd also borrowed other names, such as Melville Water and Cockburn Sound. Critics said Perth was an "obscure place in Scotland known only to geographers or reading men". He should have chosen a name that "the three countries [England, Scotland and Wales] in unison may look up to". Swan River, London Town and Wellington were suggested, but Perth it was declared and Perth it remained.

LEFT: French seamen at Shark Bay in 1818. ABOVE: Matthew Flinders and George Bass survey the Australian coast. ABOVE RIGHT: the *Swan River Job*, an 1829 cartoon by McLean, implying that the English colonist Thomas Peel was developing the Swan River settlement solely for his own financial gain. RIGHT: the presentation of her Majesty Queen Victoria's commission to the officers of the West Australian Volunteers in front of Government House, shortly after its completion.

Exploration and hard toil

The early years were a struggle for everyone in the Swan River Colony, and in 1832 Governor James Stirling sailed back to Britain and spent two years trying to raise more money and support. He had little luck, but was loaded with honours, knighted and presented with the Swan Cup (now in the Western Australian Museum). In 1834 the Stirlings moved out of their family home in Woodbridge, Guildford, and into the newly built Government House on St George's Terrace.

One of Perth's first families of residents were Adam Armstrong and his three sons, who arrived with Thomas Peel. They were lucky enough to obtain 128 hectares (320 acres) overlooking the Swan's Melville Water, where they dug a well and started Dalkeith Farm. That area is now in Nedlands, a wealthy municipality stretching across the peninsula from river to ocean. The Armstrongs were relatively lucky. Many people were forced to search for usable agricultural land, and the west was explored continuously. In 1837 George Grey landed at Hanover Bay and was driven off by Aborigines. Two years later he tried again, at Shark Bay. With 11 others he walked to Perth, losing one man and fighting off attacks all the way.

overlooking the Swan would be a suitably symbolic act. It worked, and is remembered mostly because of George Pitt-Morrison's painting, made many years after the event *(see page 34)*. According to Commander Dance of the migrant escort ship *Sulphur*, his wife won the honour of chopping down the tree because she was "the only lady who could be persuaded to venture into a savage land" (meaning the bush around the Swan).

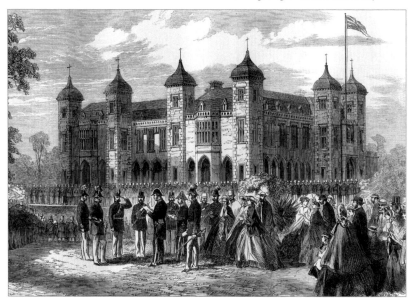

Grey discovered and named many rivers on the route south. Such explorers are now immortalised in place names. Eyre, Roe, Forrest and others are perpetuated on roads, buildings and parks across the state. But when settlers followed and moved onto traditional tribal lands and hunting grounds, there was often murderous conflict.

Although Perth's first settlers were British, since World War II waves of migration, mainly from Europe and Asia, have created a multicultural population.

Battle of Pinjarra

Perth and its environs are Noongar territory. (Bibbulmun is an alternative name for this Aboriginal tribe.) Three small tribes of Noongar (the Mooro, Beeloo and Beeliar) lived around the Swan when Europeans moved in. Yagan was a Beeliar, the son of tribal chief Midgigoroo and popular with white settlers. He became an outlaw after he and his father were accused of spearing to death two white labourers at

Maddington Farm (near Fremantle). Midgigoroo was caught and executed by firing squad, but Yagan remained free for months, protected by the lingering affection of settlers who didn't want him harmed. Finally, a £30 reward proved too tempting for two young settlers, the teenage Keates brothers. Spotting Yagan approaching a house, they pretended friendship and shot Yagan dead. William Keates was immediately speared to death by Yagan's companions, but 13-year-old James escaped to claim the reward.

Governor Stirling always strived to maintain friendly relations with the indigenous people, but after a series of violent incidents he led a punitive expedition against the Murray River people upon his return from London in 1834. The so-called Battle of Pinjarra was, in fact, an ambush. Twenty soldiers and police came across a group of Aborigines, including women and children, in a river bed. Dividing into two groups, Stirling's party attacked with crossfire that killed 30 and wounded 30 more.

Around Perth, the local Aborigine community soon declined, and by 1837 only 120 Noongar remained. The statue of Yagan now stands on Heirisson Island *(see page 80)* as a silent reminder of the times.

Missionaries

In 1834 an Aboriginal institution was opened at Mount Eliza; five years later, in 1839, the Aboriginal prison was built on Rottnest Island and a Protector of Aborigines was appointed. But it wasn't until 1846, at the invitation of Catholic Bishop Brady, that European missionaries came to the colony specifically to attend to the dispossessed people. Among the international group was Dom Rosendo Salvado, who would eventually establish the Benedictine Monastery of New Norcia (*see page 194*).

His party of five left Perth with a borrowed bullock cart, planning a nomadic life among the Aborigines at Moore River, where they would learn their language and teach agriculture and animal husbandry. Three of the missionaries perished quickly, but Salvado and his friend Dom Joseph Serra persevered until their stores were exhausted.

Salvado then walked the 130km (80 miles)

to Perth, with an Aboriginal guide, to find that Bishop Brady could spare nothing.

Resourceful as ever, Dom Salvado put his musical talents to work in a one-man fundraising concert at the courthouse, entertaining the colony's elite with piano and song. He even gave his version of an Aboriginal corroboree. The concert paid for a wagon, bullocks and fresh supplies.

A year later a cottage chapel was built on the New Norcia site by volunteers.

REVERSAL OF FORTUNE

Celebrations, parades and re-enactments marked WA's centenary in 1929, and while loyalty to the Crown was as strong as ever, faith in the Commonwealth of Australia was about to undergo a tough test with the 1930s Depression. In 1931 one in four Perth men was jobless, and a protest march, 5,000 strong, ended in fights and arrests. Many searched for work in the goldfields, while others looked to public works such as the continuing Swan River reclamation. Some building continued, including the Tudor-style London Court (*see page 88*). General discontent about the state of the economy brought about the revolutionary vote for secession in 1933.

LEFT: *The Foundation of Perth* by George Pitt-Morrison, now in the Art Gallery of Western Australia. A copy of this painting was given to every WA school in 1929 to mark the state's centenary celebrations. **ABOVE:** view of Perth from Mt Eliza in 1847.

People for a new colony

Perth's first settlers lived in an outpost of the British Empire, and independence from the old country was unthinkable. The population grew slowly until gold was found, and then it soared, from 46,000 in 1890 to 184,000 by 1901. In 1910, 282,000 people lived in the west – 38 percent of them in Perth.

In 1848 the colony was home to just 41,000 people, and there was a drastic shortage of labour. The settlers originally wanted to keep convicts out of WA, although they did compromise a little and 200 boys were sent out to a new and better life from the juvenile prison at Parkhurst on the UK's Isle of Wight. Ironically, one of them became a murderer and was the first migrant to be hanged in the colony, when he was just 15 years old.

The settlers petitioned Britain to make WA penal colony, and the first convicts arrived in 1850 (transportation to the eastern states had ended in 1840). In WA's convict era (1850–60) much of the early infrastructure was built, including the Government House, Perth Town Hall, the Cloisters, as well as police stations, court houses, roads and bridges in the state's southwest. Convict labour also built Fremantle jail, and a smaller jail in Perth. But the presence of the convicts made the settlers nervous; many began to carry guns by day, and they didn't venture far at night.

During this time Queen Victoria granted Perth city status (1856), and a local Perth council was established two years later.

HOME THOUGHTS

Migrants who arrived as recently as the 1960s say they never really expected to see "home" again. But in the 1960s it was at least possible, at a price, to phone home. Connecting Western Australia to the rest of the world began when convicts installed poles for the colony's first electric telegraph line, from Perth to Fremantle, in 1869. In 1877 the first international link to London by overland telegraph was made, via Eucla and Adelaide.

Perth's local telephone service started in 1887, for just 17 subscribers who each paid £15 annual rental. International calls were unknown until 1911, when a submarine cable linked Perth and London.

LEFT: gold prospectors at Coolgardie in the 1850s.
RIGHT: dry-blowing for gold, East Murchison, 1910.

Gold fever

Gold discoveries from the late 1880s finally made Perth into a real city. Mining became the bedrock industry for city and state, and remains so today, contributing 75 percent of WA's multi-billion exports.

In 1854 a surveyor's expedition to the north assured the state government that WA probably had "one of the finest goldfields in the world" at Mount Magnet (so named because the area sent compass needles swinging wildly). The governor offered a £5,000 reward for the discovery of a payable goldfield. Pay-off was made in the 1880s with a strike in the far north (Halls Creek in the Kimberley region).

The Kimberley boom was short-lived, but it inspired prospectors to scour the state. They made rich discoveries in the Pilbara, Yilgan and Murchison, but all were topped by Paddy Hannan and his partners, Tom Flanagan and Dan Shea. Hannan had migrated from County Clare, Ireland, as a 20-year-old and spent a lifetime searching for elusive riches in the goldfields of Australia and New Zealand. At the age of 50 his luck finally changed, with an 1893 strike that opened up Kalgoorlie and made the area world-famous as "The Golden Mile". In Aussie vernacular, Hannan was a "battler" who made no personal fortune from his find, though he did receive a small pension from the state, in recognition of its importance to the state's economy.

Australia's eastern states were in depression and, with the Kalgoorlie boom, Cinderella WA became the queen of colonies. Migrants flooded into Perth and business prospered. In 1890, £87,000 worth of gold was exported. Ten years on it reached almost £4 million, and gold paved Perth's progress. People spilled out into new suburbs, some linked to the city by trams, as more roads, drains, sewerage and lighting were installed. People strolled and shopped at night under street lighting, and enjoyed the Esplanade leisure area reclaimed from the Swan.

A modern city

Building accelerated in keeping with prosperity. The *London Evening Standard* in 1906 praised Perth for its "modern appliances for expediting communication either by road or car", and said, "Perth put to utter shame the roadways of many far more pretentious and incomparably older towns and cities... both in the motherland and the United States."

In 1834 St George's Terrace, Perth's first (and there most prestigious) street, was a narrow

clay-base strip. A few years later the first rickety timber Causeway stretched across the Swan via Heirisson Island. Even in the late 1870s only parts of central streets were macadamised and all the rest made of unsealed stone.

By 1907 Perth had 145km (90 miles) of made roads, many sealed with tar, and by 1913 the number of motor vehicles just about equalled the carts and carriages on its streets. The era also created many of the neoclassical facades preserved today, such as His Majesty's Theatre, and the Palace Hotel (now a bank). Created by a Californian, John de Baun, the latter boasted 130 guest rooms, 12 baths (with hot and cold water), a library, smoking/reading room, billiards, a post and telegraph office, electricity and electric elevator, plus 70 staff.

Government and politics

Western Australia is vast. Outside of Perth and a handful of other towns, the state is barely populated. By 1901 all the Australian colonies were independent states with self-government under the British Crown. They didn't need to give up a shred of independence unless they chose to do so – but they united and made Australia a single country, with a two-chamber Parliament,

In 1962 orbiting US astronaut John Glenn dubbed Perth the "City of Lights" as it gleamed out of its isolation, a beacon surrounded by thousands of kilometres of darkness.

a House of Representatives and a Senate, based on the systems of Britain and the US. In the Senate all the states have equal representation, regardless of population size. Members of the House of Representatives are elected directly by the people.

Six separate states became the single Commonwealth of Australia, and remained part of the British Empire with allegiance to the monarch, who is represented by a governor-general. The new federal parliament took charge of all national affairs and controlled the armed forces, but the states retained their own local governments and power. They are still fiercely proud of this independence, none more so than WA. It's partly due to physical separation by thousands of kilometres of desert, but also partly due to a friendly rivalry with the other states.

Above: a view of Hay Street in the late 19th century, with electric tram and horse-drawn transport.

WA was always hard to please. Its leaders initially refused to put federation to the vote, and held out for a transcontinental railway to link WA with the eastern states, and for their state to impose its own customs and excise duties. They were forced into the vote by "t'othersiders", the nickname for the thousands of men drawn to WA from the east by the lure of gold. The miners were firm federationists, and threatened to petition the British government for a new goldfields state unless WA put federation to the vote.

So the people voted and said yes, although in 1933 they flexed their muscles again, voting to opt out of the Commonwealth of Australia. The UK imperial government stymied the idea, ruling it unconstitutional. A few Western Australian separatists still claim that their booming mining and farming industries support the rest of Australia, and want WA to secede.

The transportation revolution

At least moving around the state became much easier from the 1880s with the advent of the railway. In 1879, the first government railway line opened north of Perth, carrying copper and lead from Northampton's mines to Geraldton's port, and two years later railways linked Perth, Fremantle and Guildford. In 1898 they radiated south to Albany, north to Geraldton and, of course, east to Kalgoorlie and the Golden Mile.

Railways revolutionised the act of disaster aid as well. When the Pensioner Barracks in Perth caught fire in 1887, the Fremantle fire engine was loaded onto a train and rushed to aid the Perth brigade in their fight to save the soldiers' quarters. In 1907 a "Rescue Special" train set a line speed record that stood for 47 years. Divers based in Fremantle were able to dash east to Coolgardie and save a miner trapped for nine days in a flooded gold mine at Bonnievale.

Travel to the eastern states also became easier in 1917 when the Trans-Australian Railway ran from Kalgoorlie to Port Augusta in South Australia.

Road travel, right across Australia as well as in Perth, improved dramatically throughout the 20th century. In Perth a 1930s Depression-fighting project created Langley Park and Riverside Drive by reclaiming some of the river,

ALAN BOND

When Bond Corporation, the business empire of the high-flying WA tycoon Alan Bond, collapsed in 1989, investors lost almost AUS$2 billion. It was a far cry from the heady days of the 1980s when Bond Corporation seemed invincible.

Alan Bond had all the right stuff to be the archetypal Aussie hero: the common touch (a migrant signwriter from Hammersmith, London), sociability (he married into a respected Perth family) and ambition (he began Bond Corporation nine years after migrating). He was declared Australian of the Year in 1978, a top businessman whose yacht *Australia II* won the America's Cup and brought a new lease of life to Fremantle. He bought and sold television stations,

took over major companies, gold mines and breweries, and founded the country's first private university.

But by 1996 he was in prison. His first sentence involved a AUS$15 million charge over the Édouard Manet painting *La Promenade*, and in 1997 he received another four years for using AUS$1.2 billion from his company Bell Resource to prop up Bond Corporation.

Today Alan Bond has a home in Perth and is still active in business. With AUS$12 million held in offshore trusts, he and his family bought Bond out of bankruptcy. The agreed payout gave creditors, owed some AUS$1.8 billion, around half a cent on the dollar.

and in 1954–8 the Narrows Bridge and the Mitchell and Kwinana freeways were built. The Graham Farmer Freeway followed at the turn of the 21st century.

Western Australians were quick to grasp the value of air transport in such a large and remote continent. In 1911 Joseph Hammond took off from the Belmont Park racecourse in a Bristol Boxkite to make the first-ever significant Australian flight – lasting for 45 minutes.

Langley Park on the Perth foreshore became the unofficial airport, taking over from the racecourse (which was liable to flooding), and

in 1920 the first transcontinental flight from Melbourne landed there.

Australia's first scheduled service began in 1921 when West Australian Airways flew from Derby to Geraldton and then from Perth to Wyndham. Even today helicopters and the occasional small plane touch down at Langley Park, within walking distance of the CBD.

Twentieth-century Perth

By the early 20th century Western Australia was able to raise taxes, sell Crown land and control day-to-day government. Britain had

granted such independence to other Australian colonies in 1852 and was finally persuaded, in 1890, that WA deserved the same. The imperial government had been wary of handing over control of such a huge amount of land to so few people. When it finally accepted WA's draft constitution it retained the power to subdivide the state if it ever felt the need.

Under its first premier, one-time explorer Sir John Forrest, the independent state was able to enact some forward-thinking legislation for a new century, the most notable of which was the right to vote, for both men and women. WA became a pioneer of female suffrage, ahead of Canada (1917), Britain (1918) and the US (1920).

The 1901 vote to join the other states in the Commonwealth of Australia marked the start of party politics in WA. The Australian Labor Party, formed in 1891, is the country's oldest political party, but in Western Australia, Tasmania and Victoria there were no strong and coherent labour parties until 1901. After becoming a federal party, Labor's power grew across the country, and the WA Labor Party won office first in 1904, and again in 1911.

Empire loyalty

Allegiance to the British Empire remained strong, and throughout the 20th century many Australians took up arms in its defence. In World War I Anzacs (the word coined for the Australian and New Zealand combined forces) joined Britain in the fight. Western Australians favoured conscription, and more recruits came from WA than any other part of the nation. Six

---

FAR LEFT: examination candidates in Perth, c.1900.
LEFT: Cottesloe beach, c. 1900. RIGHT: cars take over, Barrack Street, c.1910. ABOVE: Australians cheer King George V, in France in 1916, during World War I.

thousand of them died in the conflict and thousands more were wounded.

Australians served again in World War II, as they would in Korea, Malaya and Vietnam. Thousands of Australians were captured in

> *Many Australians were upset when their troops were sent to fight in Africa rather in the Pacific theatre where they could help protect against Japanese invasion.*

the 1942 fall of Singapore, and Perth feared invasion for the first time, especially after the bombing of Darwin in Australia's north. HMAS *Sydney* was sunk off the west coast; Broome and Wyndham suffered air attacks. Air-raid shelters were built, alerts rehearsed and children given gas masks in preparation for the worst.

Fremantle was essential to the war effort, the secret base for 170 allied submarines. Sunderland and Catalina flying boats took off from the Swan.

Victory in the Pacific – VP Day – was celebrated wildly in Perth on 15 August 1945. But everyone knew that Britain could no longer be relied on to defend WA as she had done in the past.

A new wave of migrants

After World War I a new influx of migrants tried to carve a living in the southwest under a joint UK–Australian Group Settlement Scheme. Just like Peel's early party of settlers, many foundered in the difficult conditions.

It finally took oil and big industry to make the area succeed. In 1954 the town of Kwinana was built to house the men and women who built and then ran the BP oil refinery there. Dozens of industrial and commercial businesses followed, and today Kwinana is an industrial powerhouse equal to any in Australia.

The 1950s saw a new construction boom in Perth. The Causeway and Narrows Bridge spanned the Swan, and better roads boosted traffic. By 1958 parking meters were needed in the city, and trams were scrapped in favour of buses, which could run on flexible routes.

Communication

New entertainments were welcomed too. Black-and-white television on commercial Channel 7

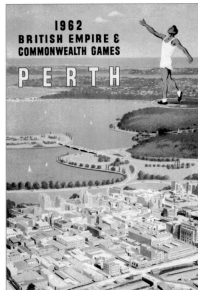

came to Perth in 1959, three years after Sydney. On day one there were just 3,387 licensed sets, and crowds jammed the footpaths around store windows to watch the new wonder. Colour followed in 1975.

Public entertainment has come a long way since 1902, when the first "kinema" opened. In 1919 a record played into a transmitter in Sydney was the first music broadcast heard in Perth. Perth's own radio service began in 1924 with broadcasts by 6WF. Today, 720 6WF is part of the ABC (Australian Broadcasting Corporation) in Perth.

Better communications and access to other cultures, especially America, whose servicemen had been prominent in Australia during World War II, began changing Perth's character. The 1960s brought anti-Vietnam War marches to the streets and rock 'n' roll music to the radio. Hip young men became "bodgies" dancing with their "widgies" at

Perth's hottest teen spot, the Snake Pit at Scarborough. Perth became the Harley-Davidson capital of Australia.

Strength to strength

The 1970s ushered in a new period of confidence. Skyscrapers sprang up alongside the few 19th-century buildings that escaped the developers. Fortunes were made in new mineral booms, such as nickel. At the same time massive industrial/commercial development created new jobs, and demand for houses doubled the size of Perth's suburbs.

LEFT: child immigrants to WA in 1933. ABOVE: St George's Terrace in the 1960s with new skyscrapers.
ABOVE RIGHT: poster for the 1962 British Empire & Commonwealth Games. RIGHT: Queen Elizabeth II inspects Royal Australian naval personnel in 1954.

Important public buildings of the era included Perth Concert Hall (1971), an important symbol of Perth's modern sophistication, just as the Town Hall had been in 1870. New universities Murdoch, Curtin and Edith Cowan expanded the role of higher education begun in 1911 by the University of WA.

Days of sail

New building spread to Fremantle, too. It was the first part of WA to be settled, and in the early years outgrew Perth as a thriving port city. Aptly, Freo's new life was borne in by sail, when Alan Bond's *Australia II* won the America's Cup off the coast of Rhode Island in 1983.

Some say winning the America's Cup was Australia's greatest sporting achievement. In a nation famous for sporting success that's doubtful, but the cup brought crucial attention to Western Australia, and specifically to the port city of Fremantle, where the cup was defended (unsuccessfully) in 1987.

The cup may have been lost, but Fremantle was reborn. Historic buildings were restored, and new businesses and services were created in preparation for the huge influx of visitors. Fremantle is now well and truly on the nauti-cal map as the home port for round-the-world sailors, visiting yacht racers, cruise liners and giant American aircraft carriers. Fremantle has also become a desirable and charismatic place to live on the western coast.

In the 21st century Fremantle's days of sail are still celebrated. A replica of Captain Cook's *Endeavour* was built in the harbour to sail around the world before settling in the Australian Maritime Museum in Sydney. Another replica, of Dutch sailor Willem Jansz's 1606 *Duyfken*, remains in home waters and is regularly seen sailing on the Swan and in coastal waters.

In the new millennium Perth and WA prosper and grow ever faster. Exploration and discovery continue. Offshore gas reserves are tapped, fresh iron deposits exploited, and academics continue searching the outback for signs of our prehistory. As the old millennium ended, WA Museum experts returned to the capital from outback WA with a slab of 3,500-million-year-old stromatolite fossils, the earliest proof ever found of life on Earth. ❑

ABOVE: Alan Bond's ship *Australia II*, winner of the America's Cup in 1983 off the coast of Rhode Island, USA.

People in Power

Australians love talking politics and everyone should have an opinion, since voting is compulsory for the nation

Australians are triple-governed – by local councils, state and federal parliaments. Everyone votes in national (federal) elections because they have to. Federal law made it compulsory in 1924.

The worth of the three government tiers might be assessed by the level of coercion and remuneration involved. Local councillors earn nothing, and most of the electorate ignores them. There's no compulsion to vote at state government level either, but the MPs are paid. Western Australia's state premier earns more than the prime minister of Australia.

WA has sent some notable figures to Canberra, beginning with Sir John Forrest, who became a cabinet minister in Australia's first federal parliament. An explorer who led three expeditions into the interior, he became WA's surveyor-general, and in 1890 became the first premier. He promoted big public works and land settlement, and pulled Western Australia into the 1901 federation of Australian states.

Only two WA-based politicians, John Curtin and Bob Hawke, have held the country's top job. Curtin, the World War II leader and 14th prime minister, is regarded as one of its greatest; Hawke, longest-serving Labor PM, its most charismatic.

Curtin made some hard choices during 1939–45. He rejected the British strategy for Aussie troops, and, with a successful defence of New Guinea, protected Australia's north. Although opposed to conscription in the 1914–18 war, he sent conscripts to fight overseas and took the bold decision to give leadership of Australia's defence force to US General Douglas MacArthur. John Curtin died in office, on 5 July 1945, six weeks before the end of the war in the Pacific.

Successful trade union president Bob Hawke became prime minister in 1983 after only two years in parliament, and one month leading the opposition. He had joined the Labor Party in 1947 and went to Oxford University as a Rhodes Scholar six years later. There, his academic achievements (Bachelor of Letters with a thesis on wage-fixing in Australia) were balanced by the notoriety he achieved by setting the world record for the fastest consumption of beer: 2½ pints in 11 seconds. Hawke later wrote that this feat did most for his

political success in a country "with a strong beer culture". Out of office since 1991, he became a businessman and is still a powerful Labor Party presence.

In June 2010, Australia swore in its first female prime minister, Julia Eileen Gillard, when Kevin Rudd stood down after losing his Labor Party support. Her election was a landmark event for the country. ❑

RIGHT: Julia Gillard, Australia's new prime minister, and the country's first female leader.

AN OUTDOOR CITY

A love of sport, a sunny climate and a wealth of attractive
public spaces draw everyone outdoors. Even domestic life
often revolves around the deck or the pool, the two
most coveted features in suburban homes

Surrounded by the sail-flecked waters of
the Swan River and framed on one side
by the sparkling Indian Ocean, Perth's
enviable geographical location makes it the ultimate outdoor city. Landscaped parks and playgrounds on virtually every corner, an endless
stretch of pristine coastline and a well-developed network of cycle and walking paths provide the locals with numerous ways in which to
make the most of the city's appealing year-
round climate. Whether on foot or on two
wheels, in the water or on land, being outdoors
in Perth is, quite simply, a pleasure.

Good sports

Sport is a religion in most of Australia, and
Perth is no exception. It doesn't matter what
sport you follow, just as long as you're prepared
to spin a yarn about it in endless depth down
at the pub.

For cricket fans, the WACA (the ground of
the Western Australian Cricket Association) is
the scene of many triumphs and tears. Its light
towers are an iconic part of Perth's river-front
skyline, as well as serving the more practical
purpose of enabling play to continue when
the daylight has gone, so no chance of "light
stops play". The ground has verges at both ends
where spectators can sprawl on the grass to
watch the game with a hamper full of food, and
the kids have space to run around, re-enacting
their heroes' winning moves. Passionate, vocal

crowds make this version of the game a very
different experience from the genteel, village-
green cricket played in England in front of
politely applauding spectators, and is all the
more fun for it.

In winter, all attention switches to Australian
Rules Football, a fast and furious game of bone-
crunching tackles that inspires reverence among
its followers but can be somewhat bewildering
to outsiders. Aussie Rules was conceived in the
1800s as a means of keeping cricketers fit during the off-season, explaining why it is played
on most of Australia's cricket grounds. Perth has
its own league, the WAFL (Western Australian
Football League), consisting of nine teams, but

PRECEDING PAGES: mixing business with pleasure.
LEFT: outdoor performance, Matilda Bay.
RIGHT: a friendly game of cricket at Houghton Winery.

it is the national competition, the AFL, that is most closely followed, with teams from all over the country – including Perth's own Fremantle Dockers and West Coast Eagles – vying for glory. You can catch an AFL match every winter weekend at Subiaco Oval *(see page 125)*.

Fancy a flutter?

It's often said that Australians will bet on two flies crawling up a wall, so it's perhaps little surprise that horse racing enjoys year-round popu-

> The Rottnest Channel Swim is a 19.7km (12¼-mile) annual ocean swim from Cottesloe Beach to Thompson Bay in Rottnest and runs every February.

larity, from lively Friday nights at Gloucester Park's trotting track to the fashion and finery of the Perth Cup, held at Ascot Racecourse on New Year's Day and one of the biggest events in Perth's social and sporting calendar. During winter, flat racing is held at Belmont Park and always attracts a good turnout.

Golfers are spoilt for choice in Perth, with a number of world-class greens all boasting beautifully landscaped surrounds and abundant bird- and wildlife – don't be surprised if you're teeing off next to an inquisitive kangaroo or two. Ranked among the best public courses are Kennedy Bay (Port Kennedy), 40 minutes south of Perth and running alongside the Indian Ocean, and Collier Park (Hayman Road, Como). Members of overseas golf clubs can usually pay an appropriate green fee at any of the private clubs to gain access, but check their requirements well in advance.

In other sports, the Hopman Cup sees some of the big guns of the tennis circuit representing their country at the Burswood Dome, while motorsports enthusiasts should visit during October for the Telstra Rally Australia.

Beach life

People from Perth are not as body-conscious as their Sydney counterparts, so going to the beach is less about being seen and more about making the most of the fabulous outdoor lifestyle that Perth enjoys. And with beaches as stunning as these, it's little wonder that the locals spend every available opportunity at the coast. Even in winter the beaches are popular with water-sports enthusiasts, cyclists and the ever-present surfers and joggers, as most find it too cold for sunbathing and swimming. It is in summer, however, that the coast really comes into its own, with beach-goers getting up early before the blistering heat of the day sets in. No one stays in bed when there are waves to catch, so even first thing on a Saturday morning you'll see surfers bobbing about on their boards, kids body-boarding in the shallows, windsurfers, kite-surfers and even ocean kayaks gliding past. Jogging, cycling and power-walking along the beachfront pathways are also popular activities, and you'll see many locals enjoying a leisurely stroll at dusk to catch the spectacular fiery sunsets over the ocean.

A walk in the park

With endless walking, cycling and nature trails crisscrossing some native bushland and botanic gardens, Kings Park is a physical and spiritual focal point. Whether you're looking for frogs in the water gardens, discovering the flora and fauna of Western Australia on the elevated tree-top walkway, or simply laying out a picnic in the cool shade of a towering gum tree, Kings Park is a unique space in the heart of the city. In spring, wild flowers carpet the ground in a spectacular display of colour that draws visitors from all over. Music concerts enliven summer days, while evening open-air theatre performances (held in December and January) are peppered with the laughter of kookaburras in the trees above. Year-round, the park affords stunning views over the city, and an evening drive along Fraser Avenue, with its columns of statuesque gums, provides an unmissable vista of the city lights shimmering in the river.

Messing about on the river

Away from the Indian Ocean, the Swan River represents Perth at its most leisurely. Cruise boats ply the waters en route to the Swan Valley, carrying tourists and revellers on wine-tasting and sightseeing trips. Sleek yachts lean sharply, sails billowing, as the sea breeze comes through. Flash speedboats skim along towing water-skiers, leaving creaky rowing boats rocking in

---

RIVER LOOP

A good way of exploring the riverside is to hire a bike and cycle the 10km (6-mile) loop between the Narrows Bridge and the Causeway across Heirisson Island. Alternatively, "doing the bridges" is a favourite route of many local joggers. Either way, you'll have lots of company on the very good dual-use path which takes you all the way around the city. About Bike Hire *(see page 221)* rent bikes, double bikes and quadcycles, with trailers, baby seats, etc, as well as in-line skates. Kayaks – double or single – can also be hired. Prices are reasonable, by the hour or day.

---

their wake. Families gather for picnics at sheltered spots with sandy banks where children can swim in the shallow water. Cross over the Narrows Bridge on virtually any fine weekend and you will see the river below dotted with windsurfers.

If you want to try windsurfing for yourself, head for Pelican Point on the north bank, which has the best conditions and a windsurfing school offering equipment for hire and lessons from October to April. Cruises

LEFT: a fun run along the banks of the Swan.
RIGHT: Perth has a well-developed network of cycle paths.

along the river depart from Barrack Street Jetty (see page 76), in the shadow of the Swan Bells. Lunch and dinner trips are available, as well as full days out to the boutique wineries of the Swan Valley.

The river can also be enjoyed from another angle – on two wheels. There are 50km (30 miles) of waterside pathways to explore, which are used enthusiastically by Perthites either as a means of keeping fit, getting around, taking the kids out or simply enjoying their beautiful city. Try heading out to the riverside suburbs of Crawley or Peppermint Grove, where you can spend a pleasant morning cycling along wide streets lined with vivid jacarandas, admiring the homes of the affluent families who live here, before resting on the river bank and cooling hot feet with a paddle. Even the smartest riverside neighbourhoods allow public access to the shore.

Cinema under the stars

It may sound like something out of 1950s America, but a trip to the drive-in movie theatre is still a possibility in Perth. The Galaxy cinema (closed Mondays, check local press for times and programme) is one of only two drive-ins remaining in WA (the other being at Busselton), and attracts a fair crowd on fine evenings. Whilst there's nothing terribly glamorous about sitting in what is essentially a car park with a giant screen in it, it's hard to resist the old-fashioned charm of the experience. With your car radio tuned to pick up the soundtrack on a special frequency, the smell of hotdogs and popcorn drifting across from the small kiosk, and the stars above you, the drive-in offers a real slice of movie magic.

AHOY SAILORS

With its brisk breezes and wide river, the waters of Perth are ideally suited to sailing, as the large number of boats invariably scooting across Matilda Bay testify. However, unlike many yacht clubs elsewhere in the world, there are a number of Perth clubs that are pleased to welcome experienced sailors who are visiting the city and can help crew. The nearest club to the centre is the Royal Perth Yacht Club (see page 239). If you know how to sail and want to sample this quintessential Perth experience, ask if you can join their regular Wednesday-afternoon races or, if you are invited by a member, the Thursday twilight sail.

a picnic – or sample the nightly "sausage sizzle" at Burswood – but don't forget the bug spray.

Dining alfresco

Perth's gastronomic scene has flourished in recent years, thanks in no small part to its Mediterranean-style climate. Balmy evenings are enjoyed from pavement tables, bar windows are thrown open to allow patrons to catch the longed-for evening breeze, and waterfront cafés are filled with crowds still salty from a day at the beach, tucking heartily into fish and chips.

There are barbecue and picnic facilities in virtually every park and at most beaches, while along the ocean and river, and in the trendy suburbs of Subiaco ("Subi", as it's known), Claremont, Leederville and Fremantle, there's a wide variety of places to eat, ranging from the traditional Aussie pub to chic sushi joints. Many restaurants make the most of local produce, notably the fabulous seafood freshly caught that day, and exhibit the kind of culinary inventiveness that is getting modern Australian cuisine noticed on the world dining scene. ❑

Locals do it in style, bringing picnics and setting up chairs and tables beside their cars, or lining the boot with blankets and pillows and snuggling up to watch the film. Best of all, there's no annoying person in the seat behind you rustling sweet wrappers.

> On Australia Day (26 January) people gather around the river, spending the day picnicking and playing games. In the evening a firework display sends rockets soaring into the night sky from river barges.

For other outdoor cinema experiences, during summer there's a screen in Kings Park (at Synergy Parkland; entry from May Drive) showcasing a wide range of current films and cult classics, and another at Burswood Park on the Swan River foreshore (check www. moviesbyburswood.com for programmes). Take a rug and

LEFT: sailing in Matilda Bay. **TOP:** Australia Day fireworks. **ABOVE:** open-air concert in Kings Park. **RIGHT:** eating alfresco at the Little Creatures microbrewery, Fremantle.

FABULOUS FOOD

Locals love to boast that Perth has more restaurants per capita than any other city in Australia, an abundance fuelled by a booming economy, superb local produce and a veritable passion for eating out

Stereotypically, Perth is thought of as the poorer country cousin to Australia's brashest city, Sydney. But thanks to successive waves of immigration, an abundance of fresh produce and the wealth from a resources boom, Perth's culinary personality has come into its own in recent years. Add to this a new wave of dynamic chefs wedded to local produce and to travelling the world in search of culinary trends, and you'll find a brand of modern Australian cuisine that, at its best, easily ranks alongside those of Sydney or Melbourne.

But it is important to realise that Perth does not reveal its culinary secrets easily. If you want to experience the most innovative food that Perth has to offer, you have to know where to go.

Origins and influences

Although Western Australia's first settlers went to the trouble of establishing the state's first vineyards in the Swan Valley, Western Australian cuisine remained defiantly British until well into the 1950s. The first inklings of a Mediterranean influence gained traction in the 1920s when the first Italian and Slav immigrants arrived, and flourished in the post-war immigration boom. But it's only since Asian immigration and the advent of fusion cuisine that Australia developed the dynamic cuisine that defines the country today.

LEFT: fine dining at the Blue Duck Café on North Cottesloe beach. **RIGHT:** fresh crayfish and green-tipped mussels are served at Kailis Bros Fish Café in Perth.

Such is the profusion of flavours in contemporary Perth that you'd have to scour the menu to find anything akin to an English roast with Yorkshire pudding. These days a roast of prime Western Australian lamb is more than likely to have a Moroccan or Mediterranean mien, and fish dishes will, in all probability, be accented with Thai or Vietnamese flavours. Even the good old Aussie pavlova has taken a back seat to desserts such as black sticky rice pudding or coconut fried ice cream. From risottos to rotis, sambals to sausages, almost every element of every national cuisine is reinvented on Perth menus every week. But by and large most restaurants tilt more towards one influence as opposed to many.

Local delicacies

Chilli mussels – made with locally farmed mussels – rate as an all-time Perth favourite, while char-grilled marron, served with a lime beurre blanc, as it is by Lamont's *(see page 111)* – the East Perth restaurant that first introduced these indigenous freshwater crustaceans to the national table – is considered a rare treat. Locals can't seem to get enough of slow-braised lamb shanks encased in pastry, as prepared at the Darlington Estate Winery Restaurant in Darlington *(see page 183)*.

A key feature of the local cuisine is its excellent produce. Long renowned for its high-quality lamb, beef and wheat, as well as for its fish, fruit and vegetables, the state has seen a massive increase in the production of gourmet produce. Boutique bakeries, artisan and organic butchers and speciality cheesemakers thrive, thanks to an upsurge of public interest in food. Little wonder then, that locally produced Wagyu beef at AUS\$120 per kilogram is finding its way onto Perth's most discerning tables, or that Kervella artisan goat's cheese is now a staple on many a menu. The succulent and tender White Rocks veal is beloved of the finest east-coast eateries. Farmed barramundi and trout

have joined marron, rock lobster, Patagonian toothfish, sardines, and snow crab at the table. Shellfish is abundant, and even Japanese chefs are demanding Margaret River venison.

Boutique olive oil production is at an all-time high, with almost every region in the state offering a unique blend. Locally grown persimmons, tamarillos and tropical fruits have joined a long list of staples, such as stone fruits, apples, pears and myriad Asian vegetables, that are sought-after at home and in Southeast Asia. New Norcia

FOOD AND WINE COMBOS

The Swan Valley, Western Australian's oldest wine-growing region, is just an hour's drive from the city, making it a more easily accessed option than the more high-profile and popular Margaret River Valley region. Sittella Winery is beloved by the Perth public for its relaxed ambience and affordable food, and Upper Reach is also popular for outdoor dining. Some of the nicest places to dine in a bush environment are at small picturesque boutique winery restaurants in the Perth Hills, also an hour's drive from the city. Most notable of these are Millbrook Winery Restaurant in Jarrahdale and Darlington Estate Winery Restaurant in Darlington.

panforte and biscotti are exported all over the world. Locally made chocolates and preserves can also compete against overseas imports, and there is an array of artisan yoghurts on offer. But as an example of the much-vaunted West Australian audacity, the local black truffles that are now appearing on Perth tables would have to win hands down.

Top tables

If you want to experience the most innovative food Perth has to offer, a pilgrimage to Jackson's in Highgate *(see page 119)* is an absolute must. English-born, French-trained chef Neal Jackson produces some of the most inspired and critically acclaimed modern Australian dishes in the country. Think WA scallops with black pudding, crispy pork belly and apple salad, or chestnut-stuffed rabbit baked in prosciutto for starters.

Equally renowned for its originality is Star Anise *(see page 128)*, where the chef-owner David Coomer woos food-lovers with his seamless blend of Asian and European flavours. Don't miss Balthazar in the city, and the wine bar Must *(see page 119)*, next door to Jackson's. An essential on any gourmet itinerary is The Loose Box, which enjoys an international reputation for its classical French cuisine. Owner-chef Alain Fabrègues holds France's Meilleurs Ouvriers de France: Cuisine Restauration, a title bestowed by the president of France and awarded to only 91 chefs since the 1920s.

Modern Australian cuisine takes its inspiration from many sources, including local plants and animals, as well as foreign influences from diverse locales.

French food-lovers also swear by Bouchon Bistro in Wembley.

A newcomer drawing accolades from abroad – not to mention from local customers – is Harvest in North Fremantle *(see page 143)*, where well-executed modern Australian dishes reveal subtle and refined Latin American and Moroccan flavours. Make sure you book well in advance.

LEFT: making Turkish bread in Subiaco Market.
RIGHT: Asian cafés abound.

Italian

The first ethnic restaurants to open their doors in Perth were Italian, and without doubt the influence of Italian cuisine has been the most profound in WA. As is typical with many ethnic cuisines in Australia, the influence has not been entirely a one-way street, and one of the quirks of Perth's many Italian, or Italian-inspired, restaurants is the way in which Australian tastes and preferences have helped shape the menus.

While Italian restaurants are generously sprinkled across suburban Perth, Fremantle and the Northbridge neighborhood have long been renowned for the proliferation of Italian- and Mediterranean-inspired restaurants and cafés. The fashionable suburb of Subiaco has also joined the fray with several Mediterranean-inspired eateries, including newcomer Rialto's *(see page 129)*, while just next door in Shenton Park you will find Galileo *(see page 129)*, famous for its wood-fired roast duck. Other Italian establishments, including the up-market Perugino, can be found in West Perth and in the CBD.

THE PERFECT PIZZA

While the regional characteristics of Italian food have not translated into local cuisine in a big way, gourmet pizza is flourishing in Perth.

At Il Padrino on William Street in Northbridge, for example, you can experience the delicious wood-fired creations of Sicilian-born chef Nunzio Nici, who was deemed by the International Association of Pizzaiolo in March 2000 to be the finest pizzaiolo in the world, and even summoned to cook for the pope.

More recently the award for the world's best pizza has gone to Little Caesars, located just outside the city in Mundaring *(see page 182)*. Its unique wheat-free pizzas have also won numerous accolades as far away as New York City, a place with a fine reputation for good pies.

Other places worth seeking out are Delizioso, with branches in Subiaco and in the city, which is winning over a devoted following for its authentic Roman pizza la taglio by the slice. The wood-fired offerings of Pizza King in East Fremantle, and Divido, Scarborough Beach Road, Mount Hawthorn, are also popular. And if you fancy a really good beer with your pizza, it's hard to resist Little Creatures in Fremantle, where the combination of boutique brews and fresh pizza (among many other options) is wooing the public in droves.

Chinese

Chinese immigrants were among the earliest to settle in Perth, but the first Chinese restaurants were not established until the 1960s. Since then they have flourished, and can be found in almost every suburb, with menus priced to suit most pockets.

Although predominantly Cantonese, other regional Chinese cuisines are making their presence felt. Many of the city's big hotels have

restaurants and chefs dedicated to producing Asian cuisines. Burswood Intercontinental Resort's Yu restaurant *(see page 110)*, which specialises in Hong Kong-style Cantonese cuisine, is a favourite among high-rolling Asian visitors, and the resort's The Wok restaurant is known for dim sum. Shun Fung *(see page 97)*, on the city foreshore, is highly esteemed for its Beijing cuisine.

Other Asian visitors prefer to take their pick of Northbridge's many Chinese restaurants, while younger, hipper diners gravitate towards the Grand Palace in the city.

Thai and Vietnamese

Although largescale immigration from Southeast Asia did not occur until the 1970s and 80s, its cuisines are now generously represented in Perth. Thai, Vietnamese and Malaysian restaurants are most abundant in and around Northbridge and to a lesser extent in Fremantle, but are also found tucked away in the most unlikely places in the suburbs. Among the most popular in a very long list of well-loved Thai restaurants are the Sala Thai in Fremantle and Claremont *(see page 143)*, and the award-winning Dusit Thai in Northbridge *(see page 118)*. Little Saigon in Highgate is popular for its innovative Vietnamese fare and Nahm Thai in North Perth is the most highly praised by Perth foodies and critics as it strays far from the standard green chicken curry.

LEFT: perfect pizza at Delizioso, an Italian-run café in Subiaco. **RIGHT:** variations on an English breakfast.

Indian

Indian cuisine was relatively slow to make its presence felt in the city, but it is rapidly evolving into one of the most popular, especially in the suburbs. Among the most established Indian eateries are the Royal India in West Perth, the Maya in Fremantle *(see page 143)*, the Punjab on Scarborough Beach Road and the Maya Masala in Northbridge *(see page 118)*.

Japanese

From up-market teppenyaki restaurants to stylish sashimi and sushi specialists, to casual sushi and noodle bars, Japanese cuisine is amply represented. Among those that have stepped into the culinary limelight are Tsunami in Mosman Park, for its superb sashimi and sushi; and 9 Fine Food in North Perth *(see page 118)*, which is famous for combining Japanese and European flavours in innovative ways.

The rest of the world

Less prolific, but readily accessible, are Indonesian, Burmese, Korean, German, Mongolian, Greek, Egyptian and Lebanese restaurants. And if you still hanker after good old English fare, many a café or restaurant will have their version of a roast on the menu. Some of the best English-style food on offer is at Chapter One in Subiaco *(see page 127)*, where you can even get a fix of smoked haddock with peas. And the rabbit pie is heavenly.

Fish and chips

Fish and chips are invariably delicious and affordable, though prices vary. Almost every suburb boasts a restaurant offering the catch of the day cooked in the preferred English style with lashings of batter and deep-fried chips, and maybe some deep-fried battered prawns and scallops for good measure. Cicerello's is a local institution, as is Kailis. Both are in Fremantle's fishing-boat harbour *(see pages 144–5)*. The Groper and His Wife in City Beach also commands a loyal following, while Swish n' Chips in Mount Lawley puts a gourmet spin on this Anglo-Aussie favourite.

Food with a view

Food with a view invariably comes with a higher price tag, but no visit to Perth is complete without at least one meal in one of the many places offering such an option. Possibilities include Fraser's in Kings Park *(see page*

82), Oceanus in City Beach *(see page 157)*, and stylish Zafferano's in the Old Swan Brewery in Crawley *(see page 83)*, which enjoys popularity with interstate guests, while Watershed *(see page 83)* pulls in the locals.

The Red Herring restaurant *(see page 145)* in East Fremantle combines an eclectic menu with arguably the best river view in town: extending over the river, close to its mouth, it is the ideal place to see dolphins swim by. The

---

FOOD FESTIVALS

Perthites need little excuse to stage a festival of any kind, and food festivals are particularly popular. One of the longest-running is the Spring in the Valley's month-long food festival in October, when up to 50,000 people descend on the picturesque region to indulge in food and wine. Another favourite is the Margaret River Wine and Food Festival in November. The Western Australia Wine and Food Festival is held at the Perth Convention Centre in June, while WA's crab industry holds an annual crab fest in Mandurah in March. Many local ethnic communities host smaller festivals, such as the Croatian Food Festival held in the Esplanade hotel in June.

Indiana in Cottesloe offers views of the Indian Ocean, along with a great seafood menu, while the Blue Duck Café and Barchetta combine the same view with a more informal ambience.

Eating in

If there's anything Perthites enjoy more than dining out, it's eating in, and being invited to dine to someone's home is the highest compliment you can receive. Home cooking has undergone a revolution in Perth in recent years, where dishes such as beef rendang, green curry and couscous have taken their place alongside the more traditional roasts, stews and grills. Long, hot summers ensure that the barbecue is a local institution, while picnics are an essential component of an outing to an outdoor cinema. And if someone invites you to bring a chop for the barbie, you can be assured they mean a well-marinated dozen chops or more. Understatement is as Australian as BYO (bring your own bottle) and local custom decrees you never turn up for a meal without a bottle of good local wine.   ❏

ABOVE: food tastes better in the open air.

Best Wines

When it comes to wine, Western Australians are as proud as punch of their home-grown quaffs, available in most restaurants

Australia's largest state boasts nine wine-growing regions and 350 wineries. Though they produce just 3 percent of Australia's wine production, they account for 20–30 percent of the country's premium wines.

By far the most prestigious region is **Margaret River**. Renowned as a producer of robust Cabernets since the early 1970s, it has since forged a reputation for crisp whites, notably Chardonnay and Semillon Sauvignon Blanc blends. Home to estates such as Evans and Tate, Cullen, Leeuwin and Pierro, and with more than 70 cellar doors, the region is a mecca for wine-lovers (www.mrwines.com).

Next to Margaret River, the **Great Southern** region is noted for Cabernet wines, as well as for Rieslings and Chardonnays. Its estates include Ferngrove, Alkoomi, Goundrey, Frankland and Howard Park.

Pemberton region enjoyed rapid growth in the 1990s, and is noted mainly for its Chardonnay, with some Merlot and Cabernet Sauvignons garnering acclaim. Its estates include Salitage, Mountford and Picardy (www.pembertonwine.com.au).

Manjimup is dominated by Chardonnay, Cabernet Sauvignon and Merlot plantings, and in the Blackwood Valley the main reds are Cabernet Sauvignon and Shiraz.

Geographe is noted for the softer character of its Cabernet Sauvignons, and its estates include Capel Vale and Killerby.

Closer to Perth is the **Peel** region – known for its Shiraz and Cabernet Sauvignon – and the **Swan Valley**, renowned for its fortified wines, verdelhos and warm-climate reds. The **Perth Hills** area has been cultivating grapes since colonial days, but was only gazetted as a wine

region in 1999. It now has 16 wineries and 13 cellar doors, including Darlington Estate and Millbrook.

Some leading estates

Cullen, Caves Road, Cowaramup, tel: 9755 5277; www.cullenwines.com.au. Open daily.

Howard Park, Miamup Road, Cowaramup, tel: 9756 5200; www.howardpark-wines.com.au. Open daily.

Leeuwin Estate, Stevens Road, Margaret River, tel: 9759 0000; www.leeuwinestate. com.au. Open daily.

Moss Wood, Metricup Road, Willyabrup, tel: 9755 6266; www.mosswood.com.au. By appointment.

Pierro, Caves Road, Willyabrup, tel: 9755 6220; www.pierro.com.au. Open daily.

Vasse Felix, corner of Caves Road and Harmans Road South, Cowaramup, tel: 9756 5014; www.vassefelix.com.au. Open daily.

Voyager Estate, Stevens Road, Margaret River, tel: 9757 6354; www.voyagerestate. com.au. Open daily. ❑

RIGHT: sampling wine and sunshine.

AN EYE ON ARCHITECTURE

Perth has a surprising variety of architecture. Look up as you walk around and you'll see Gothic Revival churches, Art Deco cinemas, Federation-style houses and much more

Early buildings in Perth were simple affairs that provided basic shelter. The styles introduced by rural settlers were dictated by the climate; the pitched corrugated-iron roofs and verandas kept off both sun and rain. As the colony became more established, grander architecture appeared. Gothic Revival trends dominate churches and cathedrals, such as St Mary's, built in the 1860s to a design by Pugin, architect of London's Houses of Parliament. It has since undergone major renovations and restorations completed in 2010. Second Empire Parisian style distinguishes the Central Government Offices, begun in 1874.

In the early 1900s the states joined in a federation, and Australian "Federation style" homes were built by the burgeoning middle class. Federation-style homes have brick tuck-pointing, stained glass, gables, elongated chimneys and towers. Lacelike ironwork was used, but became influenced by the work of British architect Norman Shaw. Steeply pitched terracotta-tiled roofs were *de rigueur*. Some 75 million Marseilles tiles were imported from France before Australia began making its own during World War I.

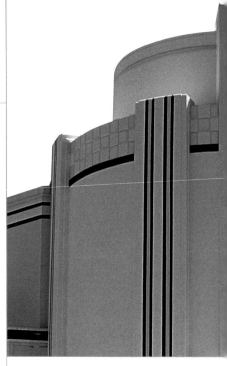

ABOVE: Perth and WA's larger towns have fine examples of Art Deco, such as the lovely Regal Cinema (1938) on the corner of Rokeby Road and Hay Street in Subiaco. The clean, elegant lines of Art Deco made a refreshing change from the excessive decoration of previous eras, of which His Majesty's Theatre (**BELOW**), on the corner of Hay and King streets, is a remarkable example. Built in 1904, it is "like a huge wedding cake iced with every classical device imaginable and topped with reclining lions".

LEFT: one of the most striking features on Perth's skyline is the tower containing the Swan Bells, given to Perth by St-Martin-in-the-Fields, London, to mark Australia's Bicentenary in 1998.

GOLD RUSH ARCHITECTURE

In many WA towns, the pubs (often known as hotels, as they originally offered accommodation) are the most impressive buildings, often dating from the wealthy Gold Rush period (1892–1900). Glowing examples are the Orient Hotel and Hotel Cleopatra (now part of Notre Dame University) in Fremantle, the extravagantly embellished Guildford Hotel in the Swan Valley, and the Palace Hotel (now a bank) in French Second Empire style on St George's Terrace, Perth.

A swelling population kept colonial architect George Temple Poole incredibly busy during this period, his team producing 300 public buildings, such as the Titles Office (Hay Street and Cathedral Avenue), the Royal Mint (the corner of Hay and Hill streets) and the Government Printing office (Murray and Pier streets). The impact of Gold Rush style lingered for some time. According to one architectural historian, Perth was "dipped bodily into a bucket of pure Victoriana and taken out, dripping plaster and spiked with towers and cupolas."

ABOVE: Fremantle has many magnificent period buildings, especially on High Street. **BELOW:** the Criterion Hotel on the downtown portion of Hay Street was built in 1937 at a cost of £40,000 for the Swan Brewery. It retains its impeccable Art Deco facade, though much of the interior has been modernised.

ABOVE: Perth is generally a low-rise city, with a small cluster of high-rises staking out the CBD. As the population has expanded, the city has spread north and south along the ocean, a suburban sprawl that planners are attempting to halt.

PLACES

A detailed guide to Perth and its surroundings, with principal sites numbered and clearly cross-referenced to the maps

The first chapter in the Places section of this book covers the two features above any other that distinguish Perth: the Swan River, the city's *raison d'être*, and Kings Park, a combination of cultivated botanic garden and native bush, where the felling of a tree in 1829 symbolised the foundation of the city. The Cenotaph on the edge of the park escarpment is the best place to get an overview of the city. From here, framed by two modern symbols of the city and its passions – the light towers of the WACA (West Australian Cricket Association) in the east and the Royal Yacht club in the west – the whole of Perth spreads out below.

This guide then explores the city centre, where the skyscrapers of the CBD are interspersed by characterful and newly renovated colonial buildings. Just north of here are the main shopping malls and the Cultural Centre, which conveniently gathers the Western Australian Museum, the Art Gallery of WA and the Battye State Library into an attractive precinct with buskers, low-key stalls, pools and more lovely views of the city.

But Perth is as much about its suburbs as its centre. Two of the older suburbs are Northbridge and Subiaco, the former a hotspot for nightlife, and

the latter a fashionable neighbourhood with a villagey feel, markets and a good restaurant scene. The other essential trip to make is to Fremantle, the port-city on the mouth of the Swan, where period architecture, an upbeat street life and a palpable pride in its working-class maritime heritage present an invigorating contrast to Perth. Travel to Fremantle by ferry instead of the train, and experience the beauty of the Swan, spotting dolphins on the way and checking out the multi-million-dollar riverside properties in Peppermint Grove and Dalkeith.

Attractive though Perth and Fremantle are, it would be a shame not to see more of WA. Dream beaches run 50km (30 miles) north of Fremantle and within a day or two of Perth is a range of enticing destinations. ❏

PREVIOUS PAGES: the skyline from Kings Park; lunching in Cottesloe. **LEFT:** a replica of the *Duyfken*, in which the Dutch mariner Willem Jansz visited Australia in 1606. **ABOVE LEFT:** street sign in Leederville, northwest Perth. **ABOVE RIGHT:** shoppers on Murray Street Mall.

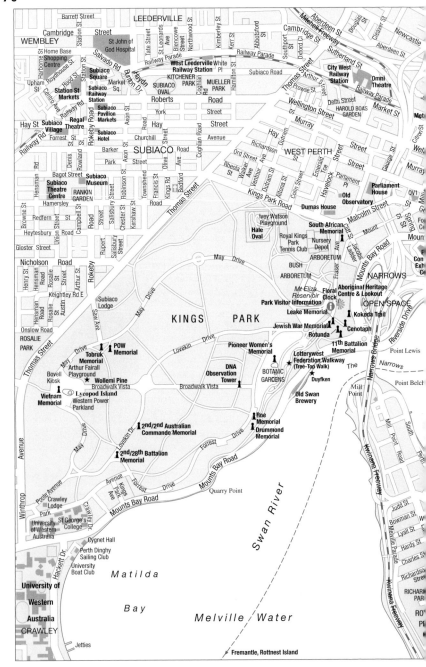

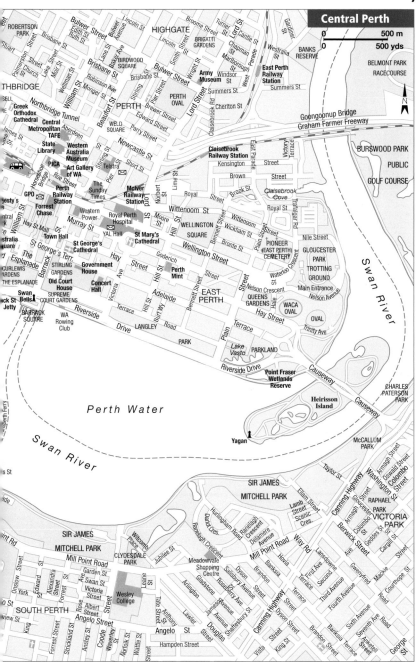

SWAN RIVER AND KINGS PARK

First-time visitors to Perth will be bowled over
by its superb location on the serpentine mouth
of the Swan River, a setting best appreciated from
Kings Park, with its splendid panoramic views

Main Attractions

THE SWAN BELLS
BARRACK STREET JETTY
KING'S PARK
BOTANIC GARDENS
ST GEORGE'S TERRACE
BARRACKS GATEWAY
PARLIAMENT OF WA
FRASER AVENUE
HEIRISSON ISLAND
PERTH ZOO

Maps and Listings

MAP OF SWAN RIVER AND
KINGS PARK, PAGES 74–5
SHOPPING, PAGE 80
RESTAURANTS AND BARS,
PAGES 82–3
ACCOMMODATION,
PAGES 223–5

Perth is synonymous with the Swan River. It was vital to the city's foundation, a secure place upstream from the ocean and the port of Fremantle. Today it forms the heart of a city where enjoyment of the outdoor life is an integral part of the culture.

The Indian Ocean, with its great swathe of beaches, is nearby, but the Swan River is another playground where Perthites can walk, run, cycle, row, cruise – or just sit back and relax while overlooking the magnificent span of shining blue water.

Strict laws against building on the river banks of the Swan guarantee public access to the shore, even in the exclusive neighbourhoods of Dalkeith, Claremont, Peppermint Grove and Mosman Park, where properties fetch multi-million-dollar sums and residents cherish both their privacy and their pricey homes.

For a first look at the gleaming expanse, take in the view from the Cenotaph in Kings Park *(see page 77)*. It offers a panoramic vista of the metropolitan area from the distant Darling Ranges to the coast. Only from here can the vastness of the Swan be properly appreciated.

The Swan Bells

Address: Riverside Drive, www.ringmybells.com.au
Tel: 08-6210 0444
Opening Hrs: daily from 10am, closing times vary seasonally
Entrance Fee: charge

The waterfront immediately south of the city centre focuses on **Barrack Street Jetty ❶** and the Swan Bells. Immense copper sails cup a green-glass bell tower. The bells, a gift from St Martin-in-the-Fields (Trafalgar Square, London), were installed in the

LEFT: view from the bell tower near Barrack Street Jetty. **RIGHT:** the Central Business District as viewed from Kings Park.

ABOVE: the red-brick Barracks Gateway at the top of St George's Terrace.

bell tower to mark Australia's bicentenary in 1988. They rang in the New Year in London for 275 years and proclaimed the coronation of every British monarch since George II in 1727. There's a small charge to see the bells and to take the lift to the outside observation level, but the lovely views of Perth and the Swan make the fee worthwhile.

The jetty is the departure point for various river cruises to Fremantle and up the river to the wineries clustered along the Swan Valley, as well as the ferry to South Perth. Right next to the Old Port is the restored clapboard boathouse of the WA Rowing Club, where you can stop off for a coffee. There are also a number of other cafés and restaurants hereabouts. The club was founded in 1868; its 1905 boathouse is National Trust-listed.

From the jetty, the Esplanade stretches up to the modern Convention Centre, the long, low building beyond Transperth City Busport. A small glass pyramid across the Esplanade is a conservatory of tropical plants and is open to the public.

WEST OF BARRACK STREET

North of the jetty, Barrack Street runs up to **St George's Terrace**, the heart of the downtown area, where the city's cluster of skyscrapers shares elbow room with a number of fine colonial buildings (*this area is covered in detail in The City Centre and Old Perth, page 87*). The west end of St George's Terrace (turn left from Pier Street) leads up to Kings Park, the best place for an overview of the city.

Where the Terrace veers up to the park (and changes its name to Malcolm Street) you'll see the **Barracks Gateway** (along the north side), all that remains of the Pensioners' Barracks. This building housed the Enrolled Pensioner Force, which was made up of British soldiers who originally arrived in WA as convict guards and stayed on to settle when army numbers were cut.

The barracks were demolished to make way for the Mitchell Freeway. Walk through the arch. The freeway is below you, crowned by the **Parliament of WA ❷** buildings and cascading fountains (visits are possible, especially when parliament is sitting, but call the information office first, tel: 08-9222 7222).

this area is covered in detail in The City Centre and Old Perth, page 87

EAT

For really amazing 180-degree views of Perth's city skyline and a spot of lunch to go with it, head to Heathcote Reserve in Applecross. The only way to get there is by car. Make sure you book a reservation if you want to dine at the restaurant, Bluewater Grill, 56 Duncraig Road; tel: 9315 7700.

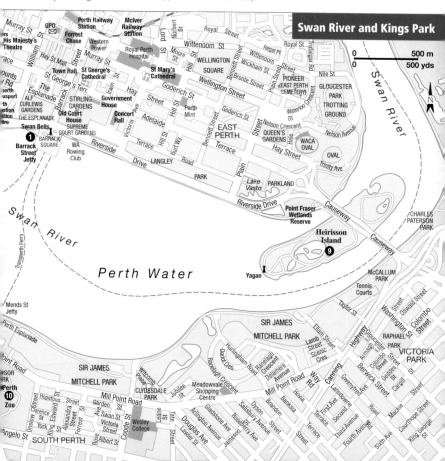

Heartbreak hill

Cross the freeway and climb "heartbreak hill" – what Mount Street feels like to the 20,000 runners and walkers who surge up it in the annual City to Surf race. From the Cloisters, it's exactly 1km (½ mile) up the hill to the Edith Cowan clocktower and the start of **Fraser Avenue**, one of the main avenues through Kings Park. From the park, runners in the City to Surf race have another 11km (6 miles) to reach their final ocean desination at City Beach.

Kings Park

Address: Fraser Avenue,
www.bgpa.wa.gov.au
Tel: 08-9480 3634
Opening Hrs: daily 9.30am–4pm
Entrance Fee: free

This city park ❸ is unique. No other city in the world has such a large area of natural bushland at its heart. The lawns, terraces and water gardens are substantial, but form only a small part of the 400-hectare (988-acre) site, which is mainly native bush. **Park Visitor Information** offers free half-day bush and wild-flower walks

ABOVE: memorial to Australian victims of the South African War of 1899–1902.
BELOW: boats at the Barrack Street Jetty.

conducted by volunteer guides.

The park is full of war memorials, and Fraser Avenue is no exception. The ranks of magnificent lemon-scented gums, known as the widow-maker's tree on account of its habit of shedding large branches during times of drought, were planted to mark WA's 1929 centenary. Individual gums lining May Drive and Lovekin Drive commemorate the fallen of two world wars. As well as the Cenotaph, other war memorials commemorate victims of the Bali bombing of 2002, Western Australian victims of the South African War of 1899–1902 (just off Fraser Avenue) and victims of the Vietnam War (near Western Power playground).

Further along Fraser Avenue is a choice of eateries with river views, ranging from the elegant Fraser's Restaurant (*see page 82*) to a family-oriented restaurant-café and a kiosk for snacks and ice cream. Also here, Aspects of Kings Park sells high-quality Australian crafts.

Aboriginal Art Gallery ❹

Address: Mount Eliza, Kings Park,
www.aboriginalgallery.com.au

Barrack Street Jetty

Various cruises and the Transperth "zoo ferry" operate from the jetty. You can book cruises and trips to Rottnest Island, as well as lunch and dinner cruises, or rent self-drive launches for up to 10 people. Self-hire is a good option if you like exploring. Travelling downriver in a smaller boat, you can follow the Canning River. Simply follow the south bank, watching for channel markers, and sail under the Canning Bridge. Good places to pull in for food and drinks are the Raffles Hotel, at Canning Bridge, and further down the Swan, towards Fremantle, Walter's River Cafe, an excellent licensed café at Point Walter (but watch out for the sandbar halfway across the river).

Tel: 08-9481 7082
Opening Hrs: Mon–Fri 10.30am–4.30pm, Sat–Sun 11am–4pm
Entrance Fee: free

This gallery sells fine indigenous arts and crafts. It usually has an Aboriginal artist in residence.

From here the path passes a memorial to the Australians who fought and died on the Kokoda Trail during the Japanese invasion of Papua New Guinea in World War II. If you stay on the road, rather than the path, you will approach the **Cenotaph** ❺ through the Whispering Wall, commemorating the various battles in which Australians have fought. The huge river gum just past here was planted by Elizabeth II in 1954, during one of her numerous Australian tours.

City views

The panoramic views from the Cenotaph are outstanding. To the left are the towers of the CBD and the Barrack Street Jetty; in the distance you can see South Perth and the Causeway to Heirisson Island, with the Darling Ranges beyond. On the north bank is East Perth, marked by the lights of the WACA (the Western Australian Cricket Association). To the right the river widens to become yacht-studded Melville Water, flowing on to join the Canning River and then surge down to Fremantle and the Indian Ocean.

The park's elevated position places it almost on equal terms with the city's skyscrapers. Though Perth has few high-rise buildings, more are springing up – particularly in the areas east around Burswood and south at Canning Bridge.

The Botanic Gardens

Beyond the Cenotaph are the heavily planted sections of the **Botanic Gardens** ❻. Any of the paths to the right will lead to exotic plants and trees, including many hundreds of native species.

By keeping to the left-hand path, with the Swan on your left, you will

ABOVE: the view of the city from the Cenotaph.
BELOW: although Queen Victoria is commemorated in King's Park, it didn't gain its royal prefix until 1901 following King Edward VII's accession to the throne.

world's first trees), and calamites (fern-like plants). In the lake, replicas of 3.5-billion-year-old stromatolites are inset with solar cells to power the misty spray.

In a steel cage near the lake is a growing Wollemi Pine, until recently thought to have been extinct. In the 1990s a grove of such trees was discovered in a secret gorge in Wollemi National Park, New South Wales. Rare examples were sent to important botanical authorities, and soon the propagation (and sale) of the pines was well under way.

Matilda Bay and the University

The administration buildings and residential colleges of the **University of Western Australia ❼** (UWA) line the road all the way to Winthrop Avenue. St George's College, whose crenellated towers and flagpole can be seen from afar, is the most picturesque.

ABOVE: yachts in Matilda Bay. **BELOW:** a bronze ballerina strikes a pose near the university's Dolphin Theatre.

come to a **Tree-Top Walk** with views across the river, and then enter an area of native bush (stay on the marked paths), eventually exiting the park on Park Avenue, an exclusive neighbourhood near the University of Western Australia, about 2km (1 mile) west. Back in the Botanic Gardens, between the riverside path and Forest Drive, is the **Pioneer Women's Memorial**, a grassy bowl with an ornamental lake and fountain that doubles as an open-air theatre in summer, featuring Shakespeare's more popular plays.

The Broadwalk

Close by is the Broadwalk, a grassy swath with a high lookout, known as the "DNA Tower" because of its twin, twisting staircases; from here you can see Rottnest Island about 30km (18 miles) away. The Broadwalk leads (after about 2km/1½ miles) to the Western Power children's playground and lake. Lycopod Island in the centre of the lake has model dinosaurs and timber-and-steel lycopods (the

Turn left at Winthrop and follow the footpath through the short subway under Stirling Highway, into the University, and go back 70 years in time. UWA was the first free university of the British Commonwealth. Across the Reflecting Pool is **Winthrop Hall**, with its undercroft, terracotta frieze of gryphons and 50-metre (164ft) clocktower. To the right across Whitfield Court, the colonnaded building is the original library (now administration), and more pillars hold up **Hackett Hall**, on the left. All were built in 1932 with an endowment from Sir John Winthrop Hackett, the first Chancellor of UWA and also the owner of Perth's daily newspaper *The West Australian*. The design was by the Victorian architects Sayce and Alsop, who won an international competition for the commission.

Cross the lawn, turn left and walk through the **Great Gateway**. Above is the Senate Room, where the university's governors meet, watched over by the *Five Lamps of Learning*, a

Venetian glass-tile mosaic by the Victorian artist Walter Napier.

Through the arch, turn right to the **Sunken Garden**, a secluded retreat and a cool, shady place in which to sit. The visitors' centre (north end of the admin building) has information on campus artworks, concerts, theatre productions and guided tours.

Walk back to Winthrop Hall, take Saw Promenade towards Reid Library, turn left at the Arts building and cross Hackett Drive to the river.

You could have coffee and a snack (during semester) at Hackett Hall, or in the refectory below the library, but 200 metres/yds downstream (turn right when you reach the river bank) are the **Matilda Bay Tea Rooms** and the adjacent restaurant, the latter more sedate and expensive, with sparkling views of the bay.

Home of the Wagyl

It is a long walk back to Perth from here, but you can easily catch a bus from Mounts Bay Road. The route passes the old boathouse of the Perth Dinghy Sailing Club and the old **Swan Brewery ❽**, now an apart-ment complex with restaurants and a pub-cum-microbrewery. Aboriginal people believe the site is sacred, home of the Wagyl, a serpent-like creature that created rivers by meandering over the land.

A replica of the ship, the *Duyfken* (Little Dove), in which the Dutch mariner Willem Jansz became the first European to record a landing in Australia, in 1606, 164 years before Cook's famous landing in Botany Bay, used to be moored near the brewery (it is now in Cairns). To mark the 400th anniversary in 2006, Dutch and Australian prime ministers looked on as the *Duyfken* left Fremantle to sail around the continent in celebration.

EAST OF BARRACK STREET

From Barrack Street, **Riverside Drive** runs down to Heirisson Island. Hundreds of palms fringe both the road and **Langley Park**, which was Perth's first airfield (small aircraft still fly in occasionally). It is used for special events, and various circuses pitch their big tops here. Helicopter trips operate from here too *(see page 240)*.

The University of Western Australia's Sunken Garden has long doubled as an amphitheatre for theatrical productions, beginning with Sophocles'Oedipus Rex in 1948. Today it is one of several university venues used during the Perth International Arts Festival held during the last three weeks of February and early March.

BELOW: joggers and cyclists take advantage of the path around the shore of the Swan River.

Point Fraser, near the foot of the Causeway, used to be a wetlands reserve. The redevelopment of this site, begun in 2003, is ongoing but, along with most of the facilities, is open for free public use. Indigenous dryland and wetland flora can be viewed from boardwalks, and there are picnic and barbecue facilities, plus a children's playground. A restaurant and function centre are expected to open by 2012.

ABOVE: statue of the Aboriginal leader Yagan on the southern tip of Heirisson Island.
RIGHT: inquisitive roo on Heirisson Island.

Heirisson Island

The walk from Barrack Street Jetty to **Heirisson Island** ❼ can be done comfortably in 30 minutes. At the end of Riverside Drive follow the path up onto the Causeway, turn right off the Causeway, and follow the track down towards an orange sign, with the river on your right. A small colony of Western Grey kangaroos is housed in an enclosure here, bringing an iconic bush element right into the city. During the heat of the day kangaroos stay under cover, but if you move quietly around the track there's a good chance of finding them grazing.

There is a 2km (1-mile) track around Heirisson Island. At the southern tip is a bronze statue of Yagan, an Aboriginal leader killed in 1833. Yagan's head, which had been removed after death and taken to the UK to be exhibited as an anthropological curiosity, was retrieved by tribal elders only a few years ago. It will be buried with the rest of his remains when a secure location is agreed upon.

Heirisson Island was named after a French sailor, midshipman François Heirisson. Long before the founding of Perth, he rowed a longboat all the way upriver to the island from his moored ship *Le Naturaliste*, which carried Nicolas Baudin's scientific expedition of 1801–4. As late as the 1920s squatters lived rough in shacks on the island, in sight of Government House. In 1984 an Aboriginal camp lasted for 40 days before its occupants, land rights protesters, were evicted.

South Perth

Over the Causeway, riverside parkland leads back downriver, with a café, boat ramp and boat hire at Coode Street. Also here is the popular Boatshed restaurant (see page 83).

SHOPPING

Kings Park is more about natural beauty than shopping, but there are a few boutiques worth taking a look at.

Crafts

Aspects of Kings Park
Fraser Ave, Kings Park. Tel: 08-9480 3900.
This store showcases high-quality, modern and contemporary Australian craft and design and offers a distinctive shopping experience that bridges the areas of art, ecology, conservation and education.

Souvenirs

Boardwalk Souvenirs
3/1 Barrack St. Tel: 08-9325 6060.
If you've admired the Swan River from all angles, then head to this small and quaint souvenir shop on the jetty.

Books

Boffins Bookshop
806 Hay St. Tel: 08-9321 5755.
An Australian-owned, independent bookseller offering an eclectic range of technical, practical and special-interest books and niche topics.

At **Mends Street Jetty** the **Transperth ferry** departs for Barrack Street every half hour during the day, and every 10 minutes at peak commuting times. Also moored at Mends Street is the paddle steamer *Decoy* (tel: 08-9524 5922; www.psdecoy.com), which can be hired as a private charter vessel. A genuine steam-powered craft, it has plied the river for many years as a pleasure craft.

Mends Street has a multitude of eating options, including the Federation-style Windsor Café *(see page 83)*, in the Windsor Hotel, at the junction with Mill Point Road. Restaurants facing the river are especially popular at night, when the illuminated skyline of Perth is enchanting.

Perth Zoo

Address: 20 Labouchere Road, South Perth, www.perthzoo.wa.gov.au
Tel: 08-9474 4420
Opening Hrs: daily 9am–5pm, including Christmas Day and Good Friday
Entrance Fee: charge

If you're feeling very energetic, the cycle/pedestrian pathway runs on from Mends Street, under the Narrows, all the way to Fremantle. To return to the north bank use the bridge. But first you might like to visit **Perth Zoo** ❿, a five-minute walk from Mends Street.

When the Perth Zoo opened in 1897, six keepers looked after two lions and a tiger. Now there are more than 1,800 animals and 120 staff. Then the zoo was a place of entertainment and leisure, with natural hot springs, tearooms and ornamental gardens. Today the accent is on animal conservation and education, though there are still evening concerts, special events and activities for the kids.

One of the highlights is the Australian Bush Walk through recreations of different Australian ecosystems, from the arid interior to a tropical rainforest. In the Australian wetlands exhibit boardwalks wind through a huge aviary and pool complex, with a thrilling array of waterbirds and freshwater and estuarine crocodiles, including Simmo, 5 metres (15ft) long and weighing 500kg (1,102lb). ❑

TIP

Talks on various species, from reptiles to orang-utans, are held at Perth Zoo throughout the day. Also look out for feeding times for the Australian Little penguins, Ghost bats and the koalas.

BELOW: feeding the river's famous black swans.

BEST RESTAURANTS AND BARS

Swan River and Kings Park

Modern Australian

Botanical Café

Fraser Ave. Tel: 08-9482 0122 Open: B, L & D daily, in winter months Sun–Thur $ ❶ p253, D4

This casual restaurant offers fresh WA produce and is fully licensed. With magnificent views to the Park, don't miss out on the sights.

Fraser's Restaurant

Fraser Ave. www.frasers restaurant.com.au. Tel: 08-9481 7100. Open: B, L & D daily ❷ $$$$ p253, D4

Executive Chef Chris Taylor is a proud advocate of top-quality Western Australian produce, and you'll find plenty of it at Fraser's. Expect a varied menu, from dishes such as roast kangaroo loin with potato and celeriac crumble, beetroot and caramelised onion, to char-grilled WA rock lobster with spicy tomato sauce. The restaurant is situated high up in Kings Park, overlooking the city and the Swan River. You can also just pop in for a

morning coffee.

Jo Jo's

End of the jetty off Broadway, Nedlands. www.jojos restaurant.com. Tel: 08-9386 8757 Open: Tue–Sat 11.30am–late, Sun 11.30am–4pm $$$ ❸ p256, A4

Restaurants with water views are a treat in Perth and you can't get closer to the Swan River than Jo Jo's. The menu offers crunchy salads and various antipasti, the freshest catch of the day as well as the comfort of homestyle pastas.

Matilda Bay Restaurant

3 Hackett Drive, Crawley. www.matbay.com.au. Tel: 08-9423 5000. Open: L & D daily. $$$ ❹ p256, B4

Situated on the banks of

the Swan River at Matilda Bay, this restaurant is popular for its beautiful views and peaceful location, making it a good option for a special occasion at reasonable cost. The dinner menu has regular rotisserie items (including kangaroo, fish and duck), fresh crayfish from the tank, plus favourites such as char-grilled sirloin and rack of lamb.

Zafferano

173 Mounts Bay Rd, Crawley. www.zafferano.com.au. Tel: 08-9321 2588. Open: L & D Mon–Fri, D Sat. $$$$ ❺ p257, D1

Prices for a three-course dinner per person with a half-bottle of house wine:

$ = under AUS$25
$$ = AUS$25–40
$$$ = AUS$40–70
$$$$ = over AUS$70

ABOVE: lunch at Matilda Bay Restaurant.
LEFT: high-quality menu at Fraser's Restaurant.

Located in the historic Swan Brewery complex, this high-end restaurant boasts some of the prettiest views of the city at night. The menu offers classic Italian seafood dishes, including melt-in-your-mouth crayfish and seafood risotto. The atmosphere and service are up-market, so it's perfect for that special dinner occasion. When booking, ask for a table with a view.

South Perth

Italian

Ciao Italia
273 Mill Point Rd. Tel: 08-9368 5500. Open: Tue–Sat 5–10pm **$$** ⑥ p258, C3
This small BYO eatery radiates traditional Italian cuisine and an atmosphere that keeps people coming back. There is a huge amount to choose from on the menu and the pizzas are particularly good with thin and crispy bases. It does not take bookings and is packed every night of the week, so get in early.

Modern Australian

The Boatshed
Coode St Jetty, Coode St. www.boatshedrestaurant.com. Tel: 08-9474 1314. Open: B, L & D daily. **$$$** ⑦ p258, B3
Waterside favourite at any time of day. Serves modern Australian fare and invites you to BYO.

RIGHT: raising a glass at The Old Swan Brewery.

Coco's
85 The Esplanade. Tel: 08-9474 3030. Open: B, L & D daily. **$$$** ⑧ p258, A2
In its heyday, Coco's was the place for a special – and expensive – meal. Perched on exclusive real estate on the South Perth foreshore, it's still a great place to eat, but with Perth's explosion of quality restaurants and global cuisines, its reputation is not what it used to be. Coco's has stuck to doing what it does best, which is elegant, traditional meals.

Mends Street Café
Shop 2/35 Mends St. Tel: 08-9367 7332 Open: B, L & D daily. **$$** ⑨ p258, A2
This is a waterside favourite at any time of day. A relaxed spot to chill out with a coffee and a snack while reading the newspapers.

Modern Mediterranean

Incontro
79 The Esplanade. www. incontro.com.au. Tel: 08-9474 5566. Open: B & L Tue–Sun, D Tue–Sat. **$$$** ⑩ p258, A2
Run by the enthusiastic

Bars

The Windsor Hotel
112 Mill Point Rd. Tel: 08-9474 2229. Open 11am–late. ① p258, A2
The Windsor Hotel has a swanky hotel bar that has been stylishly refurbished. A boutique beer list, top shelf liquors, great cocktails and a wine list make the Windsor the perfect place to enjoy a drink or evening out. There are light snacks available as well. There are both inside and outside facilities.

The Old Swan Brewery Cafe Restaurant
173 Mounts Bay Rd. Tel: 08-9211 8999. Open B Sat–Sun, L & D daily. ② p257, D1
Enjoy Swan River views and a crafted beer from the on-site microbrewery. There are plenty of dishes on the menu, such as cumin-spiced lamb cutlets, beetroot couscous and tahini mayo. Enjoy the best on tap with a light snack followed by a stroll along the river banks.

young chef Peter Manifis, Incontro offers sophisticated Mediterranean cuisine using fresh, quality ingredients. The wonderful desserts are worth saving room for.

THE CITY CENTRE AND OLD PERTH

The cluster of skyscrapers comprising the CBD
is visible from most of Perth. Less high-profile
are the pockets of Victorian buildings in
their shadow, remnants of Perth's earliest
days and well worth seeking out

Gold-rush wealth rapidly turned small-town Perth into a bonified city in the 1890s. Riches from the Kalgoorlie goldfields paid for hundreds of new public buildings, as the government of the day struggled to cope with the tide of newcomers.

Today, mineral resources such as nickel, iron and gas have fuelled a new expansion, drawing skilled migrants from around the world and regenerating the inner city with tourism-driven ventures, new homes and commercial towers. The city now has more glass-and-steel towers, entertainment and leisure centres on the river, and revitalised public buildings and cultural centres occupying former industrial sites. Key to Perth's new look is the Northbridge Link, a scheme that sank the railway line that dissected the city, separating Northbridge from the centre and the Swan River.

HISTORIC PERTH

Many historic buildings disappeared in 20th-century redevelopment, but those that remain are elegant reminders of times before the streets were paved with gold – or even tarmac. The best place to take in Perth's

architectural heritage is **St George's Terrace**, Perth's first thoroughfare, stretching the length of the CBD and centring upon Stirling Gardens, where a collection of buildings dates back to the very founding of Perth.

Perth's first brick building was the **Old Court House**, built in 1836. It's still in place, next door to **Government House** (residence of the state governor) to the rear of **Stirling Gardens ❶** on the south side of St George's Terrace. The Old Court House shares the gardens with the

LEFT: skyline meets streetscape.
RIGHT: café conversation on Hay Street.

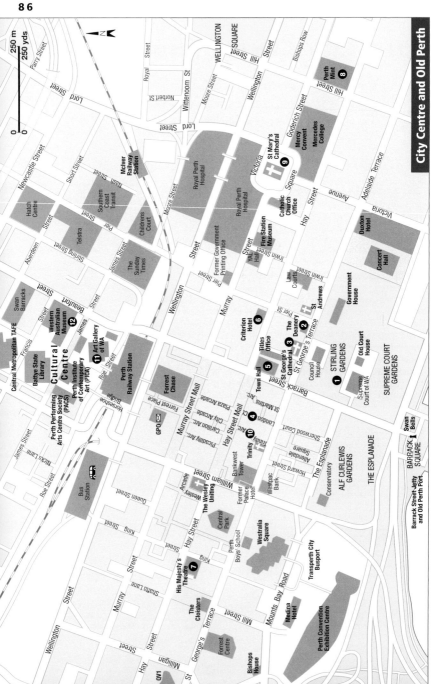

City Centre and Old Perth

Supreme Court of WA (1903). It was here that the first settlers pitched their tents in 1829. Alongside the gardens is **Council House**, the modern headquarters of Perth City Council.

CIVIC PERTH

Some public parts of the Supreme Court are accessible, and members of the public can sit in on trials (serious criminal and civil cases are tried here), mostly timed between 10am–1pm and 2.15–4.15pm Mon–Fri; entrance-hall staff will advise on the cases in progress.

Crime was rare in the early years of the settlement, and the Court House was also used for worship, entertainment and education. A piano concert given in 1846 by Dom Rosendo Salvado, a Christian missionary and talented musician, raised the money to found the Benedictine monastery at New Norcia, bringing Christian care to the Aborigines north of Perth *(see page 194)*.

The Court House architect was Henry Reveley, who would never have become famous for his simple design. Instead, history records that he saved Percy Shelley from drowning in the Arno in 1818 (sadly, Shelley went on to drown in the Mediterranean instead). Reveley later designed Perth's first Government House (1834–8) for James Stirling. Although the current house was completed in 1863, Reveley's building remained in the grounds until the 1890s, when the gardens were extended and a large ballroom built.

East of Stirling Gardens, St George's Terrace runs up to **Perth Concert Hall**, a superb auditorium whose addition to the city was, in the view of historian Dr Tom Stannage (*The People of Perth*, 1979), as important for the spirit and self-confidence of the city as Perth Town Hall was in 1870. Next to the concert hall, at No. 1 St George's Terrace, is **The Duxton**, Perth's tax office until its transformation into one of the city's finest hotels in 1996. East of here is Adelaide Terrace, the location of more hotels. In

ABOVE: the Deanery, built by "ticket-of-leavers" (convicts on parole) in 1859.
BELOW: one in a family of bronze kangaroos outside Council House near Stirling Gardens.

TIP

The London Court clock bells can be heard at noon every day while the mechanical automata depicting St George chasing a dragon and severing its head, spring to life every 15 minutes. The clocks, which are at either end of London Court, were installed in 1937 and made by London's Synchronome Company, one of the world's most famous clockmakers. The display always draws a crowd to watch the knight in action.

BELOW: London Court, a 1930s-built mall of speciality shops.

the early days of the colony, houses backed onto the water here and people swam in the Swan River straight from their gardens.

NORTH SIDE OF ST GEORGE'S TERRACE

Opposite Stirling Gardens, on the north side of St George's Terrace, is the **Deanery** ❷ (under restoration) on the corner of Pier Street, a good spot to pick up the trail of Old Perth. In the short walk from here to the corner of Barrack Street are some of the most substantial pre-gold-rush monuments to early settlement.

Matthew Blagden Hale, the first bishop of Perth and one of its most influential characters, built the Deanery in 1859. Bishops House (1858) and the Cloisters, the colony's first secondary school for boys, further west along St George's Terrace, are among his best-known buildings. Hale School, which had its origins at the Cloisters (it is now at Wembley Downs), is WA's most prestigious school.

By the time Hale arrived in Perth in 1856, the labour-starved colony was using convicts. Though he was strongly opposed to penal colonies, by the time work began at the Deanery non-convict builders were scarce, and the good bishop was forced to employ parolled prisoners, or "ticket-of-leavers". He consoled himself by deciding that the former felons would achieve moral reformation through daily contact with God-fearing men such as himself and Dean Pownall, for whom the Deanery was built. Ticket-of-leavers had something to gain, too. After working their parole for up to four years they could achieve a conditional pardon.

St George's Cathedral
Address: 38 St George's Terrace
Tel: 08-9325 5766
Opening Hrs: daily 7am–6pm, closes earlier in winter
Entrance Fee: free

A little further west from the Deanery is **St George's Cathedral** ❸. Had it been built a decade later it would have been a much grander building, but it was begun in 1879 when times were hard, and completed in 1888, four years before the WA gold rush, and the citizens of Perth couldn't even afford a spire.

The cathedral's architect was Edmund Blackett, whose Great Hall at Sydney University is said to be one of Australia's finest buildings. Blackett never travelled west to Perth to see his plans take shape. One wonders how the great Gothic Revivalist would have reacted to the square tower added in 1902, as a memorial to Queen Victoria.

Inside the cathedral, WA jarrah wood in the framed ceiling and stained glass complement the bricks and limestone that Blackett used to evoke the medieval period.

Next door and almost a block long, the **Central Government Offices** took more than 30 years to build in the Second Empire Parisian style. Inspired by Baron Haussmann,

the style was copied worldwide during Napoleon III's Second Empire (1850–70). WA's first Roman Catholic governor, Frederick Weld, began the ensemble with a Treasury building in 1874. By 1905 the General Post Office and other government departments were added.

London Court

Address: 647/649 Hay Street
Tel: 08-9325 1268
Opening Hrs: daily 9am–5pm
Entrance Fee: free

A few metres west along St George's Terrace is **London Court** ❹, one of only a few major building projects from the 1930s depression. The mock-Tudor ambience is enhanced by its narrow alley, bijou shops and decorative porticoes at each end, one in Hay Street Mall and the other on St George's Terrace, the latter topped by a St George and the Dragon clock. Of all the arcades, this is the one to comb for the out-of-the-ordinary: antique jewellery, coins and stamps, Argyle diamonds, opals and Broome pearls.

A little further along, on the corner of William Street, is the former **Palace Hotel**, now a bank, built in sumptuous style in 1895. Its French Second Empire style is in brilliant contrast to the Bankwest Tower which looms above. The latter was built by Alan Bond *(see page 40)* at the height of his success and fame.

BARRACK AND HAY STREETS

Some of the finest examples of WA's red-brick heritage can be found on the corner of Barrack and Hay streets. In busy **Barrack Street** it's possible to see what the 1890s boom in gold financed. But you need to keep your head up, because most of the historic architecture has been lost from the street level, and only a few turn-of-the-20th-century facades endure above the surf shops and travel agents.

Town Hall

Address: corner of Hay and Barrack streets
Tel: 08-9229 2965
Opening Hrs: Mon–Fri 11am–1pm
Entrance Fee: free

Although the **Town Hall** ❺ is now hemmed in by other structures, the building's early impact is not hard to imagine. Early photographs show it clear and unencumbered, its clocktower visible for many kilometres. Built from 1867–70, it was a sign to settlers that Perth was a city intent on establishing itself permanently. It was also a very useful landmark for the many citizens without a watch.

The Town Hall was built by convicts using local materials – tough jarrah timbers, Swan Valley limestone and clay bricks from the east Perth quarry that later became Queens Gardens. Local she-oak shingles were originally used on many roofs (you

ABOVE: the Town Hall
BELOW: stonework on St George's Cathedral, designed by Gothic Revivalist Edmund Blackett in a time of austerity.

ABOVE: special coins at the Perth Mint.

Millions of government dollars were spent on restoring His Majesty's Theatre in the 1970s, and much of architect William Wolf's splendid wedding-cake exterior was preserved. Unfortunately, one extravagant feature of the original theatre was lost with restoration (and the advent of air conditioning) – a dome which was winched open on hot Perth nights to offer cooling views of the night sky.

can still see examples of these at the Old Gaol in the Western Australian Museum, *see page 95*).

The renovated building and the Gothic arched undercroft – a copy of a late-medieval market – are open to visitors (Mon–Fri 11am–1pm, although hours may vary).

Three fine facades face the Town Hall (above the former McNess Royal Arcade of 1897, on the west side of Barrack). Turn right at the Town Hall into **Hay Street** and there are more at first-floor level. A little further on is the Art Deco **Criterion Hotel ❻**, and next to the Town Hall on the corner of Cathedral Avenue is the 1897 **Titles Office**, thought the best work of George Temple Poole, colonial architect in charge of public works in the gold-rush days. His team turned out 300 public buildings in just two years (1895–97). Sweeping entrances were a favourite feature of Poole's, like those further east on Hay Street at the Perth Mint.

In **Pier Street**, left off Hay, is the Salvation Army's first Perth citadel, and adjacent Milton Chambers, both fine old buildings. The citadel, designed by one of its officers, Edward Saunders, in 1899, cost around £8,000. Adjacent buildings were bought, and the Army spread around the corner into **Murray Street**. The heritage-listed Congress Hall has been converted into stylish inner-city apartments.

Hay Street

On the western section of Hay Street is one of Perth's finest buildings, **His Majesty's Theatre ❼**, a symbol of Perth's established prosperity when built in 1904 for £42,000 by entrepreneur, mayor and parliamentarian Thomas Molloy, who made his fortune out of hotels and theatres. This was his greatest project, seating 2,584 patrons on three levels around a horseshoe-shaped auditorium. The theatre opened with *The Forty Thieves* on Christmas Eve of 1904. His Majesty's Theatre is believed to be the only functioning Edwardian theatre in all of Australia, and was named a State Heritage Icon in 2004.

Perth Mint

Address: 310 Hay Street
Tel: 08-9421 7428
Opening Hrs: Mon–Fri 9am–5pm, Sat–Sun 9am–1pm
Entrance Fee: charge

At the eastern end of Hay, the **Catholic Church Office** and **Cathedral Presbytery** face the Art Deco facade of **Campbell House**. Around the corner from here, at the junction with Hill Street, is **Perth Mint ❽**, just a block away.

The Mint began in 1899 as a branch of the Royal Mint, London, and has the look of a colonial mansion – with two wings, central riser and flagpole. The elegant front lawns feature a statue of prospectors cast in bronze. Australia's oldest working mint, it is always busy producing special editions, such as one which marked the 2000 Olympic Games in Sydney.

Inside, you can experience a reconstructed turn-of-the-20th-century miners' camp, and get your hands on a 400-ounce gold bar. You can also watch a gold pour, held every hour in the original Melting House (Mon–Fri 10am–4pm, Sat–Sun 10am–noon). The guided tour (every half-hour from 9.30am) takes you through the Gold Exhibition and finishes in time to see the molten gold poured into ingots. You can conclude a visit with a cream tea in the period restaurant.

The Mint is on the corner of Hill Street, which leads (north) to Goderich Street and Victoria Square, dominated by **St Mary's Cathedral ❾** (closed for restoration work), probably based on a design by Pugin, the Gothic Revivalist who co-designed Britain's Houses of Parliament.

Facing it on your left is **Mercy Convent** (1873), designed by an Irish

political prisoner named McMahon. This was the base for six Sisters of Mercy who came from Ireland in 1846 and established schools such as nearby Mercedes College. Three distinctive gables with decorative brickwork are original; the iron lacework and veranda were later additions.

Fire Station

Address: corner of Murray and Irwin streets
Tel: 08-9416 3402
Opening Hrs: Tue–Thur 10am–4pm
Entrance Fee: free

Leave Victoria Square on Murray Street, shadowed by a magnificent Morton Bay fig tree whose canopy spans the road. Many of the buildings along here are now part of the Royal Perth Hospital precinct, but on the left you'll find the **Fire Station** (*c.*1900). It's now a Safety Education Centre and **Museum** (being refurbished; tel: 08-9323 9353 to check progress). It is worth a look for the old Dennis fire engines, which are still licensed and ready to roll.

The front elevation of this building is amazing. Architect Michael

ABOVE: for vintage fire engines, pay a visit to the Safety Education Centre and Museum.
BELOW: pedestrians on the Murray Street Mall.

Cavanagh – who also designed the east front of the Cathedral – threw everything at it: turreted gables, friezes, spires, iron lace, terracotta chimney pots, covered balconies, and pillars – there are even bright-red firemen's helmets.

After the fire station is a parade of intact historic buildings – the Young Australia League, heritage-listed Living Stone Foundation, and Salvation Army Congress Hall. Across the road is the former Government Printing Office (1891–4), next door to the Government Stores (1911). The Printing Office is architecturally interesting, starting calmly at street level and becoming progressively more daring as it rises to the sky with turrets and domes. It's more of Temple Poole's monumental output.

THE ARCADES

A warren of shopping malls and arcades lies between St George's Terrace and Wellington Street. Some of the arcades date back to the gold-rush expansion, but today all are modern and air-conditioned. Buskers are everywhere, and the action reaches a crescendo in Murray Street Mall. Outside Myer, ragtime pianist John Gill, an in-demand performer at international jazz festivals, is one to watch for among a throng of jugglers, mime artists, living statues and other performers.

During the gold rush the whole commercial centre of Perth was rebuilt. Until the 1880s it was rural in character, with just a few shops and businesses among small cottages. Hay Street was the 20th century's main commercial street, with traffic and trams, until turned into Australia's first pedestrian mall in 1970.

Every arcade has some individual character. **Trinity Arcade** ⑩ is on three levels. Below ground are essential services such as dry cleaning, shoe repairs and hairdressing for men and women. At street level you can take your own lunch into Trinity Church hall, and buy tea, coffee and cakes knowing all the proceeds go to charity. Rare books are crammed into the tiny Trinity Arcade Bookshop; Leonidas specialises in Belgian chocolates; and the very exclusive Parker & Co. men's outfitters have two shops here.

Piccadilly, **Plaza** and **Carillon City** are the other principal arcades. The five levels of Carillon City run between Murray and Hay street malls, and even include a tourist lounge at the top. Among the shops in Plaza Arcade are Outback Red and Opal Strike, as well as a Flight Centre and Transperth information centre. Piccadilly Arcade includes several specialist outlets, such as Heraldic Arms and Crests and Roc Candy, where you can watch sticks of rock being rolled, whilst the Rare Coin Company is located at 286 Hay Street. King Street and the newly developed Wesley Arcade are where you can find the luxury brands such as Louis Vuitton, Prada, Cartier and Gucci, and leading Australian fashion designers such as Alannah Hill and jewellery designer Jan Logan.

ABOVE: Forrest Chase shopping centre, off Murray Street Mall.
BELOW: the Art Gallery of Western Australia.

NORTH OF WELLINGTON

Perth's cultural centre lies just north of the railway tracks and is most easily accessed via the walkway over Wellington Street from the Forrest Chase shopping mall.

Art Gallery of WA

Address: James Street Mall, www.artgallery.wa.gov.au
Tel: 08-9492 6622
Opening Hrs: Wed–Mon 9am–5pm, free tours Tue–Sun, hourly
Entrance Fee: free

The **Art Gallery of WA** ⓫ is the main building to the right after you cross into the centre, its slab-sided face generally advertising its latest exhibition. Inside, several floors of modern, well-lit galleries display more than 1,000 works of art, including Australian and international paintings, sculpture, prints, crafts and decorative arts. On the first floor of the main building, two galleries house one of the conti-

nent's best collections of Aboriginal art – paintings, bark paintings and carvings giving a comprehensive overview of traditional and contemporary works from Arnhemland, the Central Desert and Western Australia.

Also worth seeing are the **Centenary Galleries**, contained in the former Perth Police Court building. Among the highlights here are *Down on His Luck* by Fred Mc-Cubbin, *Breaking the News* by John Longstaff, *Ada Furlong* by Tom Roberts, *Black Thursday* by William Strutt, and *The Hillside* by Arthur Streeton.

Almost as intriguing as the art is the building itself, a late 19th-century interpretation of French Renaissance style. It was unusual for Perth architecture but localised in its use of WA materials such as the pink Donnybrook stone of the facades, hard jarrah timber for floors and interior furnishings, stained-glass feature panels and Australian-made ornate

ABOVE: *The Caller,* by Gerhard Marcks.

EAT

The café in the Art Gallery of WA is good for creamy cappuccinos, large glasses of wine and light lunches. Outside tables provide views of the lively passing scene. Alternatively, the café in the Old Gaol of the Western Australian Museum is also good, with gourmet sandwiches, snacks and some outside tables.

SHOP

King Street, though home to high-end fashion labels such as Louis Vuitton and Prada, also showcases local labels. Look out for gothic-style pieces by Kings of Cabbage, stocked at Dilettante (shop 1/90 King Street), or flowing designs from Christine Tang's label Story By Tang.

pressed-metal ceilings. The courts closed in 1982; one court room and two adjoining cells are preserved.

One painting that is almost always included on the general tour of the Art Gallery is *The Foundation of Perth*, by George Pitt, depicting the moment when Mrs Dance marked the founding of Perth by felling a tree *(see page 32)*.

Placed just outside the Art Gallery is a dramatic steel sculpture, *Between 1979–1980*, by Australian-born sculptor Clement Meadmore, and, near the pool, another startling artwork, *The Caller*, by German artist Gerhard Marcks, who said he was inspired when he stood next to a man who called across a river to attract the ferryman on the other side.

Battye Library of WA History

Address: Alexander Library Building, Perth Cultural Centre, James Street, Northbridge
Tel: 08-9427 3111
Opening Hrs: Mon–Thur 9am–8pm, Fri 9am–5.30pm, Sat–Sun 10am–5.30pm
Entrance Fee: free

The **Battye Library of WA History** contains the state archives, film and photographs. The main attraction for casual visitors is likely to be the discard bookshop in the front lobby.

The black-and-white sculpture *Coalesce*, by Akio Makigawa, in front of the library, has become a popular meeting place; the stepped forms symbolise the stages of acquiring knowledge.

SHOPPING

The city's King Street and surrounding precinct is a clothing fashion mecca in the city, while neighbouring Leederville is jam-packed with edgy design stores and one-off boutiques. Between the two, you're guaranteed to find that perfect gift for yourself or someone back home.

Women's Clothing

Dilettante
575 Wellington St. Tel: 08-9226 1400 www.dilettante.net.
Stocks a range of high-end Japanese labels as well as Australian and Western Australian designer pieces such as One Fell Swoop, and has a creative art-based approach to fashion.

Varga Girl
148 Oxford St, Leederville. Tel: 08-9444 8990.
This high-end store stocks predominantly Australian designer labels and has an eclectic range of accessories and shoes.

Gifts

Black Plastic
2/226 Carr Pl. Tel: 08-9328 1236.
Interesting cards for all occasions, quirky gifts, games and odd trinkets can be found in this locally owned gift shop.

Arcades

Trinity Arcade
Linking Hay Street to St George's Tce, this arcade has services such as dry-cleaning, shoe repairs

and hairdressing for men and women

Piccadilly Arcade
links Hay and Murray streets and has a range of stores including JB Hi-Fi and the old and romantic Piccadilly Theatre, an ideal way to get out of the heat and rest those shopping shoes for a few hours.

Carillon Arcade
This is the main shoppng arcade in the city and includes one of the biggest and cheapest food halls in the city with cuisine from Asia to Italy.

Food

Jus Burgers
743 Newcastle St, Leederville. Tel: 08-9228 2230 www.jusburgers.com.au.
With its "buy west eat best" initiative it is no

wonder this burger joint has Perth's tongues wagging and salivating.
Fresh WA meat, hand-cut chips and gluten-free buns are just the tip of the iceberg. They have also opened in Subiaco and will soon be in Fremantle.

Greenhouse
100 St George's Terrace. Tel: 08-9481 8333 www.greenhouseperth.com.
What do you get when you cross a designer, a restauranteur and a cocktail professional? The greenhouse, of course. Designed and built to have a small carbon footprint, the food and atmosphere share the same ethos. The result? A restaurant that can harvest good food in a comfortable, green-friendly environment.

Western Australian Museum

Address: James Street, Northbridge,
www.museum.wa.gov.au
Tel: 08-9427 2877
Opening Hrs: daily 9.30am–5pm
Entrance Fee: suggested donation

Next to the Battye building is the **Western Australian Museum**, an elegant red-brick and sandstone building with a colonnaded upper floor. In WA scientists have access to some of the oldest land on earth, its earliest life forms, and a wealth of artefacts of early man, such as the rock paintings in the Pilbara.

In 1999 a fossil proving the earliest evidence of life on earth was discovered in WA's Pilbara region. Now on display in the Dinosaur Gallery, it looks like a slab of red rock. But it holds the oldest life-fossil known, stromatolites, estimated to be 3.5 billion years old. Living versions still grow in the highly saline water of Hamelin Pool at Shark Bay, far north of WA.

Australia began to acquire its present-day form 120 million years ago when the supercontinent of Gondwanaland began to break up, separating South America, Africa, Madagascar and India from Australia. South America was connected to Australia at its southern tip, via an ice-free Antarctica, until 30 million years ago. Isolated since then, Australia's prehistoric life forms were undisturbed and safe from man until perhaps 40,000–50,000 BC. Botanists believe Australia was the prime location of early flowering-plant evolution. Some of the weird and wonderful products of isolation survive – such as the duck-billed platypus, kangaroo and wallaby.

The museum has a pleasant coffee shop next to the **Old Gaol**, built by convicts in 1855–6 and now crammed with memorabilia of Perth life since James Stirling's expedition of 1827, including a complete original court room, a pedal radio that kept outback families in touch, a complete 1917 pharmacy, clothes, toys and furniture.

Perth Institute of Contemporary Art

Address: Perth Cultural Centre, James Street, Northbridge, www.pica.org.au
Tel: 08-9228 6300
Opening Hrs: Mon–Fri 10am–6pm, gallery Tue–Sun 11am–6pm
Entrance Fee: free

WA's creative arts scene centres on the Northbridge end of the Cultural Centre, loosely drawn around PICA, the **Perth Institute of Contemporary Art**, and PACS (**Performing Arts Centre Society**; www.pacs.org.au). The soaring main gallery has studios on a mezzanine, a bar and café (open daily), and a theatre on the ground floor. Sharing space with PACS is Propelarts, a youth arts organisation encompassing everything from writing to dance. **Artrage**, Perth's alternative arts coordinator, is around the corner.

The newest attraction at PACS is the Blue Room, where around 20 shows are staged per year, each running for a two- to three-week period. ❏

ABOVE: a 1970s dental surgery reconstructed in the Old Gaol looks astonishingly antiquated.
BELOW: a peek inside the Western Australian Museum.

BEST RESTAURANTS, BARS AND CAFÉS

City Centre

Asian

Annalakshmi

4 Barrack Square at Barrack St Jetty. www.annalakshmi. com.au. Tel: 08-9221 3003. Open: L Tue–Fri and Sun, D Tue–Sun. **$** ⑪ p254, A4
You won't find many restaurants like Annalakshmi. Run by Hare Krishnas, this restaurant has no prices and no bills. When you leave, you simply pay what you can, or what you feel your meal was worth. This system has been in place for years and is very popular. All meals are vegetarian.

Matsuri

Ground floor, QV1 building, 250 St George's Terrace.

www.matsuri.com.au. Tel: 08-9322 7737. Open: L Mon–Fri, D daily. **$** ⑫ p253, E3
A great spot for a fast and tasty Japanese meal that won't break the bank. Entrées such as the beef tataki are good to share, and the set menus (choice of main such as ginger fish or chicken teriyaki, plus miso soup, rice and salad) offer excellent value for your money. The quality is also top-notch for the price. The food is flavoursome, generous, and you can BYO. The entrance is off Hay Street.

Nine Mary's

Corner of Hay and Milligan streets. www.ninemarys.com. au. Tel: 08-9226 4999. Open: L Mon–Fri, D Mon–Sat. **$$** ⑬ p253, E3
This is a light and bright restaurant serving traditional Indian cuisine. An extensive menu includes good tandoori, alongside a range of curries from mild butter chicken to the fragrant (lamb saag) and the hot (pork vindaloo). Try the mixed tasting plate for starters.

Taka's Kitchen

397 Murray St (in Shafto Lane). Tel: 08-9324 1234. Open: L & D Mon–Sat. **$** ⑭ p254, A3
You'll fight to get a table at this popular, cheap Japanese café at lunchtime. With an emphasis on speed and value, Taka's serves a range of dishes (including agedashi tofu, chicken katsu, teriyaki fish, sashimi). All meals are available in small or large sizes. There is free tea and a range of help-yourself sauces. The quality is reasonable, especially at such low prices.

Australian

No. 44 King Street

44 King St. Tel: 08-9321 4476. Open: B, L & D daily. **$$–$$$** ⑮ p254, A3
Open from early until late at night with a menu that changes daily, this is a Perth dining institution

LEFT: drop by for a coffee at No. 44 King Street.

where you'll find business people sealing deals over breakfast, locals popping in for a coffee and young couples dining at night celebrating that special occasion. The lofty, semi-industrial space allows you to watch the baristas, chefs and bakers at work, or you can simply gaze out onto the city's most fashionable street and people-watch. The food is quite innovative, and there is a large and interesting wine list.

Bar One

Lower level, QV1 building, 250 St George's Terrace. Tel: 08-9481 8400. Open: B, L & D Mon–Fri. **$$** ⑯ p253, E3
This funky bar-cum-café attracts people at all times of day. You can pop in for a coffee and have a bite to eat, a more serious pasta lunch or relax over drinks with a group of friends at the end of the day. It is popular on Friday nights with young professionals, so if you don't want shoulder-to-shoulder action choose another night to visit. There is a large wine list and excellent mixed drinks. The food is Italian-influenced.

Box Deli

918 Hay St. www.boxdeli.com. au. Tel: 08-9322 6744. Open: L Mon–Fri, D Mon–Sat. **$$$** ⑰ p253, E3
This little rectangular slice of Manhattan is quite

popular with Perth's beautiful people. The small mezzanine dining area overlooks the sophisticated lounge bar where you'll find some of the city's best cocktails. The food is classy, and is the best of modern Australian cuisine with robust flavours.

C Restaurant Lounge
St Martin's Tower, Level 33/44 St George's Terrace. www.crestaurant.com.au. Tel: 08-9220 8333. Open: L & D, every day except Sat, D only. Open until late every night. **$$$$**  p254, A3
It's worth going to C Restaurant just for the view. Located on the 33rd storey of one of the city's office buildings, this revolving restaurant offers diners a 360° view of Perth, from Rottnest Island to Fremantle and across to the Perth Hills. The food is modern Australian and is served elegantly. Even if you don't have a full meal here, reserve a table near the window in the bar area and enjoy a couple of first-rate cocktails while watching the sun set.

David Jones Foodhall
622 Hay St Mall. Tel: 08-9210 4000. Open: L daily. **$–$$** 19 p254, A3

Prices for a three-course dinner per person with a half-bottle of house wine:
$ = under AUS$25
$$ = AUS$25–40
$$$ = AUS$40–70
$$$$ = over AUS$70

Located on the ground floor of Perth's swishest department store, the David Jones Foodhall is a must-do for any foodie. Aside from the freshest produce available for purchase, there is an oyster bar serving both fresh and cooked oysters with champagne, a sushi bar, a noodle and curry bar, fresh sandwiches, a coffee and chocolate bar as well as a fresh juice bar. Take some time out from walking the shops to relax with some top-quality food.

Etro
49 King St. www.etro.net.au. Tel: 08-9481 1148. Open: B & L Sat–Thur, D daily. **$$** 20 p254, A3
In good weather you'll always find the seating around Etro's footpath jammed with trendy young people sipping strong coffees or stronger cappuccinos. Inside you can enjoy well-priced cooked breakfasts and a large range of tasty lunches and dinners. In summer, the rooftop area is sometimes open for dancing and cocktails, so keep an eye out for flyers and other promotional material. It's the perfect place for a nice evening out.

The Globe
Mill St. Tel: 08-9215 2421. Open: B, L & D daily. **$$–$$$** 21 p254, A3
Part of the Hilton Hotel, The Globe is an elegant

RIGHT: a quiet corner in Leederville.

and modern place to enjoy a quiet dinner. The flavours here are a blend of traditional European fare and local Asian influences, with a focus on fresh, top-quality produce. The wine bar is a great spot to relax, and there is a small but interesting tapas menu served from 5–8pm.

Chinese

Grand Palace
3 The Esplanade. www.grandpalace.com.au. Tel: 08-9221 6333 Open: L Mon–Fri noon–3pm and D daily from 6pm. **$$$** 22 p254, A4
Situated in a beautiful 1928 heritage building, the Grand Palace offers fine dining of Cantonese cuisine with a menu that has been influenced by western cultures.

Shun Fung on the River
6 Barrack Sq. at Barrack St. Jetty. www.shunfung.com.au. Tel: 08-9221 1868. Open: L & D daily. **$$$** 23 p254, A4
Top-notch Chinese seafood cuisine is served at this well-located restaurant with views over the Swan River. Some of their more unusual dishes include whole grouper, shark fin and bamboo fungus soup and crispy king prawns with spiced salt and chilli. Live lobsters and mud crabs are kept in tanks. They also do banquet menus for large groups.

European

Belgian Beer Café Westende
Corner of King and Murray streets. www.belgianbeer.com.au. Tel: 08-9321 4094. Open: L &D daily. **$$** 24 p254, A3

This unique pub serves modern Belgian fare, including mussels, venison sausage and mouth-watering Belgian waffles. There is plenty of outdoor seating on the street or in the garden at the rear of the pub, where you can enjoy one of the many beers on tap, including Hoegaarden, Leffe and Kriek. The pub is great for dining, or you may like to join the Friday-night throng of exuberant city workers for a drink (or four). A cone of frites with aioli is a must.

Italian

Millioncino
451 Murray St. Tel: 9480-3884. Open: L Mon–Fri, D Mon–Sat. **$$–$$$** **㉕** p253, E3
Within walking distance

of many of the hotels in Perth, this dining establishment is well worth a visit. The chef and owner Mario is passionate about giving his guests top service and first-rate Italian food. Mario's signature truffle dish is highly recommended.

Modern Australian

Balthazar
6 The Esplanade. Tel: 08-9421 1206. Open: L Mon–Fri, D Mon–Sat. **$$$** **㉖** p254, A3
You won't find Balthazar just by walking past, but it's worth the effort to look for it. Conveniently located in the CBD on the corner of Howard Street, and only a short stroll across the grass from the bell tower, this dark, sophisticated restaurant serves some of the best

food in town. Known for its massive and interesting wine list – the waiters are very knowledgeable and are happy to advise. Perfect for the indecisive are the tasting plates, which change daily (they even have a dessert tasting plate). Balthazar is a must for foodies, and it is best to book.

Bouchard
42 Mount St. www.bouchard.com.au. Tel: 08-9321 5013. Open: B & L Mon–Sun from 7am. **$$$** **㉗** p253, E3
Owner Sebastien Bouchard has made his mark on the Perth dining scene with this delightful and innovative restaurant that has a varied and interesting menu such as braised pig's head ballotine, black pudding, apple purée with a Pedro Ximenez reduction, and

tempting desserts like vanilla pannacotta with beetroot jelly and burnt honey cannelloni.

Leederville

Another good area for eating out is Leederville, a short hop from the CBD by train from the Central Station.

American

Retro Betty's
127 Oxford St. Tel: 08-9444 0499. Open: L & D daily. **$** off map
This American café is done up in a traditional diner style, and has a large menu of delicious burgers, all specially cooked to order using quality meats and fresh sourdough rolls. Be sure to order the crinkle-cut fries and a milkshake too,

BELOW: drawing a pint.

or perhaps the pancakes with chocolate chips, which are to die for.

Asian

Banzai
741 Newcastle St. Tel: 08-9227 7990. Open: L Fri–Sat, D Mon–Sat. **$** off map
This funky slice of Japan is always busy with students and locals who love a bargain feed. There are set meals which are good value, as well as some tempting à la carte dishes, including fresh sashimi, agedashi tofu and mixed tempura.

Cinnamon Club
228 Carr Pl. Tel: 08-9228 1300. Open: L Mon–Fri, D daily. **$$** off map
Come to the Cinnamon Club for traditional Indian cuisine in a funky setting. The mixed tasting plate for starters is generous between two: sample dishes include lamb saag or the goat curry. Salmon fillets from the tandoor oven are moist and generous and great with mint yoghurt. The traditional Indian desserts are good, too.

Ria
106 Oxford St. Tel: 08-9328 2998. Open: D Tue–Sat. **$$** off map
If you have any interest in

Prices for a three-course dinner per person with a half-bottle of house wine:
$ = under AUS$25
$$ = AUS$25–40
$$$ = AUS$40–70
$$$$ = over AUS$70

Malaysian food, put Ria at the top of the list of restaurants to visit. From salty chunks of fish served on banana leaves to moist, caramelised duck, you'll find it difficult to choose what to order. The atmosphere is modern. Be sure to book in advance.

European

Duende
662 Newcastle St. www.duende.com.au. Tel: 08-9228 0123. Open: L Fri, D Mon–Sat. **$$$** off map
This nook of a restaurant ticks lots of boxes. Atmosphere? Definitely. Top-notch food? Certainly. Amazing wine list? Of course. Duende is a slice of Europe, serving tapas, cheese and other titbits in an elegant and funky setting. Ask for help with the wine list.

Fish

Kailis Bros Fish Market and Cafe
101 Oxford St. www.kailisbrosleederville.com.au. Tel: 08-9443 6300. Open: B, L & D daily. **$$** off map
On one side of the store is a counter selling some of the best fresh seafood in WA, and on the other side is a seafood restaurant. The Kailis family is one of the biggest local players in seafood, and you'll be guaranteed excellent quality, whether it's a fried snapper fillet or fresh tuna sashimi. There is another branch in Fremantle *(see page 145).*

Bars and Cafés

Andaluz Bar and Tapas
21 Howard St. Tel: 08-9481 0092. Open: Mon–Fri noon–late, Sat 6pm–late. ❸ p254, A3
This cutting-edge bar serves the finest cocktails in town, has a great wine and beer list and is always playing funky tunes. All this, complemented by some contemporary tapas, makes for a perfect night out.

Cino to Go
105 St George's Terrace. www.cinotogo.com. ❹ p254, A3
This is a local chain serving some of the best coffee and light food, such as muffins, coconut bread and fruit salad for breakfast, and salads and paninis for lunch.

Fibber McGee's
711 Newcastle St. Tel: 08-9227 0800. ❺ p254, A1
Fibber McGee's is an Irish pub with a good range of beers plus a menu big on comfort food. The steak-and-stout pie comes out looking like a pastry-topped football. All portions are on the large side, so beware when ordering.

Helvetica
Rear 101 St George's Terrace. Tel: 08-9321 4422. ❻ p254, A3
Perth's first whisky bar is a hidden gem. With a swanky outfit and comfortable chairs, enjoy a glass of the brown stuff. They also have a good wine selection.

Leederville Hotel
742 Newcastle St. Tel: 08-9286 0150. www.leedervillehotel.com. Open: L & D daily. ❼ p254, A1

The big nights at the Leederville are Wednesdays and Sundays, when a young crowd packs out the beer garden in summer and the indoor dance floor in winter.

The Lucky Shag Waterfront Bar
Barrack St Jetty. www.luckyshagbar.com.au. Tel: 08-9221 6011. Open 11am–late. ❽ p254, A4
This pub/bar overlooking the river has a good range of beers and wines, plus live music and DJs up to 4 nights a week. Food is available, too. In case you're wondering, shags are seabirds, and they are often seen perched by the water drying their wings.

Niche Bar
Off Oxford St (city end). Tel: 08-9227 1007. ❾ p254, A1
You'll find this hip bar by walking through the car park at the end of Oxford Street. Think 1970s – white shag pile and lots of couches.

The Paddington Ale House
141 Scarborough Beach Rd, Mount Hawthorn. ❿ p254, A1
Traditional and popular pub, this place is known to the locals simply as "the Paddo".

Steve's Nedlands Park Hotel
171 Broadway, Nedlands. Tel: 08-9386 3336. Open: daily. ⓫ p256, A4
Recently refurbished, this waterfront bar pulls out all the stops. With a tapas-style menu and a big wine list, sitting in the courtyard or inside by one of the fires in winter is a pleasant way to spend the day.

EAST PERTH

This former industrial area is being transformed into an attractive landscape with a contemporary feel and great leisure facilities, creating positive first impressions for visitors arriving from the airport

East Perth is becoming a spectacular gateway to the city, a sporting riverside precinct for living and socialising that is taking shape out of an industrial wasteland. Its main area, Riverside, is set to develop further over the next decade, but the rebuilding of East Perth is already a sight to see.

RIVER VIEWS

The deck of a boat on the Swan River is the ideal place to stand and take a first look at East Perth. Cruisers from Barrack Street Jetty motor past the north bank, where the slender light towers of the WACA (Western Australian Cricket Association) are prominent. Closer to the foreshore and its pilot wetlands area is the heritage-listed police headquarters; behind the WACA is the Gloucester Park harness-racing track.

Boats sail under the Causeway, passing Heirisson Island and its little colony of native kangaroos, before sighting the distinctive, pyramid-shaped Burswood Hotel and Casino complex on the south bank. But the best of East Perth is to come, on a northerly diversion off the Swan and into Claisebrook Cove, a stream of fresh water found and named by

Captain Stirling in his 1827 exploration of the river. He called it Clause Creek, after the ship's surgeon, Clause. When the city expanded, the area became the "East Ward" of Perth, and Clause Creek evolved into Claisebrook.

Leisure grounds at the mouth of the inlet give way to houses and apartments, with restaurants and cafés fringing the waterway. A footbridge, Trafalgar Bridge, crosses Claisebrook, and footpaths and cycle paths run around it. One of Perth's

LEFT: Trafalgar Bridge over Claisebrook.
RIGHT: boating in Claisebrook Cove.

TIP

To get to East Perth from the city centre, you can take the free Yellow CAT bus from Wellington Street to Trafalgar Road.

best restaurants, Lamont's East Perth, looks over the water to Burswood.

Cruise boats can go no further along the waterway, but you can proceed on foot. The elimination of motor traffic and the encouragement of walking and bike riding is part of the East Perth ethos.

VICTORIA GARDENS

Start at **Victoria Gardens ❶**, at the mouth of Claisebrook on the city side (access is from Royal Street). Free barbecues, picnic tables under the trees, a pavilion looking over the inlet and free parking make this a popular spot for families at weekends. Grassy slopes lead down to the river and inlet.

An interesting architectural mix is a vital element of the new East Perth. Influences range from oriental, Regency and traditional European to concrete and steel with a broad spectrum of materials and colours to match that diversity. This is inner-city living with style. Everyone has a veranda, patio or terrace, but there's no space for private gardens. This makes public areas like Victoria Gardens all the busier.

Like so much of Perth, Claisebrook is an ancient area with powerful Aboriginal links. This river-bank area is known as Nganga Batta's Mooditcher (Sunshine's Living Strength) and is a place of hope and friendship for Aboriginal people. The standing stones on the foreshore form a winding trail – the *Illa Kurri Sacred Dreaming Path* – that describes the chain of lakes and wetlands spanning the land before Perth was built. An inscription tells us that this is the route home walked by initiates through the Claisebrook Valley, leading from one freshwater lake to another. Each of the granite stones is named after an individual lake.

Also on the foreshore is the *Charnock Woman* ceramic pavement, which tells the story of an evil woman who

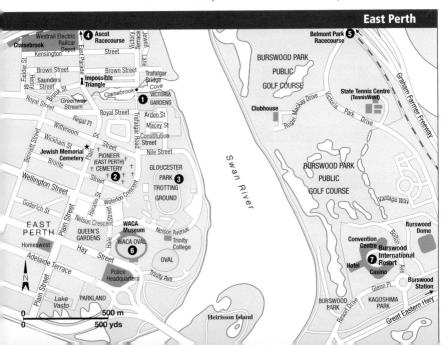

stole children in the Dreamtime, and the Yoondoorup Boorn, an old river gum that was removed, treated and returned to the site at the request of the Noongar people. Their ancestors who camped here used its burnt and split trunk as a hiding place for messages and goods.

ART TRAIL

These icons are a good starting point to explore East Perth's Art Trail. When redevelopment started in the early 1990s, state government allocated one percent of the cost of landscape and architectural projects to public art. The results are dotted along the banks of the inlet and throughout East Perth.

EPRA (East Perth Redevelopment Authority; www.epra.wa.gov.au) can provide detailed information and leaflets on the Art Trail and other aspects of the continuing development.

Follow the path up Claisebrook Cove by the waterside, fringed with sand washed clean by the Swan. A colonnade of ochre-stained limestone pillars cut into the hillside of Victoria Gardens houses the 14-metre (46ft)-long *Niche Wall Mural*. This powerful relief, in fiery colours, is an allegory by artist Joanna Lefroy Capelle on the history and redevelopment of East Perth.

Stone steps alongside – adorned with steel swans – lead up to Victoria Gardens Shelter, an iconic European folly that pays tribute to the graceful 19th-century creations of architects such as Richard Roche Jewell.

The waterside path continues under the footbridge spanning Claisebrook, around well-kept gardens of native shrubs, and into the main cove where a few select cafés and restaurants provide the opportunity to sit, eat, drink and enjoy the

ABOVE: Claisebrook Cove. **BELOW:** *The Impossible Triangle*.

To prevent indiscriminate Burials and unpleasant consequences arising there from in a warm climate, a Burial Ground will be set apart in Every Township or Parish... Burials will take place in them only and a Register will be kept... all Burials by the Chaplain will be restricted to times as soon after sunrise as possible, or an hour precisely before sunset...

Colonial Secretary's Office, Perth, 13 February 1830

ABOVE RIGHT: a stone angel watches over the Pioneer Cemetery.

view. In front of a Korean restaurant built into the Victoria Cove apartment complex is one of artist Mark Cox's sculptured seats. Three of these around the inlet recall industrial history, using recycled jarrah timber on a theme of pulleys, beams and rollers. A wooden jetty within a few steps of the restaurants allows patrons to sail in, tie up and enjoy the amenities.

A trickle of water flowing over rough-hewn stone blocks marks the point where the brook flows into Claisebrook Cove. Follow the path through an archway along the trickle (you'll barely notice the busy East Parade road above). Stone turtle shells in the stream are another artwork – *Turtle Walk*, symbolic of the Noongar people's journey to ceremonial grounds at Mount Eliza (Kings Park).

Past the archway, the water widens into the Greenway Stream, with a fountain in its centre. Look right, up to East Parade and the most spectacular of East Perth's public art pieces. *The Impossible Triangle* is a landmark in gleaming steel set on a large traffic roundabout. Made by artists Brian McKay and Ahmad Abas, it was inspired by a 1950s concept of mathematician Sir Roger Penrose, and only appears as a complete and perfect triangle from two perspectives.

Further on, in Boan Place, is the *Red Surveyor*, a carved wooden figure atop a pillar. The restored red-brick building behind the sculpture, now used for art events, was once the warehouse of Boans, Perth's foremost department store.

Turtle Walk continues as the stream narrows again and passes two small paperbark trees growing out of the water. Many of the pieces on the Art Trail celebrate the importance of water, such as *Drinking Fountain* and *Spring*, marking the end of the route after Brook Street.

Return to Victoria Gardens by retracing your steps, or walk along **Royal Street**, a commercial and residential mix that has the feel of a new town, setting the tone of Riverside and new Perth precincts of the future.

The Graves of Pioneer Cemetery

Church records, copied years later from faded sheets, show the first person interred in the Pioneer Cemetery was John Mitchell, a 22-year-old private of the 63rd Regiment who died on 6 January 1830, a few months after the foundation of the settlement. In 1831 William Stirling, the infant son of Governor Stirling, who died in an epidemic, was also buried here. It's the first of many names inscribed on headstones in the cemetery. Also here is the grave of Walter Padbury, a destitute orphan who became WA's first millionaire and the first mayor of Guildford, one of WA's earliest settlements.

Like Padbury, many of the cemetery's occupants are commemorated in WA place names. There's John Septimus Roe, first surveyor-general; Sir Luke Samuel Leake, first speaker of the legislative council; John Burdett Wittenoom, first colonial chaplain; Frederick Durck Wittenoom, sheriff of the colony; and Bishop Hale, first bishop of the colony and founder of Hale School. Goldwyer, Harding and Panton are less famous names – "three young surveyors who were speared to death while sleeping on a headland of Lagrange country Roebuck Bay, with Maitland Brown, who risked his own life to recover the bodies..."

Pioneer Cemetery

Address: corner of Plain and Bronte streets
Opening Hrs: Sun 2–4pm
Entrance Fee: small donation

A short walk up Plain Street off Royal Street presents an intriguing paradox. East Perth, the newest, fastest-growing locality in the city, also contains the colony's earliest link with its own history.

Two new town houses on Plain Street have unique back gardens. Peer through their iron gates, and you'll find the **Jewish Memorial Cemetery**. The houses are built over the original Hebrew burial grounds that opened in 1867. About 30 people were buried here before a new cemetery opened for people of all faiths in 1899.

Strictly speaking, this and the cemetery on the other side of Plain Street make up East Perth Cemeteries. But Australians don't much like speaking strictly, and everyone calls it the **Pioneer Cemetery ❷**.

Opened at the governor's command in the earliest days of the colony, it once included separate sections for seven different religious faiths.

Perhaps because East Perth was used for industry and was therefore less desirable than other parts of the city, the graveyard survived the pressure and demands of urban sprawl. Around 10,000 people were buried here before it was closed in 1899, but only around 800 grave sites can now be identified. Some burials in vaults and existing family graves went on until 1924.

GLOUCESTER PARK AND WACA

Life on the other side of Cemetery Hill couldn't be livelier. Plain Street runs all the way down to the river and to various sports stadia. There's harness racing at Gloucester Park, cricket at the WACA, tennis and golf over the Swan at Burswood, and thoroughbred racing at the Belmont and Ascot racetracks.

Nelson Crescent leads off Plain Street to the WACA and Gloucester Park and also to **Queen's Gardens**, the first public park in Perth, created in 1899 out of clay-pits that for 50 years supplied bricks for buildings such as Perth Town Hall. Lily ponds and English trees show the gardens' British influences, as does the 1927 replica of Sir George Frampton's statue of Peter Pan. The original of

ABOVE: Peter Pan statue, a copy of the one in London's Kensington Gardens, in Perth's Queen's Gardens.
BELOW: visit Gloucester Park on Fridays for harness racing.

Know the Form at the Trots

To appreciate Gloucester Park racing it's useful to know your trotters from your pacers. Harness-racing horses are all standard-breds, trained to pull a driver in a light, two-wheeled sulky. Standard-bred horses are smaller than thoroughbreds, with heavier bones, a larger body, shorter legs and with greater endurance. They are less temperamental than thoroughbreds, which means their racing form is more predictable (many punters believe the favourite is more likely to win in harness racing than in other types of racing).

Trotters and pacers all pull sulkys, but run differently. Trotters move with a diagonal gait (left front and right rear legs move together, followed by the right front and left rear legs). Pacers have a lateral gait, which means moving both legs on the same side forward in unison. Most harness racing is for pacers, because the pacing gait is easier to teach and maintain. A collection of straps (hopples) connecting the front and rear legs on each side help the pacer balance its stride. Galloping is not allowed, and if a horse gallops or breaks stride the driver must pull up the horse and coax it back into the approved gait. Breaking is less likely with pacers because of the hopples.

Gloucester Park ❸ comes alive as crowds pack through its Indian Raj-style gateway for a full card of harness racing – known around Perth as "the trots".

Harness racing has been in Australia for more than 130 years. Racing here is a spectacle to appeal to all ages. It's advertised as a good family night out, and there are childcare facilities as well as restaurants and bars. Like many clubs, it caters for newcomers with a "meet and greet" service, if you make advance contact. Usually meetings have between six and nine races. The track is quite short at around 800 metres/yards, so the whole race can be followed from the stands.

Ascot Racecourse

Address: 70 Grandstand Road, www.perthracing.com.au
Tel: 08-9277 0713
Opening Hrs: Sat 8.30am–5pm
Entrance Fee: charge
Transport: On race days free parking is available at both racetracks; Path Transit buses for Ascot leave from the City Busport (Stand D7)

J. M. Barrie's boy who never grew up is in London's Kensington Gardens: Perth's copy, autographed by Barrie, was bought by the Rotary Club of Perth for the children of WA.

Australia's love of horses and racing is deeply embedded in the cultural psyche. Europeans introduced the horse to the continent, along with the camel and buffalo. Henry Lawson's poem *The Man from Snowy River* is, perhaps, Australia's best-loved piece of literature; the army's light horsemen have been internationally celebrated in films such as *Gallipoli*.

Gloucester Park

Address: Nelson Crescent, www.gloucesterpark.com.au
Tel: 08-9323 3555
Opening Hrs: Mon–Fri 8.30am–4.30pm
Entrance Fee: charge

Country race meetings are social events that draw visitors for days of partying. In Perth, though, the Aussie thirst for racing and gambling is served year-round. On Friday evenings

EAT

Ascot has an alfresco barbecue restaurant, but for the full race-goer's experience the Terrace restaurant in the main grandstand offers spectacular views of the racing while you enjoy a meal from the buffet or carvery, with full tote and beverage service plus a personal TV monitor to watch the photo finishes. To book a table, tel: 08-9277 0777.

With its grand 1900s buildings and grandstand, **Ascot** ❹ is WA's principal racecourse and used for summer racing (in winter the action moves to nearby Belmont Park). Ascot's 300-metre/yd inclining straight is regarded by experts as the toughest test of stayers in Australia.

A spacious and attractive course, Ascot makes for a good day out. Weekend entry prices are low (children under 16 are free), and midweek meetings are free for everyone. Special events such as the Spring Carnival, Melbourne Cup Day and New Year's Day draw many thousands of race-goers and party-goers. Entry prices are higher for these special days, so check the Ascot website for information about special events.

On New Year's Day an acre of lush paddock is transformed into a party zone for a summer party that packs in 14,000 race-goers with more interest in hats, frocks and party streamers than racing silks. Transperth runs special buses every 15 minutes for such meetings.

ABOVE: match in progress at the WACA.
BELOW LEFT: harness racing in action.

Belmont Park racecourse

Address: Victoria Park Drive, Burswood, www.perthracing.com.au
Tel: 08-9277 0777
Opening Hrs: Sat 8.30am–5pm
Entrance Fee: charge

Belmont Park ❺ is Perth's winter racecourse. It lies on a spur of land opposite the East Perth Power Station, now being regenerated as the hub of a new cultural centre. Surrounded by the river on three sides, Belmont is accessed along the Graham Farmer Freeway, which crosses the Swan on the Goongoonup Bridge. This prime site is ripe for development; Perth Racing plans to build a massive apartment and leisure complex to take full advantage of its location so close to central Perth.

Unlike winter National Hunt racing in the UK and other countries, Belmont Park has no jumps. Good drainage makes it one of the best wet-weather tracks in Australia, which ensures racing in rain, hail or shine. Also, at Belmont everything is fully enclosed, ensuring race-goers are warm and comfortable while enjoying spectacular views. (Anyone who has trudged ankle-deep in mud and betting slips across older tracks of the northern hemisphere will appreciate the relative luxury of the Australian experience.)

Western Australian Cricket Association (WACA)

Address: Nelson Crescent, www.waca.com.au
Tel: 08-9265 7222
Opening Hrs: Mon–Fri 8.30am–5pm
Entrance Fee: charge

If gambling is an Australian addiction, cricket is another. There are few better places to experience the national sport in all its forms than the grounds of the **WACA** ❻, WA's governing cricket body founded in 1885. More than 40

SHOP

Racecourse shops at both Ascot and Belmont sell a wide range of horsey souvenirs, including full-size racing silks.

days of first-class cricket are played each summer season (Oct–Mar) ranging through international one-day matches, Test matches and inter-state contests. Some games are played at night under state-of-the-art lighting that makes night seem like day.

Variations on traditional cricket include the fast-action 20-20 competition, in which each side has only 20 overs of batting. The first time this was tried the WACA was filled to its capacity of around 24,000. But there are other times when it is as tranquil as a match on a village green, with a small crowd enjoying the laid-back ambience of a four-day game. Grandstands at each end provide ample undercover seating to keep off the sun, and on each side of the ground are grassy banks where picnickers stretch out on the turf and while away the day, and kids play their own matches.

ABOVE: the distinctive 70-metre (230ft) -high lights of the WACA are an integral part of the cityscape. **BELOW:** there is a smart-casual dress code in the members' area.

Entry prices are low (sometimes even free), except for the Test and international one-day matches, when prior booking is essential. The WACA provides special shuttles on match days, running to the ground from the Wellington Street Train Station, via the bus station; regular bus services to Nelson Crescent include the free red CAT bus.

Even if there isn't a match to watch, you may want to visit the WACA's **Museum** (Mon–Fri 10am–3pm; small charge; tours of museum and ground 10am and 1pm Tue, Wed and Thur), where you can discover more about the history of the club and many of the great international cricketers, such as Bradman, Lillee, Marsh, Sobers and W.G. Grace.

BURSWOOD

West of the Goongoonup Bridge, the **Burswood Entertainment Complex ❼** is one of Australia's best-known resort developments. The original 413-room InterContinental Burswood pyramidal hotel and the permanently inflated Dome, used for concerts and sporting events such as the annual Hopman Cup international tennis tournament, were built in the 1980s. To the north new apartment blocks have risen and are fully occupied.

Burswood Park Public Golf Course

Address: Rodger Mackay Drive, www.burswoodparkgolfcourse.com
Tel: 08-9362 7576 or 08-9470 2992
Opening Hrs: Nov–Mar 6am–sunset, Apr–Oct 7am–sunset; book in advance
Entrance Fee: charge

Burswood is surrounded by 100 hectares (250 acres) of landscaped gardens and parklands. The sports facilities are open to everyone, not just the hotel guests.

The 18-hole course is challenging, with nine lakes and two creeks coming into play on 15 holes. A

driving range and putting and chipping greens are available until 8pm Mon–Thur and until 7pm Fri–Sun. Clubs, buggies and tuition are available; as usual, neat and tidy dress standards apply.

WA's **State Tennis Centre** (tel: 08-9361 1112) is also on the Burswood peninsula. It's one of Australia's largest tennis complexes, with 15 hard courts, including a covered show court, an open Rebound Ace court and 13 Plexi-Cushion courts. Courts and equipment can be hired seven days a week, day or night. Three court-side gazebos provide a setting for a casual drink or barbecue after a game. Alternatively the centre can supply you with beer, wine and soft drinks.

Burswood's casino

Two-up is not exactly a sport – but it's certainly a traditional Australian game, a national favourite that's been played (generally illegally) all over

the country. It's unique to Australian casinos, and when Burswood was opened in 1985 two pennies were tossed into the air in the two-up ring to mark the event.

In this simple game, the spinner sets two coins on a small wooden skip, which is then used to throw them into the air above head height. Players bet on whether both coins come down heads or tails. A croupier ringkeeper decides if the spin is valid or not, and if you guess right you're paid even money.

The casino offers all the usual gambling options of course, such as blackjack, roulette, baccarat, pai gow, poker, and Caribbean stud and craps, all available 24 hours a day, except Christmas Day, Good Friday and Anzac Day. A total of 180 gaming tables is on offer, 140 located on the main gaming floor and a further 40 available for members and VIP players in the International and Pearl Rooms. ❑

ABOVE: a distant view of Burswood Entertainment Complex
BELOW: the WA state cricket team is known as the Retravision Warriors.

BEST RESTAURANTS, BAKERIES AND BARS

Restaurants

Asian

Basil Leaves
82 Royal St. Tel: 08-9221 8999. Open: L & D Mon–Fri. **$$** 28 p255, D3
Serves beautifully presented Asian cuisine, with an emphasis on Thai and Vietnamese dishes. Lots of the dishes have big fresh flavours which go well with a cold beer on a hot day. For the cooler months of the year, there are plenty of phad dishes and soups. The staff are very friendly and the atmosphere is modern and welcoming.

Joe's Oriental Diner
Hyatt Regency, 99 Adelaide Tce. Tel: 08-9225 1268. Open: L Mon–Fri, D Mon–Sat. **$$** 29 p255, C4

Picture yourself in British colonial Singapore – wicker bird cages, cane chairs and wooden tables. Joe's Oriental Diner looks the part. Joe's serves a great range of dishes from Singapore, Malaysia and Thailand, and the brown paper menus even carry a chilli rating (beware, these chilli ratings are serious, so anything sporting three chillis or more is very, very hot). The service is unobtrusive.

Viet Royal
Cnr Royal and Plain Sts. Tel: 08-9221 2388. Open: D daily. **$$** 30 p255, D3
Traditional Vietnamese cuisine showcasing the best this style of cooking has to offer. The atmosphere is calm and comfortable, reflecting owner Kim Ha's gentle and generous personality. You can also BYO, and there's a bottle shop located just a short stroll away.

Yu
Burswood Entertainment Complex. Tel: 08-9362 7551. Open: D daily, L Sun–Fri. **$$$$** 31 p255, D2
Offering some of the best Chinese cuisine in Perth, Yu's tends to take classic Chinese dishes and give them a contemporary twist. Its signature dishes include melt-in-your-mouth Szechuan sliced filet steak, Portuguese stuffed crabs and Peking duck. Service is slick and the wine list is extensive.

Australian

Amuse Restaurant
64 Bronte St. www.restaurantamuse.com. Tel: 08-9325 4900. Open: D Tue–Sun 7pm–late. **$$$** 32 p255, C3
This is one of Perth's premiere degustation destinations and has a string of awards to prove it. The nine-course menu starts at AUS$120 per person; to have dinner matched with wine, add another AUS$70. Flavours married together such as beetroot, coffee and cocoa, or snapper, hazelnut and bone marrow, should get your attention.

Ba Ba black
25/60 Royal St. Tel: 08-9221 1363. Open: B & L daily. **$** 33 p255, D3
On weekends you'll find this little café packed with locals, who come for its great breakfasts – stacked pancakes with berries, and scrambled eggs with smoked salmon. It is totally relaxed and the ideal place to spend a leisurely mealtime with friends and the weekend newspapers.

Chanterelle at Jessica's
Hyatt Centre, Adelaide Terrace. www.chanterelleatjessicas.com.au. Tel: 08-9325 2511. Open: L Mon–Fri, D daily. **$$$** 34 p255, C4
This is a fine-dining seafood restaurant, although meat eaters are looked after too. The fish-of-the-day is always outstanding, often served grilled with a butter sauce and a side of seasonal vegetables. This may sound too uncomplicated for some, but paired with the lovely views over the Swan, it is very hard to beat.

Cream
Suite 2/11 Regal Pl. www.creamrestaurant.com.au. Tel: 08-9221 0404. Open: D Tue–Sat. **$$$** 35 p255, D3
Cream is cosy, intimate, relaxed and sophisticated, all at the same time. Chef/owner John Mead is passionate about creating food that is unpretentious, yet top quality. Everything from pasta to

LEFT: for extravagant dining, visit Friends.

sauces is freshly made in the kitchen, with the exception of the New Norcia bread. Specialities include crispy-skinned Tasmanian salmon with spicy potato and aubergine salad, and passionfruit soufflé with a fabulous Belgian white chocolate sorbet.

Friends Restaurant

Hyatt Centre, 20 Terrace Rd. www.friendsrestaurant.com.au. Tel: 08-9221 0885. Open: L Tue–Fri, D Tue–Sat. **$$$$** p255, C4

This is undeniably one of Perth's poshest restaurants, featuring a massive wine list of aged, rare and simply stunning wines. The food is similarly extravagant - pheasant layered with foie gras and braised cabbage, wrapped in pastry with celeriac purée and jus; wagyu beef, mushroom ragout, gnocchi, buttered sage, broad beans with a shiraz and thyme jus. There is also a tasting menu including wine for around AUS$145 per head.

Gershwin's

Hyatt Regency, 99 Adelaide Terrace. www.gershwins.com. au. Tel: 08-9225 1274. Open: D Thur–Sat. **$$$** 37 p255, C4

This award-winning place has the feel of a New York

Prices for a three-course dinner per person with a half-bottle of house wine:

$ = under AUS$25
$$ = AUS$25–40
$$$ = AUS$40–70
$$$$ = over AUS$70

restaurant from the 1920s, with cocktail bar, lounge, three dining areas and a grand piano. The menu includes many gastronomic delicacies. These are often served in surprising combinations, such as freshwater crayfish bisque with ceviche of scallops and confit salmon.

Lamont's

11 Brown St. www.lamonts. com.au. Tel: 08-9202 1566. Open: L & D Wed–Sun. **$$$** 38 p255, D3

Kate Lamont is one of Perth's best-loved foodies, and her riverside East Perth property is a mecca for those devoted to the plate. Serving freshly prepared and tasty dishes showcasing the best in local produce, Kate has a devoted local following.

Origins

Sheraton Hotel, 207 Adelaide Terrace. Tel: 08-9224 7777. Open: D Wed–Sat. **$$$$** 39 p254, C4

Put on your glad rags and enjoy an elegant meal at Origins. With high ceilings, dimmed lights and a view across the pool, it offers a lovely setting. The style might be described as French-Australian. The menu tends to favour traditional dishes done in innovative ways - think sliced scallops with witlof and prosciutto.

Sirocco

Burswood Entertainment Complex. Tel: 08-9362 7551. Open: B, L & D daily.

Bars

The Royal on the Waterfront

60 Royal St. www.theroyaleast perth.com. Tel: 08-9221 0466. 12 p255, D3
Hand-crafted Colonial beers, waterfront views and a modern take on pub grub make the Royal on the Waterfront an easy-going drinking hole.

$$ 40 p255, D2
Located on the ground floor of the Holiday Inn at Burswood, Sirocco offers a multitude of experiences for any time of the day. The chef de cuisine Simone Bajin has designed an extensive menu, and you can pop in on a Sunday afternoon for tapas and live music, chill out on the veranda with a glass of wine and a duck confit pizza, or perhaps indulge in a dozen oysters.

Broken Hill Hotel Bar Restaurant

314 Albany Hwy, Victoria Park. www.brokenhillhotel.com.au. Tel: 08-9361 1038. 13 p259, E2
An Art Deco building with a relaxed atmosphere serving good food, a wide selection of beers on tap and a lounge in which to enjoy all.

Bakery

Le Croissant on the Cove

108 Royal St. Tel: 08-9325 9494. Open: B & L Tue–Sun. **$** 41 p255, D3
This patisserie creates sensational breads, amazing croissants and fantastic cakes. For a snack on the go, you can also run in and pick up a quick boulangerie snack to take away. It is well known as one of the best bakeries in town.

RIGHT: wise words from the American writer.

"Life is Uncertain... Eat Dessert First"
Ernestine Ulmer

NORTHBRIDGE

Cross the Horseshoe Bridge north of the CBD
to reach Northbridge. This characterful area
offers a wealth of heritage-listed buildings
and the liveliest nightlife in Perth

Main Attractions

RUSSELL SQUARE
BREADBOX GALLERY
PIAZZA NANNI
ABERDEEN STREET HERITAGE
 PRECINCT
PLATEIA HELLAS
MONEY STREET

Maps and Listings

MAP OF NORTHBRIDGE,
 PAGE 114
RESTAURANTS AND BARS,
 PAGES 118–9
ACCOMMODATION, PAGES
 223–5

Cut off from the city centre by the Perth–Fremantle railway as well as major roads, Northbridge, an old and distinctive neighbourhood, has evolved separately from the CBD, even though it is just a short hop over the Horseshoe Bridge. But all that changed in 2009 with the completion of the "Northbridge Link", which reunited Northbridge with the city centre by submerging part of the railway and linking King Street on the south with Northbridge's Lake Street in a continuous stream of galleries, cafés and entertainments. One of the most important elements of the development project is a new entertainment and sports stadium, still under construction.

Efforts are being made to preserve the distinctive architectural heritage of the area. The New Northbridge project has identified 70 significant heritage buildings in four areas: Lindsay and Money streets; Aberdeen Street; Parry Street; and the Talbot Hobbs Heritage Precinct (an information booklet and self-guided walking trail on each area is available from http://epra.wa.gov.au).

The people of Northbridge

The longest-established communities of Perth, after the Aborigines and the British, are Mediterranean Europeans, who began arriving in WA after World War II. The dome of the Greek Orthodox Cathedral in Russell Square is a striking symbol of the times. The next significant wave of immigrants was Asian, and the little Chinatown at the east end of James and Roe streets shows its influence.

A Mediterranean atmosphere prevails in Northbridge on long summer

LEFT: Danny Moss plays a guest spot at the Perth Jazz Club in Northbridge's Hyde Park Hotel. **RIGHT:** the Horseshoe Bridge separates the CBD from Northbridge.

ABOVE: sunglasses, bush hat and a towel – one of the cast-iron artworks on Russell Square.

evenings. The area is ideal for strolling in the early evening, alfresco dining, and dawdling as you watch the passing parade. The intersection of Lake and James streets, the hub of the entertainment district, is a good place to sit over a bottle of wine or a coffee and take Northbridge's pulse. Almost every restaurant makes use of the pavement, and on a warm evening they're all bustling.

Heritage walk

When colonists first arrived, the area was swampy lakeland, but in the 1840s it was drained, and market gardens flourished in the rich soil. Building spread north from the river and central Perth, and in 1861 the railway was taken through. After this, people began talking about "north of the line" and, eventually, Northbridge.

West along **James Street**, opposite Rosie O'Grady's, is leafy **Russell Square ❶**, a traditional meeting place for Aboriginal people and now,

with its elegant town houses and new builds, a meeting place for everyone. Central to the rejuvenated square is the Pagoda artwork and bandstand, where concerts are regularly held. The cast-iron artworks represent WA's development and Northbridge's diversity: the granite galleon symbolises European influence; the pagoda the Asian community's impact on the area; the bronze snake and bearded dragon represent the natural environment; and a child's school bag, hope for the future. Fun and entertainment are represented by a bush hat, towel and sunglasses.

Walk further along James Street, checking the **Breadbox Gallery** on the way to **Fitzgerald Street**. Part of Artrage, an alternative arts organisation based near the Western Australian Museum *(see page 95)*, this gallery often has avant-garde shows.

A right turn on Fitzgerald leads to St Brigid's Church and the **Piazza Nanni ❷**, named in honour of

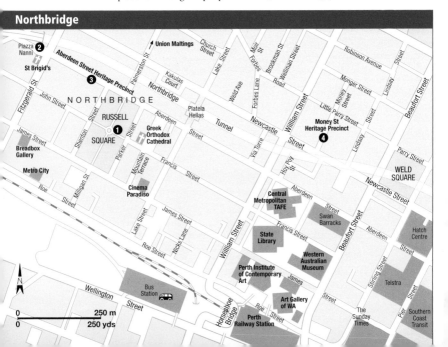

Father Nanni, St Brigid's parish priest for many years. Built on land reclaimed when the Graham Farmer tunnel cut through Northbridge, the granite piazza contrasts with the traditional red-brick and sandstone church buildings.

Look down onto the freeway emerging from the tunnel. This was Perth's biggest road-building enterprise in years. It cut a swath through Northbridge, taking out many old buildings, but also opening up new areas such as Piazza Nanni, and Plateia Hellas on Lake Street.

New streets bearing the names of notable local citizens reflect the international diversity of the area: Kakulas Court, Hoy Poy Street, Via Torre, Grigoroff Road and Zempilas Road among them. Edie Hoy Poy received an Order of Australia Medal for work in the Chinese community; the Kakulas family was a pillar of the Greek community; the Torre Italian family was renowned for its traditional butcher's store. Most notable of all was Bulgarian doctor Bogoslav Grigoroff, whose multilingual skills enabled him to serve many sections of Perth's migrant population. In

hard times he accepted bags of vegetables as payment for his services.

Opposite Piazza Nanni is the start of the **Aberdeen Street Heritage Precinct ❸**, with colourful houses and shops in a range of architectural styles. Many eminent early Perthites chose to live here, away from the bustle of the city and close to Russell Square.

The shops and houses at the west end of Aberdeen were less grand, generally built as matching pairs in Federation Queen Anne, Bungalow or Free Classical style. Most striking of these (No. 182) is the bright blue-painted antique shop of Vincenzo Rizzo, built for Braddock's Dispensary in the 1890s (the name remains in the upper masonry).

A modern Art Deco-style iron fence and gate, incorporating aircraft, cars and plant motifs, is a later addition to the well-balanced double-fronted No. 176. Victorian Italianate style is in evidence at Nos 162 and

ABOVE: leafy, laid-back Northbridge.
LEFT: Cinema Paradiso on James Street is an independent cinema that shows arthouse films.

ABOVE: an emblematic monkey hangs outside the Brass Monkey, one of Northbridge's best-known bars and restaurants. **RIGHT:** the area takes on a different flavour at night.

166, both dating from the gold boom and prosperous early 1890s.

The first owner of No. 162, now a backpackers' hostel, was Frederick Monger, a merchant and parliamentarian. (His family's mausoleum is one of the grandest in East Perth's Pioneer Cemetery, *see page 104*). His former home was a private hospital in World War I; apartments in the 1930s–50s; and a girls' refuge run by the Daughters of Charity in the 1960s, when the front room was turned into a chapel for prayers.

The first building on Aberdeen Street, a fine Victorian house at No. 156, was built in 1883 for WA's postmaster general, Richard Shollis. The south side of Aberdeen is entirely commercial now, but there is a splash of colour at the van-hire yard of Wicked Campers *(see page 221)*, aimed at the touring backpackers living over the road. Each vehicle comes ready-daubed with choice graffiti.

Palmerston Street (north, off Aberdeen) is filling with new apartments. At the far end, the historic Union Maltings has been restored, turning rambling factories into 300

new homes around a central lawn, pool, barbecue and gym area. Some units retain huge steel girders running through the walls, and solid jarrah floors. There's a small **Museum** of artefacts and photographs of 1900s maltings operations, and sculptures made from industrial bits and pieces spread around the complex.

On the east corner where **Newcastle Street** crosses Palmerston is a small heritage precinct of cottages by the Perth architect Sir J. J. Talbot Hobbs. A Londoner, Hobbs emigrated to WA in 1887 and soon became a leading figure in his field, winning an 1891 competition to design the Weld Club (Barrack Street). He was president of the WA Institute of Architects by 1909, and created substantial buildings across Perth and Fremantle.

But it was as Major-General Hobbs that Talbot gained his highest honour, when knighted for wartime service. The young architect first volunteered for Britain's 1st Cinque Ports Artillery, and on arrival in Perth joined the Volunteer Field Artillery.

Club Land

Northbridge is known for its vibrant nightlife, and in particular the area has a reputation for its vital and thriving music scene. Most clubs and late-night bars are aimed at the young twenty-somethings with cash to splash, and the hot-spots evolve, move and change names quite frequently. For all current music venues and gigs, check out the music section in the *West Australian*, which is published daily, or *X-Press*, a free magazine that lists all the latest happenings on the town.

Well-established clubs include **Metropolis** on Roe Street, a spectacular building designed with multiple levels to view the thrust stage; major touring artists usually appear here. Other possibilities include **Geisha** (135a James Street, above Novaks Tavern), featuring up-and-coming local acts; the **Mustang Bar** (46 Lake Street), specialising in live swing and funk bands; **Bar Open** (234 William Street) is a quality bar with DJ music.

Lastly, if you want to hang out with the bands, the **Moon Café** (323 William Street) is a late-nighter much favoured by musicians winding down after their own gigs in other Northbridge clubs.

In 1916 he went to France with the AIF, rose to Major-General and was knighted in 1919.

The small houses on Newcastle Street recall the start of Hobbs's career as an architect, when the population boom of the early 1890s inspired building in some unlikely locations. Hobbs built his cottages in modest Federation Bungalow style as investments to rent out. The contrast with his great works – such as the WA War Memorial in Kings Park, the Weld Club and the Savoy Hotel, couldn't be greater.

Plateia Hellas

A right turn on Newcastle leads to Money Street Heritage Precinct. En route, turn first into Lake Street to the substantial **Plateia Hellas** and its Nexus artwork formed from seven ribbed terrazzo columns, polished concrete pillars based on classical Greek architecture, interspersed with seven illuminated water jets. The square, which is especially attractive at night, was completed in 2003 to celebrate Northbridge's Greek community.

Money Street

In **Money Street ❹** English plane trees meet in a leafy canopy above early cottages and the (closed) Mackays Mineral Waters factory.

Little Parry Street, behind the factory, leads to Lindsay Street's 1893 flour mill and bakery. The restored building is next door to EPRA (www. epra.wa.gov.au), the government agency overseeing the East Perth and Northbridge redevelopment and a good place for current information on both areas. Little Parry Street ends at Beaufort Street at an 1897 Federation Free Classical building, with tuck-point brickwork and unpainted rendering. Its first occupants are named in the moulded top parapet – Manchester Dye Works and Lung Cheong Laundry.

From Beaufort, follow Newcastle back to the entertainment area via William Street. Upper parts of many Perth commercial establishments are original gold-rush-era work. A newer one in striking Art Deco with an impressive vertical clock can be seen above a pizza shop where Newcastle Street meets William Street. ❑

BELOW: Northbridge tattoo parlour.

BEST RESTAURANTS AND BARS

Restaurants

Asian

9 Fine Food
227–229 Bulwer St. Tel:
08-9227 9999. Open: D
Mon–Sat. **$$$** 42 p254, B1
Chef-owner Muneki Song
creates elegant, modern
Japanese cuisine with a
European influence. Bis-
tro-style ambience.

Dusit Thai
249 James St. www.dusitthai.
com.au. Tel: 08-9328 7647.
Open: L Thur and Fri, D
Tue–Sun. **$$** 43 p254, A2
One of the best Thai res-
taurants in Perth. The
dishes are flavoursome.
Favourites include mas-
saman curry and prawns
in tamarind sauce.

**Gogo's Madras Curry
House**
556 Beaufort St. Tel:
08-9328 1828. Open: D
Mon–Sat. **$$** 44 p254, C1
The Indian cricket team
dine here when in town.
Gogo cooks seriously
good food, with the menu
extending beyond the
obvious fare.

Little Saigon
489 Beaufort St. Tel:
08-9227 5586. Open: D
Tue–Sun. **$** 45 p254, C1
This little restaurant has a
groovy red-and-white fit-
out and serves authentic
Vietnamese food. Try the
prawns on sugar cane
starter and the goat-and-
aubergine curry. Good
value and you can BYO.

Maya Masala
49 Lake St. www.mayamasala.
net. Tel: 08-9328 5655.
Open: L & D daily. **$** 46
p254, A2
Serves authentic South

Indian cuisine, including
filled dosas and good-
value thali plates – mini
servings of curries, rice,
poppadom, naan bread,
pickle and a rice dessert.

The Red Teapot
413 William St. Tel: 08-9228
1981. Open: L & D Mon–
Sat. **$** 47 p254, B1
It's small, funky and
serves great Hong Kong-
style Chinese. Signature
dishes include honey king
prawns and salt-and-chilli
squid. Cash only, BYO.

Sparrow
434 William St. Tel: 08-9328
5660. Open: L Fri–Sat, D
Mon–Sat. **$** 48 p254, B1
Sparrow serves Indone-
sian food – not top quali-
ty, but good enough and
ridiculously cheap. The
most expensive dish is a
yellow curry fish fillet at a
whopping AUS$7.50. You
can BYO. Cash only.

**Toba Oriental Dining
House**
340 Beaufort St. Tel: 08-
9227 1191. Open: L Thur–
Fri, D Tue–Sun. **$$** 49
p254, B1
Serves excellent Thai,
Malay and Indonesian
food. Try the tom yum
soup with king prawns.

Viet Hoa
349 William St. Tel: 08-9328
2127. Open: L & D daily. **$**
50 p254, B2
The biggest Vietnamese
restaurant in Northbridge.
It's not fine dining, but

the food is reasonable
and cheap.

Australian

**BrassGrill at the Brass
Monkey**
209 William St. Tel: 08-9227
9596. Open: D Tue–Sat. **$$**
51 p254, A2
The Brass Monkey is a
well-loved Northbridge
watering hole, with the
upstairs chargrill restau-
rant showcasing fine pro-
duce from WA, including
Mt Barker chicken, kan-
garoo and seafood.

The Brisbane Hotel
292 Beaufort St. Tel:
08-9227 2300. Open: L & D
daily, drinks available until
late. **$$** 52 p254, B1
Possibly the most stylish
hotel in Perth, the Bris-
bane is relaxed and funky.
You can pop in for a drink,
but the food is worth staying for, so grab a table in
the shady garden. The
pizzas are excellent, as
are the more substantial
mains, such as grilled fish
on Asian greens and
prawn fettucine.

The Flying Scotsman
639 Beaufort St. Tel:
08-9328 6200. Open: B Sat
and Sun from 11am, L & D
daily. **$$** 53 p254, C1
An English-style pub serv-
ing top-notch burgers and
pizzas. Thursday karaoke
has a cult following.

Grapeskin
209 William St. Tel: 08-9227
9596. Open: D daily. **$$$**
54 p254, A2
Part of the Brass Monkey

LEFT: fish and chips at
The Brass Monkey.

hotel but operates separately. On weekends it buzzes with people dropping in to buy wine from the cellar, others chatting over drinks at the front bar or enjoying dinner at the rear. Sample fare includes Japanese scallops, Tenderidge eye fillet and cheese boards.

Jackson's
483 Beaufort St. Tel: 08-9328 1177. Open: D Mon–Sat. **$$$$** ⑤⑤ p254, C1
Considered one of Perth's top places to dine, Chef-owner Neal Jackson specialises in unusual combinations, such as apple risotto with grilled chorizo and seared scallops.

The Moon Café
323 William St. Tel: 08-9328 7474. Open: L Wed–Sun, D daily until late. **$** ⑤⑥ p254, B2
While the food isn't particularly special, the quirky atmosphere makes it a great place to hang out. The dark, retro interior leads through to a large courtyard.

Must Winebar
519 Beaufort St. Tel: 08-9328 8255. Open: L & D daily. **$$$** ⑤⑦ p254, C1
Enjoy a glass of wine in the funky front bar, or settle down for a serious French bistro-style meal in the restaurant. Has a

Prices for a three-course dinner per person with a half-bottle of house wine:
$ = under AUS$25
$$ = AUS$25–40
$$$ = AUS$40–70
$$$$ = over AUS$70

500-bottle wine list.

Soto Espresso
507 Beaufort St. Tel: 08-9227 7686. Open: B & L Mon–Sun, coffee and cakes daily until midnight. **$** ⑤⑧ p254, C1
Soto Espresso serves light meals and breakfasts throughout the day until 3pm. The tomato and feta on toast is a tasty bargain.

Tarts Café and Home Providore
212 Lake St. Tel: 08-9328 6607. Open: B & L daily. **$** ⑤⑨ p254, A2
Nestled amongst the terrace homes on Lake Street. For breakfast, try the scrambled eggs with feta, wilted spinach, oven-roasted tomatoes and rosemary-flavoured Turkish bread.

Italian

Il Padrino
198 William St. Tel: 08-9227 9065. Open: L Tue–Fri, D Tue–Sat. **$$** ⑥⓪ p254, A2
The walls of this pizzeria tell the story – everyone has acknowledged just how good Nunzio's pizzas are. The Pizza Association of Sicily have even declared him the best pizza-maker in the world.

Maurizio
235 Fitzgerald St. www.mauriziorestaurant.com. Tel: 08-9228 1646. Open: L Tue–Fri, D Tue–Sat. **$$$** ⑥① p254, A1
Fine dining inspired by regional Italian food. Menus are created sea-

RIGHT: The Brass Monkey, a Northbridge favourite.

Bars

The Brass Monkey
209 William St, cnr James St. Tel: 08-9227 9596. www.the brassmonkey.com.au. Open: daily. ⑭ p254, A2
The Brass Monkey is a well-known Perth landmark. It has several bar areas and a range of Australian beers.

Luxe Bar
446 Beaufort St, Mt Lawley. Tel: 08-9228 9680. www.luxe bar.com. Open: Wed–Sun 7pm–late ⑮ p254, C1

sonally, but dishes such as the roast baby goat and braised rabbit are staples on the menu.

Romany
105 Aberdeen St. www.romanyrestaurant.com. Tel: 08-9328 8042. Open: L Mon–Sat, D Mon–Fri. **$** ⑥② p254, A2
The decor might be faded, but this is a

Luxe has mastered the art of cocktail couture, and employs bartenders who have won awards for their craft. It has a plush, glamorous interior.

Universal Bar
221 William St, Northbridge. Tel: 08-9227 6771. www.universalbar.com.au. Open: nightly Wed–Sun. ⑯ p254, A2
Universal gets in some great jazz and blues bands. Excellent finger food, too.

favourite with locals who come for the traditional trattoria-style food.

Veritas
484 Beaufort St. Tel: 08-9227 9745. Open: B Sat and Sun, L Fri–Sun, D Tue–Sun. **$$$** ⑥③ p254, C1
This chic restaurant serves contemporary Italian and Mediterranean cuisine and has just been renovated.

SUBIACO

Subiaco, known as Subi to locals, is Perth's most fashionable neighbourhood, the top spot for those who like to live where they play. Close to the city centre and Kings Park, it's a great place to come for shopping, culture and entertainment

Main Attractions
SUBIACO STATION
STATION STREET MARKETS
REGAL THEATRE
SUBIACO HOTEL
SUBIACO OVAL
SUBIACO MUSEUM

Modern Subiaco has long been Perth's style centre: every major city worth the tag must have one. Creative industries – advertising, publishing, design studios – tend to be based here, and city singles aspire to live in an area that is a stone's throw from the park and the city centre and yet has a distinctive village-like feel. It is also a pleasant place to visit. Saturday lunch or brunch can be combined with a look around the markets, some up-market shopping and a stroll through the park.

History

It was here, between Lake Monger and Herdsman's Lake, in 1851 that Benedictine missionaries Dom Serra and Dom Salvado set up camp. They came to Australia in 1846, charged by Pope Gregory to follow the guidance of St Benedict and his followers who "converted whole peoples and nations to the faith". The town of New Subiaco, which took its name from the Italian town of Subiaco, near Rome, the founding place of their Holy Order, grew throughout the 1850s.

The pioneering Benedictines of Western Australia would later leave Subiaco to develop their mission at New Norcia, north of Perth *(see page 194)*. The monastery eventually became a boys' orphanage and was then taken over by the Sisters of Mercy. The hilltop building above Lake Monger is still a Catholic institution and childcare centre. The gnarled olive vines planted by Bishop Serra still grow around the original limestone church.

On the ground

Subiaco's first train station was opened on 1 March 1881 on the in-auguration of the new railway line

Maps and Listings
MAP OF SUBIACO, PAGE 122
SHOPPING, PAGE 126
RESTAURANTS, BARS AND
   CAFÉS, PAGES 127–9
ACCOMMODATION, PAGES
   223–5

LEFT: the iconic clock outside Subiaco Station. **RIGHT:** flowers in Subiaco Market.

The inaugural train journey from Fremantle to Perth in 1881 did not come off without a hitch. To the embarrassment of all concerned, it was discovered that the platforms had been built too high; the carriage doors wouldn't open. The driver-engineer had to reverse the train down the line so the governor and other dignitaries could clamber down directly onto the sand.

linking Fremantle and Perth. It was a momentous day of great excitement throughout the colony. Two years earlier, when fewer than 6,000 settlers lived in WA, 4,000 of them assembled just to watch Governor Harry Ord start the project by turning over the first shovel of earth.

In the early days, Subiaco was only a "request" stop, and passengers had to flag down the train. Some people soon learnt a less formal way of boarding, by simply jumping on and off the running boards of the slow, rumbling train. A hundred years later there was no denying that the line, though still essential, was also a bit of a nuisance. Cut off by the railway, the area north of the tracks became a wasteland, as industry declined or moved to better premises outside Perth.

A stop on the Perth–Fremantle railway, **Subiaco Station ❶** was sunk below ground in 1998 in a daring piece of planning designed to create spectacular Subi Centro, a complex of houses, apartments and offices that has transformed the area.

The process of sinking the rail line was complex and controversial, but what the America's Cup did for Fremantle, Subi Centro has done for Subiaco. Drab, empty factories were replaced by smart apartments, offices and restaurants. The station square is spotless, and the trains, unseen, glide noiselessly in and out.

For WA the concept of a sunken station was revolutionary. This is the country with room to spare, where the Australian dream home has always been a spacious bungalow set on a quarter-acre block, with garden front and back, and maybe a pool.

The renovation of Subiaco is now complete, and most people agree that it has been a resounding success. Above all, it makes sense in today's Perth, where the population is fast expanding and city planners want to contain the relentless sprawl up and down the west coast.

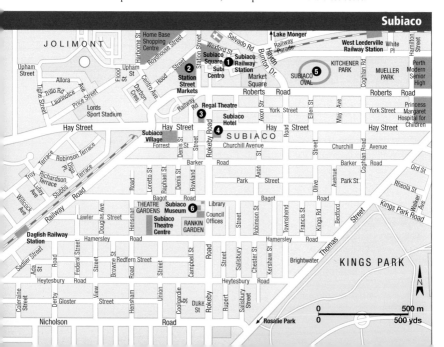

Station Street Markets

Address: 41 Station Street, Subiaco
Tel: 08-9382 2832
Opening Hrs: Fri–Mon 9am–5.30pm
and public holidays
Entrance Fee: free

On the western side of Subiaco Square are **Station Street Markets** ❷. This covered market is a Perth institution that has somehow survived the gentrification all around. Locals come here every weekend for the big spread of exotic fruit and vegetables produced by local family businesses. In addition, home-made and natural organic produce, art and crafts are spread across 100 colourful stalls. Vintage clothes, old vinyl records and second-hand books vie for attention with brand-new furniture, furnishings and expensive jewellery. Native trees by Replants (www.replants.com), an environmentally aware group that salvages and transports plants, make a striking entry statement at one end of the markets; thumping African drums are likely to greet you at the other. Railway goods wagons converted into consulting booths line the periphery, offering massage, tarot-card

readings, souvenirs (including gems, wild flowers, Aboriginal artefacts and gifts), hand-crafted jewellery, pottery, rugs, candles and more. Indonesian furniture and artefacts attest to WA's proximity to Asia.

International food, mostly Asian, is provided by individual traders around an alfresco dining area and central garden courtyard. This is substantial and inexpensive food adhering to the "big Aussie serve" principle, often accompanied by the live music of local entertainers.

ABOVE: sunken Subiaco Station.
BELOW: Station Street Markets.

The much-loved Subiaco Pavilion Market, which was in operation on the corner of Rokeby and Roberts Road for more than 25 years, closed its colourful doors in 2009. While locals wanted to keep the Subiaco icon that had once been described as the "spirit of Subi", increasing property values made it hot property and the 3,749-sq-metre (41,250-sq-ft) site was eventually sold for AUS$25 million. The new owners plan to build a AUS$130 million high-end residential and retail development.

The hub of Subiaco

A few metres south of here is the Rokeby/Hay crossroads, the hub of Subiaco. The Subiaco Hotel faces the **Regal Theatre ❸**, neighbours since the 1930s. The Regal opened as a hard-top cinema in 1938, replacing the open-air Coliseum Picture Garden, one of many in its time. While many Subi theatres closed down, the trend was reversed at the Regal, where live performance replaced film in 1977.

The interior of the Regal is as stunning as the Art Deco exterior

ABOVE: Subiaco Hotel is a landmark on the Rokeby/Hay crossroads, offering good food, cracking cocktails and an ever-popular sports bar. **BELOW:** the restaurant Chutney Mary's.

(see Architecture, pages 62–3). The original chrome-and-jarrah fittings are still in place, as is Paddy's Bar (and his chair), named after Paddy Baker, who bought the cinema in 1946. Paddy also installed the love seat in the balcony, and the Crying Room, so that parents could attend to their offspring while still watching the show. Paddy died in 1986, leaving his beloved building to the people of WA. The Regal is now listed with the National Trust.

Also on the Rokeby/Hay crossroads is the **Subiaco Hotel ❹**, which has been transformed from a standard pub into a cosmopolitan entertainment spot, with an award-winning restaurant that often features live jazz. The Llama Bar (opposite the Regal) is owned by the same proprietors and hits the same high standards.

At the crossroads, first go east on Hay Street, a continuous road to the centre of Perth. It's less than 5km (3 miles), but there was no proper link for the first 70 years of the Swan River Colony.

Among the fashionable boutiques a few old Subi shops survive, among

them G.P. and M.J. Guest's **Fine Art Services** (433 Hay Street), occupying a 1930s delicatessen. The chequered tiling, gilt lettering on windows topped with mosaic and copper, and a pressed-tin ceiling have been carefully restored by the artists within.

Across the road, the Art Deco style of the 1920s is perpetuated in the Doric Constructions arcade. Near by is The Colonnade, selling leading designer labels from Australia and the rest of the world.

Just around the corner from here, look out for **Catherine Street** and its peaceful row of Victorian terrace cottages. Eight are original (two with verandas), trimmed with ornate plasterwork and frilly iron lace; four are modern copies.

At last count, Subi had almost 100 cafés and restaurants, homeware stores, health and beauty outlets, jewellery stores and bookshops. The Subi section of Hay Street reaches beyond the stylish Vic pub, refreshed now as an apartment hotel, and finishing at the children's hospital on Kings Park Road. South from the crossroads to Kings Park, stylish shops are interspersed with several notable restaurants – Witch's Cauldron, the Buddha Bar and Curry House, and, in Forrest Walk, Zen Sea Gourmet Seafood *(see restaurants, pages 127–9)*.

Subiaco is also home to the **Subiaco Oval ❺**, WA's headquarters of AFL, otherwise known as Aussie Rules Football, the unique Australian football game. The Oval is also the home base and grand final venue for the Western Australian Football League, as well as being the home ground of local WAFL side Subiaco.

Watching a bit of AFL is a must, if only to confirm it as the most violent of all the football codes. Millions of fans would contend it is also a dynamic and exciting contest requiring superb athleticism.

In the long winter season there's an AFL match every week, plus WAFL

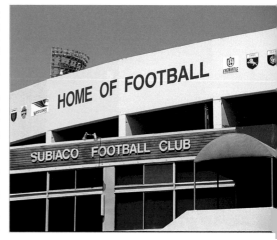

ABOVE: Australian Rules Football is not football as any other nation knows it.

matches at the Oval and elsewhere around Perth. A striking example of sporting architecture, the Oval has all-seater modern stands with a capacity of 43,000.

Towards the park

Back on Rokeby Road and heading towards the park, look out for the **library** on the corner with Bagot Road. It provides up-to-date local information and runs guided walks in the area on Sundays. Also near here is the **Subiaco Theatre Centre**, which stages regular free concerts in summer (some in the precinct) and is home to the Barking Gecko company.

The small **Subiaco Museum ❻** (239 Rokeby Road; Tue–Sun 2–5pm; free) is strong on local history and a contact point for the Subiaco Historical Society.

Further along Rokeby Road at the Nicholson Road corner are the **Mediterranean Offices**. Once the most prestigious dining spot in Perth, it is now the office of federal politician Julie Bishop. In the 1980s the Mediterranean was virtually a second home for the in-famous tycoon Alan Bond and his associates at the Bond

The local newspaper, Subiaco Post, started here as a part-time occupation in the proprietor's home, is considered one of Australia's best weekly newspapers. It often breaks news ahead of the state-wide press.

TIP

One Sunday in November Rokeby Road holds a street party featuring music, street entertainment and refreshments.

Corporation *(see page 40)*. Like many institutions, and Mr Bond himself, the Mediterranean failed in the wake of a series of corruption scandals that became known as WA Inc. and led to disenchantment with the Labor government.

From here it is a 15-minute walk to the Saw Avenue entrance to **Kings Park** *(see page 73)*, which has 400 hectares (1,000 acres) of natural bush as well as lakes, lawns, children's playgrounds and botanical gardens. Walking is easy.

Several streets connect Rokeby Road to **Shenton Park**, which con-

tains **Lake Jualbup**. A painting by the Aboriginal artist Shane Pickett on the lake's east side features wetlands flora and fauna, and the nearby picnic and barbecue area is a delightful spot. Jualbup, meaning a place where water rises in spring, was the original name of the whole area.

Walking to Shenton Park, you'll pass the substantial houses that characterise this area of Subiaco. Now a private residence (in William Street, between Nicholson and Keightley), **St Aloysius Church and Convent School** was run by the Sisters of Mercy from 1909 to 1973. ❑

SHOPPING

Subiaco and Claremont are Perth's shopping haven. Head along Rokeby Road or the Colonnade on Hay Street in Subiaco and the newly developed Claremont Quarter and Bayview Terrace for high-end Australian fashion retailers.

Jewellery

Linneys
37 Rokeby Rd. www.linneys.com.au. Tel: 08-9382 4077. Linneys specialise in selecting the finest pearls, diamonds and gold from WA and around the world to create unique pieces of world-class jewellery.

Food

Simon Johnson
169 Rokeby Rd. www.simonjohnson.com. Tel: 08-9489 3888.

High-quality gourmet food from rose and lemon Turkish delight to a range of jams and chutneys and a huge selection of Australian cheeses.

Antiques

Bloomsbury
222 Onslow Rd. Tel: 08-9381 6541. Established in 1984, specialising in English antique jewellery, accessories and furniture.

Annabelle's Antiques
54 Nicholson Rd. 08-9382 1011. Housed in a quaint corner shop specialising in English jewellery and beads with a small collection of china, linen and dolls.

Women's Clothing

Chateau Clothing
2a/205 Nicholson Rd. Tel: 08-9388 3673.

A tasteful collection of WA, Australian and international designer clothes suitable for day and cocktail wear.

Empire Rose
431 Hay St and 26 Bayview Terrace. www.empirerose.au. Tel: 08-9388 8276. This homegrown style contrasts men's tailoring with a feminine sillouette that focuses on volume, texture and playful detailing.

Megan Salmon
Corner of Bagot and Rokeby roads. Tel: 08-9382 8866. Artistically driven, edgy and directional, Megan Salmon is a label concerned with providing uniquely beautiful textiles, sophisticated cutting and construction to enhance the female form.

Men's Shoes

Highs and Lows
Rear 21 Bayview Terrace. Tel: 08-9284 3633.

For the ultimate range of men's sneakers there is nowhere else that has a comparable range of options.

Women's Shoes

Zomp
2 Bayview Terrace. Tel: 08-9384 6250. Zomp is a privately owned boutique women's shoe store that started in Perth 30 years ago. Twice a year buyers travel the world sourcing the latest looks and emerging brands.

Gifts

Petticoat Lane
531 Hay St. Tel: 08-9381 7005. This Subi favourite is stuffed full of vintage collectibles and bric-a-brac china, silver, crystal, glass, cutlery and porcelain with pieces dating back to the 1800s.

BEST RESTAURANTS, BARS AND CAFÉS

Restaurants

Asian

Cheers
375 Hay St. Tel: 08-9388 2044. Open: L Mon–Fri, D Mon–Sat. **$** 64 p252, B2
This authentic Japanese restaurant is hidden behind a group of shops on Hay Street, but it's worth it to make the search. If you're with a group, make sure you ask for one of the traditional tables where you take off your shoes and let your feet dangle into the well under the table. Order a range of things to share.

Chutney Mary's
67 Rokeby Rd. Tel: 08-9381 2099. Open: L Wed–Sat, D daily. **$$** 65 p252, B2
The fragrant smells wafting out of this Indian restaurant on the corner of Hay and Rokeby streets will entice you off the pavement. The thali plates are a popular lunch option, and at under AUS$15 each is excellent value: choose between meat, fish or vegetarian curries; you'll also get rice, naan, dahl, soup and dessert.

Prices for a three-course dinner per person with a half-bottle of house wine:
$ = under AUS$25
$$ = AUS$25–40
$$$ = AUS$40–70
$$$$ = over AUS$70

Jimmy's Noodle & Rice
Shop 4/375 Hay St. Tel: 08-9388 6337. Open: L Mon–Fri, D Mon–Sat. **$** 66 p252, B2
This is the place for good-value food in the heart of Subiaco. Most dishes are Indonesian, Malay, Thai or Vietnamese. The salty edamame beans starter can be hard to find elsewhere – if it's your first time, suck out the beans and leave the skin behind. They have good nasi goring and phad thai as well.

Lanna Thai Cuisine
375 Hay St. www.lannathai.com.au. Tel: 08-9381 2766. Open: D daily. **$$** 67 p252, B2
The extensive menu features soups, entrées, lots of vegetarian options, dry and wet curries, noodle dishes and desserts. The best things about Thai cuisine – fresh herbs, chilli, lime, light ingredients – are all evident in owner Kitty's food. The ambience is good, too, with a warm Thai welcome for all guests.

Nippon Food
479 Hay St. Tel: 08-9388 2738. Open: L Mon–Sat. **$** 68 p252, B2
This postage stamp-sized eatery offers sub-AUS$6 teriyaki chicken to busy office crowds all week. It also has a range of inexpensive sushi. It has just three tables out front, so you might be better off taking away and heading for one of the nearby parks.

Wagamama
Corner of Roberts and Rokeby roads. Tel: 08-9388 6055. Open: L & D daily. **$** 69 p252, B2
Wagamama needs no introduction to many visitors. This popular global chain, which opened this branch in Perth in 2006, does a roaring trade in all kinds of noodles and rice dishes, served in big bowls at communal tabes. All the favourites are on this menu – chicken katsu, miso ramen and fresh juices, too.

Australian

Chapter One Brasserie
292 Hay St. www.chapterone brasserie.com.au. Tel: 08-9388 1323. Open: L & D Tue–Sat. **$$$** 70 p252, B2
It's easy to walk past this restaurant without noticing it, but Chapter One Brasserie is actually one of the nicest dining options in the area. The food is sophisticated – think succulent marinated beef with potato stacks, followed by a choice of delicate desserts. There is a little courtyard area at the back, too.

Oriel Café
483 Hay St. Tel: 08-9382 1886. Open: B, L & D daily, open till midnight Mon–

RIGHT: a star act on Onslow Road.

Thur, until 2am Fri–Sat. **$$**  p252, B2

The Oriel is an institution in Perth. The menu is extensive, and there's something for everyone.

Star Anise

225 Onslow Rd. www.star aniserestaurant.com.au. Tel: 08-9381 9811. Open: D Tue–Sat. **$$$$** ⑦ p252, A4

This is one of Perth's best restaurants, located on the quiet shopping strip of Onslow Road. Chef-owner David Coomer changes the menu constantly, depending on what looks good at the local market. There is a strong Asian influence, with crispy aromatic duck always on the menu, but in winter the menu reflects a comforting French style of cooking. Dessert is worth leaving room for, as there is always something interesting to choose from – such as balls of liquorice ice cream with slabs of Star Anise meringue,

which is divine.

The Subiaco Hotel

Corner of Hay St and Rokeby Rd. www.subiacohotel.com. au. Tel: 08-9381 3069. Open: B, L & D daily. **$$** ⑦ p252, B2

Known locally as "The Subi", this pub-cum-restaurant is busy from breakfast until late, and deservedly so. On the Rokeby Road side there is a sports bar: walk through there to find a more up-market cocktail bar adjacent to the restaurant, which has outdoor veranda seating on Hay Street, as well as indoor seating and a rear garden. The inventive, inspired food ranges from Moroccan seafood tagine with spinach and feta brik pastry and twice-cooked pork belly, with prawn and scallop caramel sauce and steamed rice cake. Booking is advisable, as it's a favourite post-work hangout with the locals.

The Vic

226 Hay St. Tel: 08-6380 8222. Open: L & D daily. **$$** ⑦ p252, C2

This pub serves excellent pub grub, and its outdoor garden is ideal in good weather. There are tasty daily specials, and good lunch deals such as beer-battered fish and chips and a middy of Redback for just AUS$10. Other dishes such as teriyaki beef stir-fry, steak sandwiches and pasta dishes are always reliable. The bar packs out on a Friday night and whenever there's a game on at the nearby Subiaco Oval.

The Witch's Cauldron

89 Rokeby Rd. www.witchs. com.au. Tel: 08-9381 2508. Open: B, L & D daily. **$$$** ⑦ p252, B2

This restaurant, a short walk up from the junction with Hay, has been on the Perth scene for longer than most people can remember. It is famous for its garlic prawns, juicy steaks and succulent seafood. It might not be the most innovative cuisine in town, but it is reliable and loved by many.

Zen Sea Gourmet Seafood

Forrest Walk, 91–7 Rokeby Rd. Tel: 08-6380 1166. Open: L & D daily. **$** ⑦ p252, B2

Zen Sea is an up-market fish 'n' chippery that produces excellent take-home seafood as well as standard fare. Try the marinated prawns, sea-

food chowder, sashimi, or one of the large range of fillets, all in a nice environment.

European

Bistro Felix

118–120 Rokeby Rd. www. bistrofelix.com.au. Tel: 08-9388 3077. Open: Mon–Sat noon–late. **$$$$** ⑦ p252, B2

If you have time for a long lunch or dinner, then Bistro Felix is a great choice. Its changing European-style menu uses only seasonal produce, and the vintage art and feature wine wall make for a pleasant ambience.

Boucla

349 Rokeby Rd. Tel: 08-9381 2841. Open: B & L Mon–Sat. **$** ⑦ p252, B3

Boucla is a Byzantine treat. Fight your way past Turkish rugs and Greek statues to the counter where there are no menus and no price lists. All food is cooked fresh that day, and whatever is on display is what's left. There's often spanakopitas, roast veg salads, kotopita and lamb pies, plus lots of Greek shortbreads and cakes.

Italian

Delizioso

94 Rokeby Rd. Tel: 08-9381 7796. Open: B & L Mon–Sat, D Wed–Sat. **$** ⑦ p252, B2

The best thing about this little daytime café is its Italian pizza served by the

ABOVE LEFT: fine dining, artfully presented.

slice. Tasty toppings include aubergine and chilli, potato and rosemary, and straight cheese and herbs. There's enough seating to kick back and relax with a coffee, too.

Ecco!
23 Rokeby Rd. Tel: 08-9388 6710. Open: L Fri–Sun, D Tue–Sun. **$** ㊿ p252, B2

A sophisticated little café in the Rokeby Road shopping strip that serves fantastic pizza, coffee, panini and a small range of mains. This restaurant is worth a visit just for the potato, rosemary and mozzarella pizza.

Funtastico
12 Rokeby Rd. Tel: 08-9381 2688. Open: B, L & D daily. **$$** ㉛ p252, B2

If you could get up-market casual, this would be it. Favoured by folk about town for its good pastas and sensational pizzas, it has great alfresco seating.

Galileo
199 Onslow Rd. Tel: 08-9382 3343. Open: L Tue–Fri, D Tue–Sat. **$$$** ㉜ p252, A4

Galileo serves well-executed Italian cuisine. Those who like more unusual combinations will be kept happy along with the

Prices for a three-course dinner per person with a half-bottle of house wine:

$ = under AUS$25
$$ = AUS$25–40
$$$ = AUS$40–70
$$$$ = over AUS$70

more average palates. Not an easy balance to maintain, but they pull it off admirably.

Rialto's
424 Hay St. Tel: 08-9382 3292. Open: L Tue–Fri, D Tue–Sat. **$$$** ㉝ p252, B2

Offering a modern take on Italian food. Owner Albasio La Pegna has created a luxurious interior with refined food to match. The rare yellowfin tuna salad, mixed with avocado, lime, tabasco and spring onions, is sublime.

Bakery/Coffee

Chez Jean-Claude Patisserie
333 Rokeby Rd. Tel: 08-9381 7968. Open: B & L Mon–Fri. **$** ㉞ p252, B3

This is a little slice of baking heaven at the far end of Rokeby Road. It does a roaring trade in rolls, sandwiches, pies, sweet treats and cakes produced by French-Swiss baker Jean-Claude. There's no seating, but it's so good you won't mind taking away.

The Grind on Hay
65 Hay St. Tel: 08-9489 7033. Open: B & L Mon–Fri. **$** ㉟ p253, C2

With great coffee, tasty muffins, a big range of sandwiches and panini, and a choice of freshly prepared salads, the Grind on Hay is a great stop any time of day. All food is fresh and made on the premises.

RIGHT: a Llama Ice Tea at Llama Bar.

Bars and Cafés

Brownhaus Espresso
55 Rokeby Rd. Tel: 08-6380 1519. Open: B, L daily. ⑰ p252, B2

The coffee is strong, the chocolate is sweet, and the mood is friendly, whether you're sitting inside or out. The sandwiches are good, too.

Café Café
Subiaco Square Shopping Centre, 29 Station St. Tel: 08-9388 9800. Open: B, L daily. ⑱ p252, B1

Serving some of Perth's finest coffee, this café is packed on weekends, when Perthites come for freshly baked muffins and croissants and cooked breakfasts. They also serve panini and a tempting selection of cakes.

Fire and Ice Bar
Subiaco Train Station. Tel: 08-9381 1400. Open: L & D daily. ⑲ p252, B1

Situated in the Subiaco Train Station, Fire and Ice Bar is a great place to unwind. Their grazing menu complements an extensive cocktail menu, and the Champagne Bar is a classy alternative to the typical Subiaco bar scene.

Llama Bar
1/464 Hay St. Tel: 08-9388 0222. Open: Tue–Sat til late. ⑳ p252, B2

With a cocktail list as long as your arm and a small but tasty list of snacks and nibbles, you can be guaranteed a great night at Llama Bar. The featured drink is the Llama Ice Tea, which pairs excellently with the crispy skin pork belly. The entrance is on Rokeby Road.

FREMANTLE

A short hop from Perth, on the mouth of the Swan, the port of Fremantle has shed its workaday image and emerged as a lively and confident city proud of its period architecture and maritime heritage

The vibrant port city of Fremantle is often called WA's second capital city, although Freophiles like to say it's the first. Historically that's about right, because Fremantle was a fully fledged settlement while James Stirling was still camped on Garden Island waiting to found Perth.

The port city was named after Captain Charles Fremantle, the man who planted the union flag on Arthur Head in 1829 and claimed WA for the Crown and Britain. This, and his resourcefulness in saving the passengers of the *Parmelia* after Captain Stirling ingloriously grounded the ship on a harbour-mouth sandbank *(see page 32)*, earned him the honour.

Fremantle has a wealth of 19th-century architecture, but Freo, as it is known locally, is no living museum; it has the friendly, confident feel of a modern community, with a Mediterranean flavour.

Fremantle's period architecture might well have been demolished, like most of Perth's, had developers thought it worth the effort. But until the America's Cup in Fremantle in 1987, the city was off the radar. The old buildings remained more or less intact because there was no profit in

knocking them down. And by the time preparations for the America's Cup were under way, the redevelopers had missed their chance. Renovation began in earnest, and has never stopped since.

Getting there

Fremantle is a 30-minute train ride from Perth Central, and Transperth buses to Fremantle leave from St George's Terrace. But try to arrive by boat if you can. The ferry from Barrack Street Jetty takes about an hour.

PRECEDING PAGES: Fishing Boat Harbour.
LEFT AND RIGHT: modern and future mariner.

TIP

The Fremantle CAT – a free, air-conditioned bus service – makes a circuit around the city calling at places of interest. Buses run every 10 minutes, and Victoria Quay and the railway station are on the route.

Several companies (ticket offices at the jetty) offer this service. Captain Cook Cruises (*see page 240*) cost around AUS$20 one way, including commentary, tea/coffee, and, if returning, wine-tasting, and offers several cruises a day. Slightly less expensive are Golden Sun and Oceanic, both with ticket booths on the jetty.

Vessels cruise down the Swan past some of the state's most desirable waterfront suburbs – Dalkeith, Peppermint Grove and Mosman Park. Blackwall Reach leads into the Fremantle stretch of river; beyond Stirling Bridge lies the Inner Harbour, WA's most vital port.

Don't expect grimy docks and mouldering warehouses. Fremantle port is clean, with colourful mountains of containers and gantries. Even the distant oil-storage tanks look scrubbed white and silver. Day and night, cargo containers waiting clearance to enter and unload linger off the coast near Rottnest Island.

Ferries tie up at **Victoria Quay**, near the berth used by the *QE II* and other ocean liners, as well as *Greenpeace Warrior* and vessels making scientific expeditions to the Antarctic. The quay is also a departure point for the ferry to Rottnest Island (*see page 163*), as well as the location for the main maritime sights.

Maritime Museum ❶

Address: Slip Street, Fremantle, www.museum.wa.gov.au/maritime
Tel: 08-9431 8334
Opening Hrs: daily 9.30am–5pm
Entrance Fee: charge

This newly built museum is an imaginatively executed exploration of Fremantle's many and varied maritime industries and associations (*see pages 146–7*). Nearby is the sail training ship *Leeuwin*. When in port, the 55-metre (183ft) three-masted barquentine is open to visitors, who can also book a half-day sail (tel: 08-9430 4105; www.sailleeuwin.com).

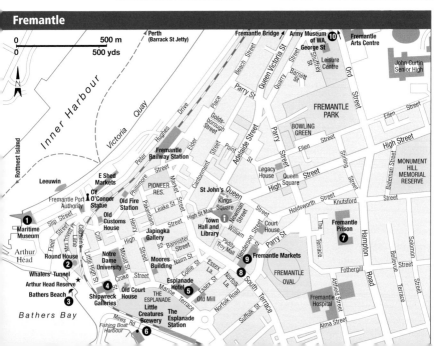

Fremantle

Also on the quay, next to the Motor Museum, are **E-Shed Markets** (Fri–Sun 9am–5.30pm), containing more than 100 speciality shops, an international food court (open till 8pm) and live entertainment.

The Round House

Address: Western end of High Street on Arthur Head, Fremantle, www. fremantleroundhouse.com.au
Tel: 08-9431 7878
Opening Hrs: daily 10.30am–3.30pm
Entrance Fee: donation

A circular CAT bus service linking the main sights *(see margin tip)* stops at the port, but it is easy enough to get around on foot. A short walk from Victoria Quay is **Arthur Head**, site of the **Round House ❷**. This is WA's oldest public building and its first gaol, built in 1830 where Captain Fremantle landed to claim Western Australia for the Crown. It was designed by H.W. Reveley, the colony's first civil engineer.

WA soon outgrew the capacity of the Round House and its eight small cells. A series of bigger prisons replaced it, but the Round House was used as a police lock-up until 1900, when it became the living quarters for the chief constable, his wife and their 10 children.

Below the jail is Whalers' Tunnel (closed for the last few years due to safety concerns), which was cut through the rock in 1837 to connect **Bathers Beach ❸** and the jetty with the settlement. Hunters of the Fremantle Whaling Company used the tunnel to move their kill. It was WA's first tunnel, and it is the only remnant of the whaling industry that was so crucial to the young colony, as documented in the Maritime Museum. Opening these few metres linking the High Street and the Indian Ocean was a huge government project. Mining technology was called on to build a steel frame to support the roof and a combination of 52 ground anchors

drilled 4 metres (13ft) into the limestone. A unique treatment developed by Australian scientists stabilised the porous limestone.

A small side tunnel, built when the Whalers' Tunnel was used as an air-raid shelter in World War II, leads up to Gunners Cottage, one in a row of cottages built alongside the Round House on Captains Lane. A tearoom occupies one of the cottages built for harbour pilots in 1906. More cottages are found along the quaintly named **Mrs Trivett Place**, which leads to an artists' gallery and looks down on an oceanside collective of sculptors' studios.

The Round House is oceanside of a rarely used spur of railway, across which is High Street, a handsome avenue of fine Federation-style buildings, running up to Market Street, which in turn leads to South Terrace, a café-lined promenade otherwise known as Cappuccino Strip *(see page 139)*.

Shipwreck Galleries

Address: Slip Street, Fremantle, www.museum.wa.gov.au/maritime

ABOVE: the Round House viewed from High Street. **BELOW:** the Fishermen's Monument at the Fishing Boat Harbour pays homage to Fremantle's fishing community.

Fremantle Prison

Fremantle Prison is a heritage site with exceptional cultural significance, as it is the most intact of all Australian convict sites

The 1858 prison was built by some of the 10,000 convicts transported from Britain to WA. At any one time, hundreds of felons (both men and women) were incarcerated in Victorian conditions that persisted until 1991, when the last 600 men were moved to a new prison at Casauarina, 20km (12 miles) south of Perth. Forty-four people – including one woman, Martha Rendell – were sent to the gallows in Fremantle Prison. All were convicted murderers; the last of them was the serial killer Eric Edgar Cooke, who was hanged in 1964.

The granite building, the biggest jail ever constructed in the southern hemisphere, has now become a heritage attraction with a visitor centre, café and a range of tours. Visitors can walk the echoing corridors and exercise yards, then step into the stark two-man cells. Incredibly, the cells were originally half this size, but were enlarged between 1870 and 1920 when the adjoining walls were removed (bear in mind that in the 1850s people were small by modern standards: according to prison guides the tallest convict ever transported was only 1.57 metres/5ft 2ins).

Furnished with no more than a hammock, fold-down table, stool and toilet bucket, the cells had no ceiling and an outward-opening door; if the door opened inwards it could be barricaded shut.

A few cells are a little more cheerful, with convict artwork on the walls; some inmates painted the furniture, too. In one, religious frescoes in the style of Michelangelo are now protected by a perspex cover.

Twenty metres (65ft) below Fremantle Prison is a system of tunnels built by the convicts, not as escape routes but as part of an 1894 project to channel fresh water to the jail and port of Fremantle. The tunnels, hacked out with hand tools, extended beyond the prison boundaries, but there was no chance of escape. After six years of hard labour that killed several men and injured dozens more, a kilometre (1½ miles) of tunnels ran through the limestone.

Water still flows through the tunnels, which were recently reopened to take visitors on an underground adventure tour. (Be prepared for an alcohol breath test before you're allowed underground!) It's possible to walk through some parts, but the tunnels are mostly flooded and accessed by wooden punts, replicas of those used by the convict diggers in 1894.

Other tours include the Great Escapes Tour and the Torchlight Tour. For full information on the tours, tel: 08-9336 9200; www.fremantleprison.com.au. The website also offers the intriguing opportunity to "find the felon in your family" by searching its convict database. ❑

ABOVE AND LEFT: a working jail until 1991, the Prison is now one of the port's top tourist attractions.

Fremantle Festival

Fun and entertainment, vital elements of Fremantle's upbeat character, are expressed in its festivals. The festival calendar, running from spring to late autumn, kicks off with the annual Festival of Fremantle, in late November. A tradition that began in 1905, it is a 10-day round of concerts, exhibitions and dance, culminating in the Carnival and Festival Parade on South Terrace. Other festivals include the Fremantle Street Arts Festival, showcasing buskers from all over the world, held at Easter, and Fremantle Children's Fiesta, in April, featuring dance, theatre, activities and workshops. For information, visit www.fremantlefestivals.com.

Tel: 08-9431 8334
Opening Hrs: daily 9.30am–5pm
Entrance Fee: charge

From here, walk along Cliff Street (right off High Street). At the end of Cliff is the original WA Maritime Museum, now known as the **Shipwreck Galleries ❹** (9.30am–5pm; free but donations welcome; guided tours available), devoted to marine archaeology. Original timber (partially reconstructed) and treasures from the *Batavia*, a famous Dutch shipwreck *(see page 137)*, are on display alongside relics from other ancient wrecks.

The Esplanade

From the Shipwreck Galleries, proceed along Marine Terrace, passing Croke Lane and the **Old Court House**, which operated from 1884 until 1897, and the 1903 **Water Police Barracks** (No. 10 Marine Terrace), to reach the prominent **Esplanade Hotel ❺**. Modern extensions are well blended into the original facade, built in the gold-rush 1890s style found in many Fremantle hotels. Across the Esplanade lawns is the harbour, a lively entertainment hub night and day.

One of the main attractions here is the harbourside **Little Creatures Brewery ❻** (bar and restaurant as well as brewery), whose output is sold around the state and widely exported *(see page 137)*.

The boatyards nearby are dominated by the boathouse in which a replica of the *Endeavour* was constructed in the 1990s. A project of Alan Bond *(see page 40)*, it was planned as a gift to the nation. Times and fortunes changed, however: the replica of Captain Cook's ship was finally completed with government aid and, after numerous round-the-world voyages, is now on permanent display in Sydney.

North of the brewery and boatyards a host of restaurants, ice-cream parlours and cafés lines the **Fishing Boat Harbour**, a working harbour for a 500-strong fleet.

Fremantle Prison

Address: The Terrace, Fremantle, www.fremantleprison.com.au
Tel: 08-9336 9200

ABOVE: the Shipwreck Galleries contain the remains and cargo of some of the ships that have foundered off WA's coast over the centuries. **BELOW:** Little Creatures Brewery.

ABOVE: Fremantle Markets are an ideal place to buy fish. For a good choice of fish restaurants, visit the Fishing Boat Harbour.
RIGHT: busking on South Terrace.

Opening Hrs: daily 10am–5pm
Entrance Fee: charge

Before exploring the centre of Fremantle, with its characterful architecture and lively cafés and shops, it is worth taking a tour of **Fremantle Prison ❼**, built by convicts in the 1850s, decommissioned as a maximum-security prison in 1991, and now one of the city's top tourist attractions.

Coffee and architecture

Fremantle claims to be the world's best-preserved example of a 19th-century port streetscape. Some of its finest architecture lies in the grid of streets inland from the Round House: High Street, Cliff Street, Henry Street, where many of the buildings now comprise Notre Dame University, and Phillimore. On Phillimore, look out for the Old Fire Station at No. 18, the Chamber of Commerce at No. 16, and the Old Customs House on the corner of Cliff Street. A short walk up Phillimore Street leads to the magnificent station built when the Perth–Fremantle railway opened in 1881. Fast trains back to Perth leave from here.

At 46 Henry Street the heritage-listed **Moores Building** is now a contemporary art gallery featuring changing exhibitions of Western Australian art (10am–5pm; free). There is also a groovy café, Moore and Moore Food and Drink, which is popular with students from Notre Dame, and an ideal spot to sip a cappuccino while perusing the art. In 1868 the Moores Building was a general merchant business, comprising a family cottage, stables, warehouse, factory and offices typical of the times when owners lived and worked on site. The fine classical facade was constructed at the height of the 1899 gold rush to unify a number of the earlier buildings into one cohesive frontage.

An unusual enclave on Essex Street, facing the Esplanade Hotel, is the **Old Mill**. Scattered across the commercial centre of the city are a few unobtrusive residential patches like this one, mostly of period cottages. Built in 1862 as the Port Flour Mill, it was converted in the 1990s to seven residential units, with an underground garage and a flagstone courtyard. For visitors who want to experience life in the hurly-burly of Freo, one of them is a bed-and-breakfast establishment, Port Mill Bed and Breakfast (*see Accommodation, page 222*).

Music in Freo

Live music is easy to find in Freo, in pubs, restaurants and clubs and from buskers on the streets. Although many pubs have been converted to backpackers' hostels, clubs or galleries, there are still plenty left, where live performance flourishes. Some of the best are **Clancy's Fish Pub** (51 Cantonment Street), **The Newport Hotel** (2 South Terrace), the **Norfolk Hotel** (47 South Terrace) and **Bar Orient** (39 High Street). Among the clubs, the **Fly By Night Musicians' Club** (Parry Street) hosts international jazz and blues, and classical performances. **Kulcha** (13 South Terrace) features world music, jazz and blues, and the **Navy Club** (High Street) has Sunday-afternoon jazz (4–7pm) organised by the Fremantle Jazz Club.

Occasional concerts (baroque, classical, romantic and 20th-century) by the **City of Fremantle Symphony** (tel: 08-9287 1874 or 04-18 933 870), a not-for-profit amateur orchestra comprising some 60 musicians, are staged at venues around town. Details of concerts and gigs of all varieties are listed in the Friday edition of the *West Australian*.

Essex Street leads to **South Terrace** ❽, also known as the Cappuccino Strip. Dining alfresco is de rigueur on South Terrace. It feels like a pedestrian mall, and, with low kerbs and flattened central islands, is designed for easy conversion for the regular street events, festivals and parades. People saunter along in a continual parade anyway; bike and car fans like to cruise, too. A long-established Italian influence, and so much competition, mean you'll find better coffee on South Terrace than anywhere in the state. There's also some of the best beer. The Sail and Anchor boutique pub brewery serves many excellent brews, including Redback and the Beez Neez.

A wide range of buskers entertains along the strip. They usually draw a crowd in the wide mall between the Sail and Anchor and the Fremantle Markets building.

Fremantle Markets

Address: corner of South Terrace and Henderson Street
Tel: 08-9335 2515

Opening Hrs: Fri 9am–9pm, Sat 9am–5pm, Sun 10am–5pm, Mon and public holidays 10am–5pm
Entrance Fee: free

First opened as a market hall in 1897 and now splendidly restored, **Fremantle Markets** ❾ is National Trust-listed. Provender spread across more than 150 stalls includes fresh fish and crustaceans, fruit and vegetables, cheeses, freshly baked bread, coffees, herbs, spices and health foods. Crafts and Australiana also abound: sheepskin and leather goods, jarrah and cane products, dried wild flowers, opals, local shells and pottery are all here. Antiques, gifts, clothing and jewellery share the hall, and there's also a bar with live music.

Back towards Victoria Quay and the railway station, along South Terrace and in arcades leading off, there are numerous shops and boutiques, as well as plenty of opportunities to stop for refreshment. Look out for specialist shops such as Purely Australian and Bob's Shoes. Leather shoes are a real bargain in Australia, and in stores such as Bob's and Bodkins Bootery on

ABOVE: browsing in Fremantle Markets.

SHOP

For second-hand and out-of-print books, visit Elizabeth's, opposite Fremantle Town Hall on William Street (Mon–Wed 9am–6pm, Thur–Sun 9am–9pm). As well as a vast choice of reduced-price books, it has a good range of Australiana and a book exchange.

ABOVE: Fremantle-born Sir Hughie Edwards is commemorated on St John's Square.

High Street, you'll find lines that are not in the chain stores.

Fremantle Village Art Markets

Address: Kings Square
Tel: 08-9432 9999
Opening Hrs: Thur 10am – 5.30pm, Fri 10am – 7.30pm
Entrance Fee: free

Further along the Terrace, Bannister Street and High Street have several specialist art shops. A right turn on High Street leads to **Kings Square**, the scene of the **Fremantle Village Art Markets** under the fig trees that includes a lunch-time concert (12.30–1.30pm) and an evening concert at 6pm on the Friday. DJ music at other times, kids' craft workshops and stalls selling food, arts and crafts, as well as tai chi lessons, also feature.

Further down **High Street**, towards the Round House, Indigenart, at the Mossenson Galleries, is filled with high-quality Aboriginal artwork. Opposite is Record Finder, where around a quarter of a million new and second-hand records and tapes are on sale. This is the best place in WA for hard-to-find albums, rarities and collectors' editions of original pressings.

Further on, at Desert Designs, the Japingka Gallery (47 High Street) specialises in paintings and limited-

SHOPPING

Fremantle is jam-packed with quirky stores, whether it be for food, clothing or antiques.

Markets

E-Shed
11 Cliff St. www.eshed markets.com.au. Tel: 08-9430 6393.
These markets have been part of Victoria Quay for almost 100 years. You'll find a selection of local fine arts and crafts. The food court sports Australian and Asian foods, a licensed bar, coffee shops, juice bars, ice-cream parlours, produce stalls and restaurants.

Fremantle Markets
Corner of South Terrace and Henderson St. www.fremantle markets.com.au. Tel: 08-9335 2515.
Get lost among the 150 stalls littered throughout this WA icon and marvel at the local crafts, food and entertainment on offer. Established in 1897, these markets are the heart and soul of Fremantle.

Food

Old Shanghai Food Court
4 Henderson St. Tel: 08-9336 7676.
Just across from the Fremantle Markets is the Old Shanghai, offering nine cheap and cheerful international food stalls.

Abhi's Bread
270 South Terrace. www.abhisbread.com. Tel: 08-9430 4373.
A favourite with Freo locals, Abhi's bread is handmade organic and sourdough bread. They also have a good selection of sweet and savoury delicacies. Try the organic panini, or, for something on the sweeter side, Abhi's chocolate and beetroot muffins are to die for.

Women's Clothing

Eros
79 Market St. Tel: 08-9335 2141.
Australian labels dominate this high-end fashion house with names like Ginger and Smart, Camilla, Sasha Drake and White Suede. It also has an eclectic range of women's accessories.

Men's Clothing

Terrace Men
65 Market St. www.terracemen.com. Tel: 08-9430 4140.
This up-market men's store provides superior quality in classic and directional clothing from local and international designers.

Antiques

Matilda's Antique Centre
222 Queen Victoria St. Tel: 08-9335 6881.
Housed in the heritage-listed old North Fremantle Town Hall (c.1902), this is Perth's largest antique centre specialising in the 19th and early 20th centuries.

Churchill Antiques and Collectibles
229 Queen Victoria St. www.antiquesperth.com. Tel: 08-9335 8889.
Deceiving from its small frontage, this store houses seven antique dealers touting specialities of the trade including collectibles, silver, glass, jewellery, furniture, prints, porcelain, tribal, military, European and English ceramics and clocks.

edition prints by Aboriginal artists, with exhibitions of the works of specific artists and communities changing every six weeks. Contemporary Aboriginal artists of all styles and major Australian regions feature. The ground-floor gallery includes paintings, prints, works on paper, didgeridoos, books and artefacts, and hand-tufted pure-wool rugs with designs by Jimmy Pike and Doris Gingingara. More can be seen further along High Street, in Bellamy's Aboriginal Art Gallery at No. 43 and Creative Native, No. 32 King Street.

On **Bannister Street**, running parallel to High, Craftworks (No. 8) occupies one of Fremantle's original bond warehouses. Here, resident crafts workers can be seen practising their crafts – woodwork, glass engraving, wildlife painting, textile printing, stained glass and pottery.

Pearls from Broome, in the state's far north, are a speciality of WA. Kailis Pearls (corner of Marine Terrace and Collie Street) has heritage displays and a video on modern pearling, as well as a good range of pearls to buy. Pearling is now a legitimate industry, but in the early days of the state Aborigines were forced to dive for pearls by white traders. By 1886,

when the Aborigines Protection Act was passed, 700 were working on the pearl luggers.

Art heritage

Artists thrive in Fremantle. Generations of writers, actors, painters, musicians and crafts workers have found inspiration (and low-cost studios) in the old port buildings.

The city's own art collection has grown to more than 1,000 works – paintings, prints, drawings, ceramics, photographs and sculpture, mostly by Australian artists. There is no single gallery for this collection; instead, exhibitions drawn from the collection are staged at the **City of Fremantle Library** and the **Fremantle Arts Centre**. Many works can be viewed at the **Town Hall** and the **Fremantle Justice Building**; others are displayed at public buildings in Fremantle and Perth.

A bequest by Claude Hotchin (1898–1977), an enthusiastic patron of the visual arts, started the city collection in 1958. He donated 41 valuable paintings by Hans Heysen, Margaret Preston, Arthur Streeton, Rupert Bunny and other Australian artists. Hotchin's generosity was echoed 20 years later when the fam-

ABOVE: keeping a beady eye on the port.
BELOW: Fremantle is a popular yachting centre.

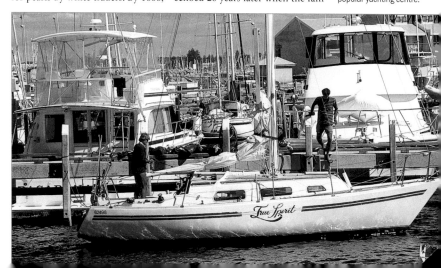

ily of the WA artist Kathleen O'Connor (1876–1968) donated 43 of her works to Fremantle.

O'Connor is one of the most famous names of Western Australia. Kathleen's father was C.Y. O'Connor, the visionary engineer responsible for the pipeline supplying water to the goldfields of Kalgoorlie. He lived with his family in Fremantle and supervised construction of the new harbour, which ultimately made Freo the state's premier port.

Army Museum

Address: Burt Street, Fremantle
Tel: 08-9430 2535
Opening Hrs: Sat–Sun 11am–4pm
Entrance Fee: charge

In nearby Burt Street is WA's longest continually occupied military base, the historic Artillery Barracks and **Army Museum** ❿. Among the pre-World War II displays is a substantial collection of tanks and other armoured vehicles.

George Street

Queen Victoria Street continues up to Fremantle Bridge, which crosses into North Fremantle, but a right turn on Canning Highway and a right on East Street leads to **George Street**, a delightful city village, where bougainvillea trails over garden walls and blue-flowered jacaranda trees drop their blossom in summer. A good reason for visiting George Street is the distinguished George Street Bistro (see page 144).

The enclave, with distant views of the Inner Harbour, has its own local character. There are restored period buildings, with stone foundations, tin bullnose awnings over verandas and a wealth of lacy wrought iron. Little Glasson Park holds an occasional local produce market. Also here, on the corner of Duke and George streets, is the green-and-ochre-coloured Old Royal George Gallery, converted from a Federation-era pub.

North Fremantle

In North Fremantle, across Fremantle Bridge, a short stretch of Queen Victoria Street retains its original charm, despite heavy traffic, with period buildings and two antiques centres, Churchill Antiques (No. 229) and Matilda's Antique Centre (No. 222), in a grand building with Corinthian columns. Both are open seven days a week. In Harvest Road several surviving cottages look as though they should be in tiny country towns.

Also on this stretch, by the bridge, is the Federation-style Swan pub, well-known for its weekend jazz gigs. Facing it is a maze of new streets filled with Mediterranean-style villas, town houses and apartments running down to the riverside to meet WA's insatiable demand for homes with water views. ❑

ABOVE: rumba at the Fremantle Festival.
BELOW: time out on a terrace, a favourite Freo pursuit.

BEST RESTAURANTS, BARS AND CAFÉS

Restaurants

Asian

Maya
75–7 Market St. Tel: 08-9335 2796. Open: L Fri, D Tue–Sun. $$$
This multi-award-winning restaurant combines a modern, elegant interior and classic Indian food. The flavours range from intense to subtle – if you prefer heat, you'll find it, and if you like fragrant you'll be satisfied too. Try the speciality goat dish or the chilli whiting fillet and hot Tawa scallops.

Old Shanghai at Fremantle Markets
4 Henderson St. Tel: 08-9336 7676. Open: L & D Wed–Sun. $
This food hall, with its range of Asian cuisines, represents good value for your money. Taka's Kitchen is budget Japanese at its best, while Ray's Curry House produces a fantastic fish curry served with roti, and there are a number of good places to get Thai and Chinese food. You can also buy alcohol and freshly squeezed juices.

Prices for a three-course dinner per person with a half-bottle of house wine:
$ = under AUS$25
$$ = AUS$25–40
$$$ = AUS$40–70
$$$$ = over AUS$70

Sala Thai
22 Norfolk St. Tel: 08-9335 7749. Open: D daily. $$
Sala Thai offers authentic Thai flavours in a relaxed setting. The food has a lovely fresh zing so typical of Thai. Good-quality ingredients and attentive service.

Australian

Benny's Bar and Café
10–12 South Terrace. Tel: 08-9433 1333. Open: B, L & D daily. $$
Serves café-style dishes and fusion food, as well as filling Italian. Pop in for oysters, cocktails and live jazz or settle in for some people-watching on the Cappuccino Strip.

Char Char Bull
44b Mews Rd, Fishing Boat Harbour. Tel: 08-9335 7666. Open: L & D daily. $$$
Offering a surf and turf experience, Char Char Bull serves seafood and meat. Its large menu encompasses prime beef, kangaroo, seafood and pizza. There's also a popular cocktail bar for pre-dinner drinks.

Flipside Burger Bar
239 Queen Victoria St. Tel: 08-9433 2188. Open: L Thur–Sun, D Tue–Sun. $
Light and airy burger bar serving gourmet burgers, including some original creations such as chicken, pear and Parmesan

RIGHT: South Terrace, aka Cappuccino Strip.

as well as the classic beef, egg, bacon, beetroot and cheese combo. The menu also caters to vegetarians with chickpea patties. Using fresh ciabatta rolls, home-made relish and mayo, these are burgers with a difference.

Harvest
1 Harvest Rd. Tel: 08-9336 1831. Open: B Sat and Sun, L Fri–Sun, D Wed–Sat. $$$
Located in a quirky cottage with mismatched furniture, Harvest takes diners on a culinary journey, exploring all sorts of styles and flavours along the way. The breakfasts are delicious, and it's worth trying the rustic-style dishes at lunch and dinner, such as pine nut and sage-filled pork loin. Well worth a visit.

The Left Bank
15 Riverside Rd. Tel: 08-9319 1315. Open: B Sun, L daily, D Mon–Sat. $$
With a bar and relaxed café downstairs and a more up-market restaurant upstairs, this venue has something for everyone. The large courtyard is popular on Sundays and is a good choice for a lazy lunch in the sun. A younger crowd hangs out downstairs, so if that's not your bag, head upstairs and ask for a balcony table.

The Norfolk
47 South Terrace. Tel: 08-9335 5405. Open: B Sun, L & D daily. $$
The Norfolk's limestone-walled courtyard is a wonderful location to while away a warm afternoon. Although the leafy out-

door area is often busy, you'll find plenty more room inside. The food is good-quality pub grub.

European

George Street Bistro
73 George St. Tel: 08-9339 6352. Open: B Sun, L Wed–Sat, D Fri–Sat. **$$$**
The walls at the George Street Bistro are brightly coloured and adorned with artwork, while the food is robust German-Euro fare. There are some big flavours here, especially in the signature duck with braised red cabbage and sauerkraut. Very popular with locals.

Italian

Capri Restaurant
21 South Terrace. Tel: 08-9335 1399. Open: L & D daily. **$**
The Capri has been a part of the Fremantle eating

scene for over 20 years. It still gives diners a complimentary bowl of minestrone soup and bread on arrival. The atmosphere is homely and the food basic but tasty.

Pizza Bella Roma
14 South Terrace. Tel: 08-9335 1554. Open: L Fri–Sun, D Tue–Sun. **$**
Always busy, this well-situated pizzeria offers family-friendly food. There is a large pizza menu to choose from, as well as lots of pastas, salads and extras. It is often loud and chaotic, but you'll feel right in the middle of the Fremantle action.

Pizza Palace
133 George St. Tel: 08-9319 8524. Open: D daily. **$**
Small restaurant where the chef creates sensational thin-crust pizza. Well worth trying if you can get a seat.

Mexican

Mexican Kitchen
19 South Terrace. Tel: 08-9335 1394. Open: L Fri–Sun, D daily. **$$**
An old-school Mexican restaurant that is family- and group-friendly. The portions are very large, and the only way to drink cocktails here is by the jug. Prepare for a siesta the next day.

Spanish

Gypsy Tapas House
Shp3/124 High St. Tel: 08-9336 7135. Open: Mon–Wed, Fri, Sun 9am–5.30pm, Thur–Sat 11am–11pm. **$$**
If you are looking for a real Freo experience, head to this fun-filled tapas bar where live music on a Saturday night is guaranteed. Try the Gypsy Tapas Banquet – an unlimited chef's selection for a bargain AUS$40 per person.

Seafood

Cicerello's Fish and Chips
44 Mews Rd. Tel: 08-9335 1911. Open: L & D daily. **$**
A family favourite that has been serving fish and chips for longer than anyone can remember. Recently refurbished, Cicerello's has several magnificent fish tanks (the fish are merely decorative, and are not for dinner) which you can watch while you queue. Food comes wrapped in traditional paper here, and the portions are often big enough to share. The kitchen closes around 8.30pm.

The Essex
20 Essex St. Tel: 08-9335 5725. Open: L Wed–Fri and Sun, D daily. **$$$**
This restored limestone cottage on Essex Street is home to a restaurant that has won several awards for both wine and food. The seafood – prawns, scallops, crayfish, salmon and Balmain bugs – is some of the best in town. For those customers who aren't into fish or other seafood, there is also Harvey beef, spatchcock and kangaroo.

Joe's Fish Shack
42 Mews Rd. Tel: 08-9336 7161. Open: L & D daily. **$$**
The decor at Joe's is nautical, to say the least. They serve delicious light bites such as stuffed tiger prawns, crumbed Freo sardines, plus a mouth-watering seafood platter

LEFT: behind the bar at The Sail and Anchor.

for two. There are also pasta, vegetarian and meat mains, and a takeaway area outside if all you want is fish and chips.

Kailis' Fish Market & Café

46 Mews Rd. Tel: 08-9335 7755. Open: B, L & D daily. **$**

Kailis has been providing Perth and Fremantle with seafood for more than 75 years. Tourists and locals alike flock to its waterside location. The fresh seafood market resides at one end of the large store, and the restaurant functions at the other, with ample seating outside on the jetty. There's basic fish and chips, plus a variety of salads, grills and desserts.

The Mussel Bar

42 Mews Rd. Tel: 08-9433 1800. Open: L Tue–Sun, D daily. **$$**

The atmosphere here is bright and cheerful during the day, and a touch more intimate and refined in the evenings. There is a strong wine list of more than 175 wines and a creative menu that makes the most of the fresh local seafood.

The Red Herring

26 Riverside Rd. Tel: 08-9339 1611. Open: L & D daily. **$$$**

Prices for a three-course dinner per person with a half-bottle of house wine:
$ = under AUS$25
$$ = AUS$25–40
$$$ = AUS$40–70
$$$$ = over AUS$70

The Red Herring restaurant projects out over the Swan River, giving diners a spectacular scene to behold, day or night. The sashimi is a house speciality, and the dozen oysters prepared six ways are a gastronomic treat. It offers a well-thought-out menu, plus first-rate service, resulting in what will be a fabulous night out.

Little Creatures

40 Mews Rd. Tel: 08-9430 5555. Open: B Sat and Sun, L & D daily. **$$**

Once a crocodile farm, this huge shed now houses one of Perth's best local breweries. Serving its own beer and a range of wine, its semi-industrial yet welcoming interior draws huge crowds. The food is good, too – try the frites with aioli, the mussels or any of the pizzas. A favourite of Fremantle's young and funky set.

The Sail and Anchor

64 South Terrace. Tel: 08-9431 1666. Open: L & D daily. **$$**

This was the first microbrewery in Perth. Still producing great beers, it has recently had a facelift and now has a funky courtyard to complement the grand building. The upstairs area has a chilled bar feel, while downstairs the atmosphere is like that of a traditional pub. The menu includes a wide range of tapas as well as more substantial mains.

East End Bar and Lounge

189 High St. www.theeastendbar. com.au. Tel: 08-9335 3331.

Inspired by the decadent bars of the 1920s and the gangster style of New York City and Chicago, the East End Bar and Lounge offers a stylish environment in which to sip those snazzy cocktails and listen to live music.

The Norfolk Basement Lounge

47 South Terrace. Tel: 08-9335 5405.

This bar, located in the basement of the Norfolk Pub, is both an intimate performance space and well-stocked bar featuring original entertainment from Thursday to Sunday nights.

Fly By Night Musicians Club

1 Holdsworth St. www.flybynight.org. Tel: 08-9430 5976.

This unique Freo venue is a not-for-profit community musicians' club and music venue. The club has a rich history of musicians, actors and comedians who have showcased their talent here over the past 20 years. There is always something to see. Artists John Butler Trio, The Waifs, Eskimo Joe, The Flairz and The Panics all started their careers at Fly by Night.

Mrs Brown

241 Queen Victoria St. www. mrsbrownbar.com.au. Tel: 08-9336 1887.

Small and intimate with mismatched furniture, this bar heaves on Friday and Saturday nights, so if you don't like crowds, come another night. With an extensive wine and beer list presented in an old-school children's story-book cover, it is an ideal place to start out the night before hitting the town.

X-wray Café and Bar

Lot4/ 3-13 Essex St. Tel: 08-9430 9399.

Distinctly in a Fremantle style, this edgy, hidden bar is only known to locals. It's a cool café by day and a rocking cocktail bar by night with live music four nights a week.

Gino's

1 South Terrace. Tel: 08-9336 1464. Open: B, L & D daily.

Gino's is a fixture of the Fremantle dining scene. You'll find families, couples, tourists and locals all sitting down for a cappuccino. The menu caters for all tastes with typical café-style fare. It is open late, and you'll find lots of people from nearby pubs and clubs grabbing coffee and cake before heading home for the night.

Sandrino Café

95 Market St. Tel: 08-9335 4487. Open: L & D daily.

A popular Fremantle eatery influenced by the flavours of the Adriatic, Sandrino prides itself on the authentic wood-fired pizza and fresh local seafood. The service is fast and friendly, with an atmosphere that oozes Fremantle charm.

FREMANTLE MARITIME MUSEUM

The futuristic-looking Maritime Museum celebrates a seafaring heritage, from whaling and pearling to hosting the America's Cup

Due to its maritime history, Fremantle is a fitting setting for the Maritime Museum, which opened on Victoria Quay in 2002. Just a few hundred metres along the waterfront is Arthur Head, where Captain Fremantle planted the Union flag and claimed WA for Britain in 1829. For more than a century Fremantle was the first sight of Australia for thousands of hopeful migrants. Wartime service turned the port into the biggest Allied submarine base outside Pearl Harbor.

The museum covers everything from whaling, pearling, fishing and trade to immigration, recreation and globalisation. There are many details to be discovered along the way, such as the importation of the Mediterranean "blessing of the sea" festival, introduced to WA by Sicilian fishermen.

ABOVE: 1.5 tonnes of high-explosive torpedo in one of six launch tubes in the submarine HMAS *Oxley*, commissioned in the 1960s.

ABOVE: the sail-like roofs of the Maritime Museum form a striking background to the sail training ship *Leeuwin*.

BELOW: the "Tin Canoe to Australia II" gallery celebrates human enjoyment of water. *Parry Endeavour* carried WA's Jon Sanders on his solo circumnavigation of the globe between May 1986 and March 1988. Here the tiny yacht hangs at the acute angle taken by Sanders as he rounded Cape Horn and survived a wall of water.

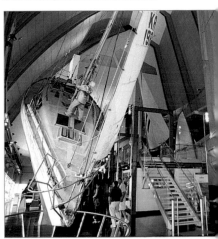

The Essentials

Address: Slip Street, Fremantle
Tel: 08-9431 8334
Opening Hrs: daily 9.30am–5pm
Entrance Fee: AUS$10 adults, AUS$5 concession
Transport: the museum is in walking distance of Fremantle Station

[Map showing: Leeuwin, Fremantle Port Authority, Slip Street, Maritime Museum, Fleet Street, Mrs Trivett Lane, Captains Lane, Arthur Head, Round House, Whalers' Tunnel, Arthur Head Reserve, Bathers Bay, Bathers Beach]

THE STORY OF THE *BATAVIA*

The Maritime Museum also includes the Shipwreck Galleries on Cliff Street. Their star exhibit is the stern of the *Batavia*, a Dutch ship wrecked off the Abrolhos islands in 1629, famous for her tragic history. Part of a Dutch expedition to the East Indies, she became separated from her companion ships on 4 June 1629, when she struck a reef. The crew escaped to two small islands, with provisions and treasure, but little water. While the captain, Francois Pelsart, and a few men, set off to find help, the ship's officer Jorome Cornelisz mutinied, leading to a blood bath among the remaining crew.

In September, Pelsart returned. The mutineers were put to death, apart from two, who were marooned near Champion Bay to become the first-known white inhabitants of the continent. Nothing was heard of them again.

The *Batavia* was raised from the depths by marine archaeologists between 1972 and 1976.

ABOVE: ships remain the cheapest way to transport goods across the world. The museum's re-creation of an Arabian souk relates the history of trade on the Indian Ocean, from the dhows of the medieval spice trade to today's container ships.

ABOVE: a guided tour of the museum's 90ft (28-metre) -long submarine HMAS *Ovens* (extra charge) reveals the cramped working lives of its 62-man crew on its 18-week tours.
LEFT: "beetle" boats, made by the US builder Charles Beetle, were carried by whaling ships in WA waters from 1792. Whaling, like pearling, was an important local industry in the 19th century.

PERTH'S BEACHES

Beginning on the doorstep of Fremantle and stretching to Hillary's Boat Harbour, some 50km (30 miles) north, Perth's Sunset Coast is the ultimate sand-and-surf playground, a chain of immaculate beaches swept by Indian Ocean breakers

Western Australians are proud of their coastline, and rightly so. In a state dominated by dry desert landscapes, the sparkling waters of the Indian Ocean exert an almost hypnotic appeal. For Perthites, whether gathering with friends for a picnic under the pines or taking an early-morning constitutional along the foreshore, the beach is a focal point of daily life, especially in summer. For some 50km (30 miles), pristine white sand unfurls in one long continuous stretch, creating more than 20 beaches, collectively known as the Sunset Coast.

Development, though continuous, is almost without exception low-rise and low-key. New buildings tend to be set well back from the shore and are likely to remain so. Perthites are fiercely protective of their right of public access to their shores.

Even in high summer temperatures almost never climb over 31°C (87°F). The Fremantle Doctor is the affectionate term given to the famous sea breeze that roars into Perth from the southwest each afternoon, cooling the city down a treat and whipping up the kinds of waves that get

surfers and sailboarders heading for the beach. For calmer conditions, choose a day when the wind is blowing from the east. In any case, take your own parasol and windcheater, as the beaches are exposed, with little shade apart from occasional crops of Norfolk pines.

Which beach?

The family-friendly resort of Hillary's Boat Harbour to the north, the trendy suburb of Cottesloe to the south and the surfing mecca of

LEFT: the best beaches for windsurfing are Leighton and Port beaches.
RIGHT: watching the action on the waves at Leighton Beach.

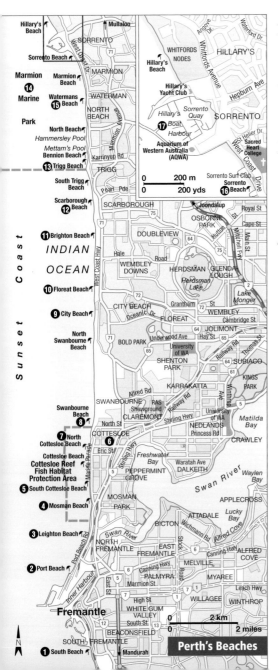

Perth's Beaches

Scarborough in the middle are the three main beaches that everybody heads for. Lively day and night, and popular with people of all ages, each has a good range of restaurants, cafés and bars, plus amenities such as toilets, changing rooms, and picnic and barbecue areas.

Elsewhere along the coast, the beaches vary from sheltered coves to rugged stretches where the wind whips up white crests on the water, making swimming unwise. If you're not a confident swimmer, or you have young children, it's best to stick to one of the busier beaches, as these are more likely to be patrolled by the Surf Life Saving Clubs (see pages 160–1). Look for their red-and-yellow outfits, watchtowers and tents. They use bright colours and red flags to mark the stretch of beach they patrol.

Although the Sunset Coast officially starts at Cottesloe, there are a few beaches further south around Fremantle which are within easy reach of the Perth CBD and good alternatives to the busier beaches to the north. It can be hard to tell when one beach has turned into another, as they all merge seamlessly, but there are signposts in every parking lot, identifying the beach, the surf and swimming conditions, and what facilities are available – invaluable if you're visiting an unpatrolled stretch. If you can't find space to park or lay out your towel at one beach, you don't have to go far to find an alternative where you can – indeed, where you may well have the sand all to yourself.

While many of the beaches have good public transport links, the best way to explore the coastline is to hire a car and hit the **West Coast Highway**, which heads north from Swanbourne Beach, becoming the **West Coast Drive** at Trigg Beach. The road runs parallel to the beach, and there are plenty of opportunities to pull in

stretch of sandy beach. Strong winds pretty much rule out sunbathing, and a sign warns swimmers of strong currents and submerged rocks, but this is a good spot to watch parasailing. Home of the Fremantle Surf Life Saving Club, **Leighton Beach ❸** is also best suited to wind- and kite-surfing, as strong currents and submerged rocks make swimming risky. There is a small car park and a kiosk.

Mosman Beach ❹ marks the start of the Cottesloe Reef Fish Habitat Protection Area, which extends up to North Street in Cottesloe. You'll see detailed signs at each of the beaches in the protected area informing you of the work being done to conserve the rare species found on this delicate stretch of reef, and what restrictions are in place (for instance, no jet-skis or spearfishing). Mosman Beach itself has no facilities other than a couple of picnic benches, while steep stepped access to the beach makes it unsuitable for people with disabilities or young children.

South Cottesloe Beach ❺ has a children's playground on a grassy area set back from the beach, but is

ABOVE: great attention is paid to maintaining a clean and safe environment. Visitors are expected to contribute to this by heeding warnings. **LEFT:** surfies training on Cottesloe sands.

and soak up the uninterrupted views, or refuel at one of the cafés along the way. You can easily cover the main section from Fremantle to Mullaloo in under an hour.

Fremantle to Cottesloe

As its name implies, **South Beach ❶** (small café, toilets 7am–9pm, good parking) is the southernmost beach in the Perth area. Owing to its proximity to the popular suburb of Fremantle, it often gets overlooked – most people come to Fremantle to shop in the markets or catch a ferry to Rottnest Island, not to swim. But South Beach is a real find, and is also a stop on Fremantle's free CAT bus as it loops around town (the railway station is approximately five minutes away on the CAT).

With views of the Fremantle Marina and flanked by a grassy area dotted with pines, South Beach is an attractive spot. Several barbecue stations and a children's playground make it popular with families. Groups play impromptu games of cricket in the shade or take to the basketball court to shoot a few hoops.

Despite the industrial backdrop of the working port of Fremantle, **Port Beach ❷** provides an enticingly long

Who Goes Where?

It can be hard to know which beach to choose, especially when they merge into one long swath of sand. These guidelines should help.

For families: Cottesloe, Mettam's Pool, Hamersley Pool and Hillary's Boat Harbour all have excellent facilities for the young ones.

For cyclists: a dual cycle track/footpath runs between Cottesloe and Burns Beach (north of Mullaloo).

For water sports: Scarborough and Trigg are best for surfing, and Leighton and Port Beach for parasailing, windsurfing and kite-surfing.

For snorkelling/diving: Marmion Marine Park (join an organised trip from Hillary's Boat Harbour) is great for diving.

For the best après beach: Cottesloe and Scarborough.

For nudists: Swanbourne, north of Cottesloe, has a strip just for nudists near the dunes at the northern end.

For rock pools: Bennion Beach, Watermans Beach.

For dogs: Whitfords Beach, north of Hillary's, has a dog beach (and an area for horses), with a dog wash service at weekends.

For visitors dependent on public transport: South Beach is served by Fremantle's CAT bus, and Cottesloe is reachable by train.

If you're planning to grab a bite to eat straight from the beach, be mindful of the fact that some places enforce dress codes banning beach attire. Bathers, flip-flops (or thongs, as the locals call them) and no shirt will see you turned away from many of the nicer cafés and bars – especially in the evening.

BELOW: fishing off the rocks at Cottesloe.

otherwise lacking in amenities. All the facilities of Cottesloe, however, are moments away, so if you like to lose the crowds but not venture too far from facilities, this is a good spot. Access to the beach is by steps only, although you can walk back along the sand to Cottesloe itself.

The trendy suburb of **Cottesloe** ❻ is the main hub on this section of coast, popular with visitors and locals alike who come to soak up the cosmopolitan vibe. Trains run out to Cottesloe from the city centre (from Cottesloe station, cross over the railway line, head down Jarrad Street and turn right onto Marine Parade). If you're driving, parking is plentiful and free but in high demand – try the parking lot on Marine Parade, but if you have no luck there, there's a much larger car park on Napier Street, just off Marine Parade.

Dominating the beach front is the graceful outline of the Indiana Tea House, an elegant, colonial-style restaurant housed in a wooden pavilion right on the beach, the perfect place for a sundowner. The bars and cafés that line Marine Parade may be set slightly back from the water, but they enjoy great ocean views and fling open their windows to let patrons make the most of it. On a hot summer's day the lively atmosphere floats out onto the street.

Most of the beach action takes place on the sand in front of the Indiana restaurant, as this is where the lifeguards keep a watchful eye. Swimming conditions are generally good here, and surfboards are banned during the height of summer (Oct–Mar) so swimmers have the water to themselves. Surfing is allowed on the artificial reef on the other side of the groyne (a man-made wall built to protect the beach from erosion).

Landscaped lawns rise up behind the beach, lined with Norfolk pines – whose distinctive shape helps lend Cottesloe its character – and provide sunbathers with some much-needed shade. Lots of families come here, as there are toilets, picnic benches, barbecues, a children's playground and plenty of room for children to run around. At night, make the most of the floodlit beach and enjoy fish and chips down on the sand.

If the crowds become too much, **North Cottesloe Beach** ➐ is far quieter, and only a minute's drive along Marine Parade or a short walk along the beach away from Cottesloe. There are no facilities, limited roadside parking – you could leave your car at Cottesloe and walk – and the beach is unpatrolled, so you swim at your own risk. In a prime location overlooking the water is the Blue Duck Café *(see page 157)*, with balcony views out to Rottnest Island.

Swanbourne to Scarborough

North of Cottesloe is **Swanbourne Beach** ➑, which is best known for its nudist bathing on the far side of the dunes. Being situated right next to a military base and accessed by a no-through road, it has plenty of privacy, but swimming conditions can be rough. There are toilets and lots of parking.

Following the road around the back of the army barracks, you soon hit the start of the West Coast Highway, from which several beautiful beaches can be accessed. First is **City Beach** ➒, voted Perth's friendliest beach in 2009 and WA's best beach in 2005. A large grassy area slopes gently down to a wide stretch of sand overlooked by the Surf Life Saving Club. Toilets, a kiosk serving refreshments, and gas barbecue facilities mean you can spend a day here quite comfortably, morning until late. There are also volleyball nets on the sand and a playground for the kids. Parking is plentiful.

Floreat Beach ➓, in the lovely, affluent suburb of the same name, is a large, attractive beach popular with locals. It is patrolled only part-time, so be sure to look for the red-and-yellow flags. There's a good range of amenities, including toilets, plenty of parking, free public volleyball courts, and a café, kiosk and large children's playground set under brightly coloured shades on a grassy picnic area.

ABOVE: a huge sundial was built at Cottesloe to celebrate Australia's bicentenary in 1988.
BELOW: Scarborough's Rendezvous Observation City Hotel is the only high-rise along the coast.

ABOVE: bird's-eye view of Scarborough Beach.

TIP

The best surf beaches are Scarborough and Trigg, but listen out for local surf conditions, broadcast daily on local radio. Note that at some beaches surfboards are only allowed at certain times of the year or in designated areas.

Brighton Beach ⓫ is another good-sized stretch of sand, framed by attractively landscaped picnic and playground areas. Access is just a short walk from the large car park through the dunes. Lifeguards are on patrol, surfers have their own designated area – indicated by blue-and-white signs – and there is a kiosk for refreshments. Brighton is a good alternative for those wishing to be near the attractions and amenities of Scarborough without the crowds.

Perhaps the premier coastal beach destination in the Perth area, **Scarborough** ⓬ is certainly the largest and most developed. Offering a wide range of waterfront accommodation, it's a popular choice for holiday-makers who prefer to base themselves outside the city centre, as well as a focal point for local surfers, who come to make the most of the prime breakers on this part of the coast. The beach is patrolled, and regular surf life saving competitions and displays are held here, making for entertaining viewing.

All types of water sports are available, or you can just sit back and watch the fun from the picnic area behind the dunes. The beach-front jogging track is always in use, while for those who prefer a more sedate pace there's the **Scarborough to Trigg Heritage Walk**. As at Cottesloe, there's a good choice of bars, cafés and restaurants, and a supermarket just a short walk from the beach. On Sundays the bars can get a little rowdy as the legendary "Sunday session" kicks off late afternoon, so if you're not up for partying, it's best to stay away.

Trigg to Hillary's Boat Harbour

South Trigg Beach has toilets and a grassed picnic area, but not much else; consequently most people carry on to **Trigg Beach** ⓭ itself, another popular spot with surfers and sailboarders. The beach is patrolled, but strong rips often develop which can make swimming dangerous, so you may prefer just to enjoy the views from the Trigg Island Café, a lively place popular with locals who come for the good food and waterfront location (see page 159). Clarko Reserve, a big grassed area back from the beach, has picnic tables, barbecues and a children's playground.

From Trigg to Burns Rock (north of Mullaloo) lies the **Marmion Marine Park ⑭**, established in 1987 to protect the reefs, lagoons and small offshore islands that run for some 5km (3 miles) along this stretch of coast. A haven for fish, dolphins, sea lions and birdlife, the park – the first of its kind in Western Australia – offers great diving and snorkelling opportunities. Most diving boats go from Hillary's Boat Harbour, or you can try your luck with a snorkel off one of the beaches in the park.

The beaches in Marmion Marine Park are very different from others along this stretch of coast. Gone are the dunes of Scarborough and Brighton and the wide expanses of sand at Floreat and Cottesloe; instead you'll find rocky outcrops jutting out of relatively narrow sections of sand and signs warning of the possibility of rock falls. Don't let that put you off, however, as there are some great rock pools to explore, particularly at Bennion Beach – where there is parking but little else – and Mettam's Pool. The latter is a shallow lagoon that literally forms a pool only 2 metres (6ft) deep – ideal for first-time snorkellers to practise their technique before hitting the open water. There are also toilets and a ramp to the beach for disabled access.

Hamersley Pool, another safe bay, is swiftly followed by **North Beach**, which has toilets, a fishing jetty and limited roadside parking. The North Beach shops include a supermarket, bakery and café within striking distance of the beach.

Watermans Beach ⑮ boasts a good stretch of sand and interesting rock pools to explore. The water is calm in the shallows, making it good for children and inexperienced swimmers, and there's a children's playground next to the beach under the shade of the Norfolk pines.

Marmion Beach has little sand to speak of and just a small car park, most of which is taken up by visitors to the private Marmion Angling and Aquatic Club which is based here.

Next stop on the West Coast Drive is **Sorrento Beach ⑯**. With plenty of beachside accommodation and the shops, cafés and attractions of Hillary's Boat Harbour next door, it's a good place to come for the day – should you tire of the wide expanse of sand and sparkling ocean, you can easily walk across the car park to Hillary's for a bite to eat or a browse among the shops. Sorrento itself has a beachside kiosk and toilets, and is patrolled by life savers, as winds can sometimes make conditions rough.

Locals with very small children avoid the surf beaches of the Sunset Coast altogether and go instead to **Hillary's Boat Harbour ⑰**. Despite its name, boats are actually prohibited in some parts of the marina, allowing for safe swimming in the flat calm of the harbour. The small man-made

TIP

Scarborough hosted the Australian Surf Life Saving Championships (see pages 160–61) in 2007 (the centenary of Surf Life Saving in Australia), and again in 2008. The championships normally take place in March or April.

BELOW: surfing at Scarborough.

ABOVE: family-friendly Hillary's. **BELOW:** the Aquarium of Western Australia at Hillary's is one of the state's top attractions.

beach is always busy with families, many of whom turn up early and set up camp for the day under one of the brightly coloured canvases that provide shade. There's an adventure playground on the sand itself, while further back from the beach is a small funfair, water slides, minigolf and trampolines. The beach is patrolled, although conditions are so tame that residents bring their children here for summer swimming lessons.

The surrounding precinct is filled with boutiques, souvenir shops, bars and restaurants, most of which line the timber boardwalk known as **Sorrento Quay**. Behind here is the **Aquarium of Western Australia** (AQWA; www.aqwa. com.au; daily 10am–5pm; charge), one of the state's top attractions, especially for children. Western Australia has 12,000km (7,400 miles) of coastline, and five distinct coastal environments are recreated here. The highlight, however, is the walk-through aquarium representing the Shipwreck Coast, where sharks, loggerhead turtles, stingrays and more glide smoothly overhead within centimetres of the upturned

faces watching them. Other highlights include a touch pool, saltwater crocodiles of the Far North Coast and tropical fish of Perth's Coast. The aquarium also offers the opportunity to dive and snorkel with sharks.

Hillary's to Mullaloo

Just north of Hillary's lies **Whitfords Nodes**, a large park with picnic spaces, scenic lookouts, a children's playground and a long coastal beach, with plenty of parking off Whitfords Avenue. **Pinnaroo Point** is another rugged coastal beach with a small grassed area and children's playground, while **Whitfords Beach** has parking but little else. As in many places along the coast, these beaches are linked by a beach-front dual-use cycle/pedestrian path.

Mullaloo Beach, towards the northern tip of the Sunset Coast, is a large, attractive spot, popular with families and groups of friends who take full advantage of the picnic and barbecue facilities scattered across the landscaped lawns overlooking the beach. ❑

BEST RESTAURANTS, BARS AND CAFÉS

Restaurants

City Beach

Mambo Italiano
316 The Boulevard. Tel: 08-9285 1555. Open: L Fri, D Mon–Sat. **$$**
This Italian restaurant has good-quality food and hearty portions. The menu has the usual range of pasta dishes, meaty mains, pizza and salad, but they are all well executed.

Oceanus
195 Challenger Parade. Tel: 08-9385 7555. Open: B Sun, L Tue–Sun, D Tue–Sat. **$$$**
This is the only restaurant on City Beach, and if it's high-class food you're after, you'll find it right here. Oceanus takes inspiration from modern Oz cuisine and specialises in seafood. Think grilled whole bugs, cuttlefish, Catalan black rice, and saffron aioli to get the idea.

Cottesloe

Amberjack's
94 Marine Parade. www.amberjacks.com.au. Tel: 08-9385 0977. Open: L & D daily. **$**
You can't beat the location of this fish-and-chip shop directly opposite Cottesloe Beach. Grab your paper-wrapped dinner and head over to the grass to watch the sun set. It tends to be the standard fare, but the food is made magical by the great location. There are great salads available, too.

Barchetta
149 Marine Parade. Tel: 08-9385 2411. Open: B & L daily, D Wed–Sat. **$$**
If you were any closer to the water, you'd be in it. Barchetta hangs over the dunes of North Cottesloe Beach, producing simple dishes with a European influence. Lunches include paella and spicy roast pumpkin salad, and the dinner options might include Moroccan-inspired chermoula lamb or crab spaghettini. You can also get great burgers and pizzas.

Barista
38 Napoleon St. Tel: 08-9383 3545. Open: B & L daily. **$$**
Serving simple yet tasty modern Australian food, Barista makes a concerted effort to keep healthy options on the menu, and the food is prepared fresh using the best ingredients. It also serves great coffee and wonderful cakes.

The Blue Duck
151 Marine Parade. Tel: 08-9385 2499. Open: B, L & D daily. **$$**
This eatery overlooking the ocean at North Cottesloe has become a Perth institution. Light breakfast starts from 6am, with à la carte from 7am and buffet breakfasts at the weekend. From lunch time onward it's always busy, and you'll have to book in advance to secure a table overlooking the ocean. The menu focuses on seafood, but you'll find many other options, from sweet-and-sour pork to saffron risotto and mustard lamb rack.

C Blu
Ocean Beach Hotel, Marine Parade. Tel: 08-9383 5414. Open: B, L & D daily. **$$$**
The food might not be that imaginative, but you'll always find it well cooked and tasty. Even if it's just a steak you're after, or grilled fish with tomato salsa, you'll find something to enjoy in this great location that overlooks the ocean.

Il Lido Italian Cantina
88 Marine Parade. Tel: 08-9286 1111. Open: daily 8am–10pm. **$$$**
With long, simple tables for communal dining, a stylish menu and an innovative wine list, Il

---

RIGHT: a quick coffee stop at Barista.

Prices for a three-course dinner per person with a half-bottle of house wine:
$ = under AUS$25
$$ = AUS$25–40
$$$ = AUS$40–70
$$$$ = over AUS$70

Lido Italian Cantina is a great place to relax with a group of friends. Order the pearl onion risotto with rosemary-crusted lamb chops.

Indiana
99 Marine Parade. Tel: 08-9385 5005. Open: L & D daily. Breakfast on weekends from 8am. **$$$**

This majestic building is hard to miss, as it sits perched above the sands at Cottesloe Beach. Although the decorating style is beachhouse, the food takes inspiration from all over the world – pizzas, seafood, salads and steaks. Part of the renowned Fraser's Group, it is a guaranteed oceanside bistro.

Van's
1 Napoleon St. Tel: 08-9384 0696. Open: B, L & D daily. **$$$**

This café epitomises the best that restaurants in Perth have to offer: a relaxed atmosphere, top-quality produce served in original ways, good wines, and great coffee to finish. The duck spring rolls as an entrée are top-notch, the open sandwich with organic chicken and roast capsicum is a perfect light lunch, and the dinner menu is mouth-watering.

Hillary's Boat Harbour

Ishka
58 Southside Drive. www.the breakwater.com.au. Tel: 08-9448 5000. Open: L & D daily. **$$$**

Spectacular views over the harbour and ocean

make this Perth eatery very special. The delicious food is well matched by the stunning view. The menu is predominantly seafood, but there is also a good selection of meat and vegetarian dishes.

Portofinos
Sorrento Quay, Southside Drive. Tel: 08-9246 4700. Open: B Sun, L & D daily. **$$**

This is one of the most popular restaurants at Hillary's Boat Harbour, located a few metres from the quay's beach. Portofinos serves oysters, pasta dishes, risotto, pizza, and a choice of steak, chicken and fish dishes. To call the portions generous is an understatement.

Mullaloo

Mullaloo Beach Hotel
10 Oceanside Parade. www. mullaloobeachhotel.com.au. Tel: 08-9401 8411. Open: B Sun, L & D daily. **$$**

This hotel overlooking Mullaloo Beach serves some fantastic food. At lunch time it offers customers an informal, just-off-the-beach dining experience, but dinner can be considerably more sophisticated. Dishes include seared Tasmanian salmon with citrus soy glaze.

North Beach

Soda
251c West Coast Drive. Tel: 08-9448 7472. Open: B & L daily, D Wed–Sun. **$$**

Soda has an innovative

menu that will delight the most jaded of taste buds. Chef-owner Ben Andrijasevich has a background in fine cuisine, and he brings his deft hand to a more inclusive environment with his own venture, Soda. Inspired dishes include Jamaican pork belly with caramelised banana, apple, coconut and lime salad. It's top-quality food with an inventive twist in a great location.

Port Beach

Salt on the Beach
42 Port Beach Rd. www.on thebeach.net.au. Tel: 08-9430 6866. Open: B, L & D daily. **$$$**

This restaurant is ideally located on Leighton Beach. You can choose to relax in the outdoor area, sandy feet and all, or opt for the plusher surrounds of the adjacent restau-

rant, which serves excellent steak and fresh fish, as well as pizza and oysters. Outside you can still order food, but the menu is more informal, with lighter options such as Turkish bread and dips. Salt on the Beach is a great spot to toast a sunset with a beer from its own Blacksalt Brewery.

Scarborough

Café del Pescatore
Corner of Manning St and The Esplanade. Tel: 08-9245 3525. Open: L & D daily. **$$**

Beautiful ocean views and fresh seafood make Café del Pescatore a popular choice in Scarborough. Don't be put off by the rather corny nautical theme of the interior decorating – the superb seafood is brought in fresh daily from all around the coast of Western Australia. In particular, try their signature crayfish dish.

Sorrento

Voyage

128a West Coast Drive. Tel: 08-9447 2443. Open: B & L Tue–Sun. **$$**

This is a great little establishment serving interesting dishes, such as Moroccan chicken with couscous and elegant open steak sandwiches. You can also buy takeaway salads and lovely bottled oils and jams. The coffee is strong, the interior light and bright, and the staff provide a warm welcome at Voyage.

White Salt

134 West Coast Drive. Tel: 08-9246 9221. Open: B Sat–Sun, L Tue–Sun, D Wed–Sun. **$$$**

White Salt's varied menu features many classic dishes prepared in new ways, such as rib eye steak with potato dauphinois and a knock-out coq au vin. There are also more unusual and unique dishes, such as succulent beef carpaccio with pesto and rocket, and seared teriyaki scal-

lops. The breakfasts are well worth considering, too: in particular, check out the fruit salad, yoghurt and muesli combo, and the generous omelettes.

Trigg

Trigg Island Café

360 West Coast Drive. www. triggislandcafe.com.au. Tel: 08-9447 0077. Open: B, L & D daily. **$$**

This is a popular standby serving tasty favourites such as scallops, chilli prawns, steak, seafood platters and a good range of salads, as well as focaccia sandwiches. Breakfast begins at 8am on weekends, 8.30am weekdays.

Ice cream

Il Gelato

88 Marine Parade. Tel: 08-9286 2800. Open: daily until 9.30pm. **$**

This is a first-rate Italian *gelato*, right on the beach at Cottesloe. Even if you are heading further along the coast, it is worth stopping here along the way. There is a range of 99 percent fat-free sorbet, plus a large selection of ice cream. The many delicious flavours – including ferrero, tiramisu, hazelnut and chocolate profiteroles – make choosing difficult. Go the double scoop: it's worth it.

Bars and Cafés

Delish Fresh Food and Coffee House

Shop 79, Floreat Forum Shopping Centre. Tel: 08-9387 1366. Open: B & L Mon–Sat.

As much as possible, the food is home-made here. Try the classic beef – spinach, mayo, thinly sliced rare roast beef and caramelised onion – or the chicken fresca – baby cos, mayo, sliced roast chicken, diced herbed tomato and marinated artichoke.

Elba

29 Napolean St. Tel: 08-9284 3482. Open: Mon–Sat noon–midnight, Sun noon–10pm.

Sleek and sophisticated best describes this salubrious new bar in Cottesloe. A selective tasting menu complements its rich wine and beer list and is a glamorous way to start the evening before heading to dinner.

Ocean Beach Hotel

Marine Parade. Tel: 08-9384 2555. Open: daily.

The OBH is a must-go for anyone wanting to experience a piece of authentic Australian pub culture. You'll fight to get space on a warm afternoon as customers jostle to secure a prime location at the front of the Saloon bar, the best place to watch the sun set over the ocean. The standard range of drinks and bar snacks is on offer.

Soda Sunlounge

Upstairs 1 North Beach Rd. Tel: 08-9203 7788. Open: Mon–Sun noon–late, Sat, Sun and public holidays 9am–late.

High up over the Indian Ocean is this uber-chic bar with good tunes, good food and drinks in a laid-back atmosphere, run by the same team as Soda.

Prices for a three-course dinner per person with a half-bottle of house wine:
$ = under AUS$25
$$ = AUS$25–40
$$$ = AUS$40–70
$$$$ = over AUS$70

ABOVE LEFT: beachside café in Cottesloe. **RIGHT:** Indiana Tea House at Cottesloe, a great place for a sundowner.

Life Savers

Some 11,000 volunteer life savers help keep WA's beaches safe. Their formidable skills (and muscles) are showcased at the many beach carnivals

Millions of beach-goers enjoy the sun, surf and sand all around the coasts of Australia, most of them wrapped up in sunsuits and hats and slathered with zinc cream. Their days at the beach are made much safer by the skill and dedication of the SLSC – Surf Life Saving Clubs.

The first club was started at Cottelsoe in 1908. Now there are 27 between Broome and Esperance, with about 11,000 members of all ages, and all volunteers. Every year they save around 500 swimmers from drowning, deal with 10,000 incidents, and administer first aid to 5,000 beach-goers.

To be effective, members must be both extremely fit and good swimmers. Each of the big beaches has its own club, whose members train regularly and compete against other clubs at local, state, national and sometimes international level.

ABOVE: spectacular displays of Surf Life Saving can be seen at beach carnivals held throughout the summer. With its emphasis on teamwork, a sense of victory over the elements and a dash of gung-ho heroism, the sport appeals to many Aussie values.
BELOW: although women have been allowed to participate in WA's Surf Life Saving Clubs since the 1920s, they were not allowed to patrol as life savers until the 1970s.

BELOW: youngsters get the beach bug early in WA, and Surf Life Saving Clubs have members of all ages who enjoy the comradeship and challenging physical activity.

NATURAL HAZARDS

Shark attacks are rare in WA and fatalities even less frequent, but after a swimmer was taken by a white pointer shark off Cottesloe a few years ago a new sea and air patrol began. Every summer, from October to March, volunteer aviation students from Edith Cowan University (ECU) fly low over Perth's beaches from Dawesville (south) up to Two Rocks (north) and also around Rottnest Island.

Flying the university's two Cessna Cutlass planes a few hundred metres above the waves, the pilots search the water below for any lurking danger and alert the fisheries and police boats to take action. Swimmers and surfers are called in from the ocean by life savers and rangers.

Before swimming on a remote beach, ask the locals for any advice, and check with the police and rangers. Hazards can include rips, undetectable currents that carry swimmers offshore (if you get caught in one, swim parallel to the shore until free, then swim back to the beach) and dangerous marine life such as stone fish and blue-ring octopus, mainly found in WA's north.

ABOVE: championship events are designed to improve and test the life savers' skills. They include sprint races in soft sand, swimming contests, iron man events (combining several different categories), board paddling and ski paddling (similar to kayaking). The surf skis are about 5.5 metres (18ft) long and weigh about 18kg (40lb).

BELOW: the boat events are often the most exciting part of the life-saving competitions. Each boat comprises four rowers plus a fifth person to "sweep" – look for the safest and quickest passage through the surf. Effective teamwork is essential.

ROTTNEST ISLAND

Perthites have a string of spectacular beaches within easy reach, but when they really want to get away from it all, they head for the pristine island of Rottnest, just 19km (12 miles) from Fremantle

Main Attractions

WADJEMUP LIGHTHOUSE
ROTTNEST ISLAND RAILWAY
OLIVER HILL
THOMSON BAY

Maps and Listings

MAP OF ROTTNEST ISLAND,
PAGE 165
RESTAURANTS AND BARS,
PAGE 167

Rotto, as the locals affectionately call **Rottnest Island**, lies a mere 19km (12 miles) from Fremantle, yet feels as though it is a completely different world. In its chequered history the island has gone through many incarnations, including as a penal settlement and a military occupied zone, before emerging as the holiday island it is known as today. Rottnest is loved by Perthites, who escape to its shores for weekends of lazing on picture-postcard beaches, snorkelling in azure waters and diving among the shipwrecks that litter its coastline. Strict environmental policies keep the developers out and the traffic to a bare minimum, helping to preserve the island's sense of timelessness for future generations to enjoy.

History

Dutch cartographer Willem de Vlamingh first put Rottnest on the map when he came across the island while surveying the coast of Western Australia in 1696. Mistaking the strange creatures who roamed the island for rodents, later correctly identified as quokkas *(see page 167)*, he named the landmass "Rotte-nest" – rats' nest.

The early settlers of the Swan River Colony arrived in 1829 with plans to establish a township. They struggled to impose their ideas of private property on the local Aboriginal tribe, the Nyungar, and skirmishes became frequent, leading to the imprisonment of increasing numbers of Nyungar people. From 1838, Aboriginal prisoners from the mainland were sent to Rottnest, and in 1841 the island was officially made into an open prison.

Rottnest is known as "Wadjemup" to Aboriginals, and the island has

LEFT: Wadjemup Lighthouse, a beacon on Wadjemup Hill in the centre of Rottnest.
RIGHT: beautifully clear, still waters around Rottnest.

ABOVE: the pool at Rottnest Lodge, a former prison and barracks offering accommodation.
RIGHT: hire a bike or take your own – it's the best form of transport on Rottnest.

great spiritual significance for them. Following the appearance of a dead whale on a Rottnest beach in December 2005, Aboriginal elders believe the island is slowly reawakening after its dark years as a prison.

In 1904 the prison was closed, and the island was used by governors entertaining high society, giving rise to a fierce debate about whether it should be kept private or opened up to the public. Ultimately, the latter argument won, and in 1917 the island was declared an A-Class Reserve, ensuring the land couldn't be leased or sold. To this day, there is no private housing on the island.

During the 1920s camping sites were established, along with a general store and tearooms to cater for the increasing visitor numbers. By the 1930s, ferries were busy transporting hundreds of holiday-makers between the mainland and the island.

When World War II broke out in Europe, Rottnest was secured by the military as a forward defence position to protect the harbour of Fremantle. Guns were installed at Bickley Battery and Oliver Hill, and barracks and

a railway were built, all of which are visitor attractions today. When troops withdrew in 1945 holiday-makers once again returned to the beaches.

Facilities on the island

The island is about 11km (7 miles) long and 4.5km (3 miles) at its widest. Facilities on the island are few and far between. Hotel accommodation is limited to the newly redeveloped Hotel Rottnest and Rottnest Lodge. At peak times, accommodation is allocated by public ballot, as demand is high. If you want to stay overnight or longer, make sure you book well in advance.

Getting around

Nothing sums up the pace of life on Rottnest more than the humble two-wheeler. With virtually no traffic on the roads, cycling is a real pleasure here – and the stunning views certainly make all the hills worth the effort. Allow about 2½ hours to make the 24km (15-mile) round trip. You can either bring your own bike (they

Getting to Rottnest

Rottnest's proximity to the mainland makes it an easy day trip by ferry from Perth. **Boat Torque Cruises** (tel: 1300 467 688; www.boattorque.com.au) operate from Northport and C Shed, Fremantle, and Barrack Street Jetty, Perth. **Hillary's Fast Ferries** (tel: 08-9246 1039; www.hillarysfastferries.com.au) run from Hillary's Boat Harbour, while **Oceanic Cruises** (tel: 08-9325 1191; www.oceaniccruises.com.au) set out from B Shed, Fremantle, and Barrack Street, Perth. It takes approximately 25 minutes to get to the island from Fremantle, 45 minutes from Hillary's and 90 minutes from Perth. The cost of the ferry crossing includes an entrance fee to the island. The ferry crossing to Rottnest can get choppy. If you're prone to seasickness, or have children with you, take motion sickness tablets beforehand and avoid filling up on snacks at the kiosk before you sail!

The beauty of the island is perhaps best appreciated from the air, so why not take the **Rottnest Air Taxi** (tel: 08-9292 5027; www.rottnest.de)? Flights leave from Jandakot Airport in Perth for Rottnest Aerodrome at times arranged to suit you (cost is approximately AUS$80 return each, based on three people sharing a four-seater aircraft).

can be carried free on the ferries) or hire one from Rottnest Bike Hire (tel: 08-9292 5105) in Thomson Bay. Note that by law you must wear a helmet when riding a bike anywhere in WA.

If cycling seems like too much hard work, the Bayseeker bus is a hop-on, hop-off service that loops between all the best beaches and the main settlement at Thomson Bay. It's designed to carry everything from surfboards to fishing rods. A day pass is reasonable (tickets available from the Visitor Centre. The trip from Geordie Bay to the Thomson Bay settlement is free, and a courtesy shuttle bus also plies this route.

The strong breeze on Rottnest – as the virtually horizontal angle of some of the trees signifies – means you can't always sense the full force of the sun, so be extra careful to take the usual precautions. In summer, the north side of the island is generally more sheltered, as the wind comes from the southwest – some-thing to bear in mind when choosing your beach.

Orientation

Disembarking from the ferry at the main jetty, you'll see a small cluster of buildings ahead, known as the **Thomson Bay** settlement. The buildings here are among the oldest on the island, built by prisoners incarcerated on Rottnest during the 19th century. They were given their distinctive ochre wash because white paint produced too harsh a glare in the bright sun. Among these, the former hayshed and mill have been converted into an excellent museum (daily 10.45am–3.30pm).

Directly opposite the end of the jetty is the **Visitor and Information Centre** (tel: 08-9372 9732; www.rott nestisland.com), an excellent resource for planning all aspects of your visit to Rottnest. Behind the Visitor Centre is a pedestrian shopping mall with a general store, post office, newsagent

ABOVE: getting close to a quokka, one of the small wallabies that inhabit Rottnest Island.

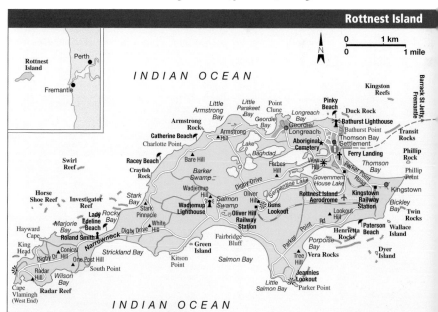

Rottnest Island

TIP

All snakes on the island are venomous, but they're not aggressive and will usually have slithered away before you even spot them. If you do see one, steer well clear – a bite can be fatal and requires immediate medical attention – and avoid walking through long grass or scrubby areas.

BELOW: Salmon Bay.

and cafés (don't be fooled by the idyllic charm of the island: chain those bikes up before visiting). To the left of the jetty are the Dome Café, the Rottnest tearooms and Hotel Rottnest – which used to be the governor's residence and is now a pub – all of which have lovely views of the bay.

Bays and beaches

With 63 beaches on the island – each equally beautiful – finding a patch of sand for yourself is never a problem. If time is short, however, the Bayseeker will take you to the most popular. The Basin, generally regarded as the best swimming beach, is only 10 minutes from Thomson Bay. Other sheltered spots include Longreach Bay, Little Parakeet Bay and Little Salmon Bay. Geordie Bay boasts holiday accommodation, shops and a picturesque bay filled with bobbing boats.

The waters around Rottnest throw up some great surfing breaks. You will find that the best conditions are at Strickland Bay, Stark Bay and Salmon Bay. The Western Cape is very salty and barren, but offers some dramatic scenery best viewed from the boardwalk that runs to the very tip of the cape.

Snorkelling and diving

Rottnest is home to some remarkable species of coral and fish, and its crystal waters create optimum snorkelling and diving conditions. Experienced divers may want to join a trip out to one of the many wrecks offshore. Enquire at **Malibu Dive** (tel: 08-9292 5111), located beneath the Dome Café in Thomson Bay. Snorkellers can pick up an underwater trail at Parker Point – a stunning beach where the crystal-clear turquoise waters offer excellent visibility. The Visitor Centre can provide pointers on the best reefs to visit.

If you want to view life below the waves without getting your feet wet, a good option is the **Underwater Explorer** (tel: 0400 202 340; www. underwaterexplorer.com.au), a semi-submersible boat that runs trips out to the reef several times a day from September to May. You'll see shipwrecks, endless varieties of coral and fish, and maybe even dolphins, turtles and rays if you're lucky. The trip takes 45 minutes, and, although it can

get choppy, you're free to go up on deck any time for a breather and to admire the island views and distant Perth skyline. Tickets can be booked at the Visitor Centre.

Tours and sights

Another nice way of exploring the island is on foot. Walking tours, run by knowledgeable volunteer guides, depart daily from the Visitor Centre. They cover a range of subjects from Aboriginal history on the island to environmental issues (most are free; some make a small charge).

If you're staying on the island for more than a day, a two-hour guided bus tour (booked at the Visitor Centre) with commentary is a good way to get orientated to the key attractions on the island. Leaving from the main bus stop behind the Visitor Centre, the tours take you around the main points of interest, with several photo and quokka-spotting opportunities along the way.

Quokkas are not exclusive to Rottnest. They can still be found at 25 sites on the mainland in the southeast of WA, but thrive in the greatest numbers on Rottnest, with a population of between 7,000 and 10,000.

Other options for a pleasant afternoon include a tour of **Wadjemup Lighthouse** (tours bookable from the Visitor Centre; children under five are not permitted inside the lighthouse). You can also hop aboard the **Rottnest Island Railway** (departure from Settlement Railway Station) for a trip to **Oliver Hill** and a guided tour of the gun and tunnels established on Rottnest as part of the defence of Fremantle during World War II.

Events

Rottnest holds a variety of events throughout the year, so make sure you check out the island's calendar (www. rottnestisland.com) to see what's of interest. The Rottnest Island Channel Swim is the most popular, with 2,300 competitors and 6,000 spectators. The Swim has the largest participation of any distance open-water swim in the world and attracts swimmers from all over the globe (see www.rottnestchannel swim.com.au). Other events include an Anzac Day service, surfing competitions and golf tournaments. ❏

ABOVE: take the Rottnest Island Railway to Oliver Hill.

RESTAURANTS AND BARS

Restaurants

Aristos Waterfront Rottnest
www.aristosrottnest.com.au.
Tel: 08-9292 5171. L & D daily. $$–$$$
The cuisine at Aristos Waterfront celebrates WA's famous seafood and has recently launched an à la carte menu to include more up-market dishes such as lobster and creamy garlic prawns. All tables have an ocean view overlooking Thomson Bay.

Marlins at Rottnest Lodge
Kitson St. www.rottnestlodge. com.au. Tel: 08-9292 5161. L & D daily. $$$
Serving modern Australian cuisine and lots of local seafood, the menu at Marlins is matched by the locale. Sample dishes include fresh Tasmanian salmon, Moroccan lamb rump, and chicken massaman curry.

Quokka Joe's
Tel: 08-9292 5777. B, L & D daily. $$
Gluten-free and organic options can be found at this cute café. Lunches include focaccia, frittata, vegetarian lasagne, curry and rice, steak, fish and salads, while dinners are more substantial with risotto, seafood dishes, steak, roast vegetables and pasta dishes. Overlooking Heritage Common, Joe's is the place to go for a healthy meal before hitting the beach.

Bars

Hotel Rottnest
Thomson Bay. www.hotelrott nest.com.au. Tel: 08-9292 5011. L & D daily. $$
At one time this hotel was the residence of the island's governor. It's the perfect place to watch the twinkling lights of Perth. Hamptons Bar puts on a good pub meal, and has both a charcoal grill and salad buffet, as well as dining options for children such as pizza and burgers.

• • • • • • • • •
Price includes dinner and a half-bottle of house wine.

$ = under AUS$25
$$ = AUS$25–40
$$$ = AUS$40–70
$$$$ = over AUS$70

AROUND PERTH

The upper reaches of the Swan Valley are characterised by lush vineyards and towns redolent of a bygone age. A little further afield are the Perth Hills, where you'll find John Forrest National Park, waterfalls and botanical gardens

Main Attractions

GUILDFORD
TOWN HALL
STIRLING SQUARE
LILAC HILL PARK
SANDALFORD
HOUGHTON WINES

Maps and Listings

MAP OF AROUND PERTH, PAGE 170
MAP OF SWAN VALLEY, PAGE 173
RESTAURANTS, BREWERIES AND BARS, PAGES 182–3

Small cities have a great advantage; you can get out of them quickly. When the surrounding country is as rich as Perth's that's a compliment, not a jibe. The western beaches and Indian Ocean, and the encircling inland hills and valleys, are as integral to Perth as the city centre and Swan River.

You need not travel far from Perth to appreciate the bush. This is not the harsh, unforgiving Outback – and certainly not the arid desert – but the kind of bush that early colonists encountered and settled nearly 200 years ago. For destinations further afield – Margaret River, Albany, Kalgoorlie, the Pinnacles and Kalbarri – see the Excursions chapter.

THE SWAN VALLEY

One of the earliest settlements in Western Australia, established in 1829, was **Guildford ❶** (*see map, page 173*) in the Swan Valley, the most accessible and appealing of the surrounding districts. If there's time for just one out-of-towner, this is the trip to make. It is only 30 minutes away by train or road (either the Great Eastern Highway or Guildford Road) from the CBD, and a further five minutes by car will take you through the vineyards of WA's oldest wine area, where wineries, breweries, restaurants and tourist attractions welcome visitors through the year.

Guildford is easily explored on foot. Close to the train station, the **Visitor Centre** (Old Guildford Court-house, Meadow Street; tel: 08-9379 9400) can provide a map of short walk trails taking from 20 minutes to an hour. Opposite the station, a parade of antiques shops

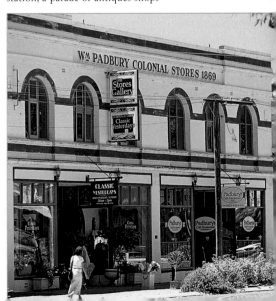

LEFT: the peaceful lake at Millbrook Winery in Jarrahdale.
RIGHT: Padbury Colonial Stores in Guildford, now an antiques shop.

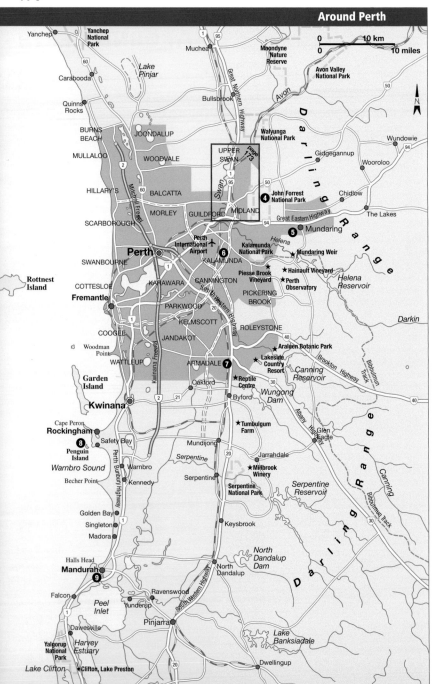

lines James Street between the once enormous Federation-style (around 1900) **Guildford Hotel** (the hotel burned down in 2008 and is currently undergoing extensive restoration) and the Art Deco **Town Hall**. Most of the period homes and public buildings are on or just off **Stirling Square**, between the railway and nearby river.

Early settlers were granted large allotments of land, and many beautiful homes were built. This part of Guildford was known as "home of the Bon Ton" or the well-to-do. Particularly stately is **Riversleigh** (132 Swan Street; closed to the public), a striking gold-rush property with deep shady verandas, turret, multi-angled tin roofs, ornamental gardens and flagpole. It was built by the surveyor Charles Crossland, who also set out the railway line to Midland.

But very close to this elegant home and the privileged lifestyle it supported is **Meadow Street**, the location of the town jail, gallows and courthouse. As well as the Visitor Centre, the courthouse contains a collection of costumes and personal

possessions, reflecting life in the town in the early 19th century. Nearby on **Swan Street** is the Rose & Crown, a Federation-period hotel, with a fine restaurant. Antiques are on sale in the one-time William Padbury Colonial Stores of 1869. Walter Padbury, the first mayor of Guildford, rose from humble beginnings to become one of the richest and most important men in Western Australia. His grave lies in the Pioneer Cemetery in East Perth (*see page 104*).

Meadow Road crosses the river at Barker's Bridge by the cricket ground of **Lilac Hill Park**, where visiting international teams play a warm-up match against a WA President's XI every year. This game is a prelude to an Australia-wide series of Test matches, and on that spring day Lilac Hill is jam-packed with hospitality tents and temporary grandstands. For the rest of the year it's a sedate riverside park where club matches are enjoyed in virtual solitude (contact

ABOVE: emblem of one of the Swan Valley's oldest vineyards.
BELOW: fruit of the vine in Swan Valley.

Food and Wine Trail

The Swan Valley food and wine trail is a 32km (20-mile) loop, leaving Guildford along the West Swan Road and returning by the Great Northern and Great Eastern highways. Wine tasting is free or at very low cost at most of the Valley's three dozen or more wineries. There are also several breweries producing handcrafted lagers, ales and pils. Drinking and driving is the only problem (penalties are severe), so either appoint a non-drinking driver, or consider joining an organised tour. Two possibilities are **Swan Valley Tours** (tel: 08-9299 6249), which will tailor trips to suit individual tastes, and **Out & About Wine Tours** (tel: 08-9377 3376).

BELOW: girls' day out in the Valley.

WACA, tel: 08-9265 7222, for further details).

Meadow Road becomes West Swan Road at Lilac Hill Park, and is the starting point of any Valley tour. Though Guildford is easily covered on foot, wheels are needed to explore the Valley, with stops at the many vineyards along the way.

The best wine estates

New wineries are opening across Australia at the rate of two a week, and Swan Valley is no exception. Growing consumption at home and abroad led countless landowners to turn their hectares over to vines in the 1990s, and the resulting glut has made everyday wine drinking extremely affordable. These bargains, known as cleanskins because they are usually unlabelled, can only be found in the bottle-shops. Don't expect such low prices at the vineyards, where you will find handmade wines of superior depth, style and quality.

Sandalford

Address: 3210 West Swan Road
Tel: 08-9374 9374
Opening Hrs: daily
Entrance Fee: free

The chance to try a wide range of wines and styles is enhanced in the Swan Valley by the diversity of vineyards, large and small, grand and humble. **Sandalford** is one of the grand ones, although most of its award-standard wine is sourced from its estate in the Margaret River wine area (see page 204). Their much smaller Swan Valley property was started in 1840 by John Septimus Roe, WA's first surveyor-general. It has won awards for its Cabernet Sauvignon and produces one, the Prendiville Reserve, which will reward the patience of anyone willing to cellar it for up to 25 years.

Lancaster Wines

Address: 5228 West Swan Road,
www.lancasterwines.com.au

Tel: 08-9250 6461
Opening Hrs: daily
Entrance Fee: free

Lancaster Wines, further along, with its unmade road and makeshift tasting shed, looks fairly humble, yet has some of the valley's oldest vines and most knowledgeable staff. Lancaster offers all the grape types that grow best in Swan Valley (Shiraz, Cabernet Sauvignon, Verdelho, Chenin Blanc and Chardonnay), including an Old Vines Shiraz, plus a late-picked Chenin dessert wine. Good strong local cheese is served, too.

Tali-jancich

Address: 26 Hyem Road,
www.taliwine.com.au
Tel: 08-9296 4289
Opening Hrs: Sun–Fri
Entrance Fee: free

Tali-jancich is a must for its fortified wines – tawny and vintage port, Muscat and Tokay. It hosts an annual international vintage Verdelho-tasting to swell appreciation of this grape. Its own Verdelho is superb, as is the Old Vine (1932) Shiraz.

Houghton Wines

Address: Dale Road, Middle Swan, www.houghton-wines.com.au
Tel: 08-9274 9540
Opening Hrs: daily
Entrance Fee: free

A rustic drive off the Great Northern Highway into the extensive grounds of **Houghton Wines** ends under jacaranda trees, heavy with blue blossom in spring. Another valley stalwart, established in 1836 by three army officers, Houghton is WA's largest commercial winery. Like Sandalford, it has an extensive stable of wines, souvenirs and a restaurant, and it even holds concerts under the trees. Its most famous winemaker was Jack Mann, whose family now runs Mann Wines. During his 51 vintages with Houghton he produced their White Burgundy, Australia's best-selling bottled wine.

ABOVE: wagons roll – a leisurely way of exploring the Swan Valley. **BELOW:** concert-goer at Houghton Wines, WA's largest commercial winery.

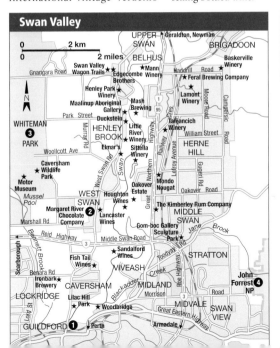

Sweet treats

Many visitors concentrate their tour on comparing as many wines as possible, but along the trail are dozens of other attractions. A sweet one is the **Margaret River Chocolate Co. ❷** (5123 West Swan Road; tel: 08-9250 1588; daily 9am–5pm), near Lancaster Wines. It sells all kinds of delicious confections – handmade truffles, hot drinks, sauces, cakes, novelties, chocolate bars and more, and offers free chocolate tastings.

Sweet cravings are also satisfied at **Mondo Nougat** (640 Great Northern Highway; tel: 08-9296 0111; www.mondonougat.com.au), a factory outlet producing eight varieties of nougat free of gluten, lactose and cholesterol. More unusual, perhaps, is the Muscat ice cream at **Edgecombe Brothers** (corner of West Swan Road/Gnangara Road; tel: 08-9296 4307), where the Edgecombe family complement their long-established vines with asparagus, honey, table grapes, preserves and wine-derived speciality ice cream.

A neighbour of Edgecombe Brothers, **Swan Valley Wagon Trails** (tel: 0412-917 496; www.swanvalleywa.com; Wed–Sun) transports visitors in pioneer-style covered wagons, drawn by Clydesdale horses, through the olive groves and pine forests of the region. Tours vary, but a half-day "Tastes of the Valley" option meanders around the wetland bird sanctuary of Lake Yakine (Nyungar for "turtle dreaming"), home of the native long-neck turtle, visits WA's oldest church, All Saints (1839), and stops for refreshments on the verandas at Edgecombe Brothers as well as Oggie's ice-cream café. The programme is flexible and can be tailor-made for vineyard tours, or evening trips.

Whiteman Park

Address: entrance off Lord Street or Beechboro Road, www.whitemanpark.com.au
Tel: 08-9209 6000
Opening Hrs: daily 8.30am–6pm
Entrance Fee: free

Just past Margaret River Chocolate Co., Woolcott Avenue offers a diversion from the food-and-wine trail: **Whiteman Park ❸** and **Caversham Wildlife Park** (inside Whiteman Park), the best place for kangaroo-spotting (excluding Perth Zoo and Heirisson Island) for visitors too short of time to go to the bush.

Here you can see Australian wildlife of all kinds. As well as the grey and red kangaroos, look out for the rare white kangaroo (albino versions of the red) and white Dama wallaby. Caversham aims to represent wildlife from all corners of Australia. The southwest section features the walleroo, rock wallaby and quokka; the southeast has gliders, potteroos, wombats, Tasmanian devils and koalas.

Whiteman Park includes many other lures, and visitors with children could find that their Swan Valley tour grinds to a halt here. Attractions include a carousel, bouncy castle, mini-electric cars and bikes, and a big blue swimming pool.

Motor Museum

Address: Lord Street, Whiteman Park, www.motormuseumofwa.asn.au
Tel: 08-9249 9457
Opening Hrs: daily 10am–4pm
Entrance Fee: charge

The **Motor Museum** (daily 10am–4pm; charge) has some fine vintage models, including a Bugatti and a 1894 Benz, displayed alongside classic Ferraris, a gull-winged De Lorean (as seen in the film *Back to the Future*) and Australian rarities such as the ill-fated 1974 Leyland Force Seven, built by Leyland Australia to compete with high-performance Aussie muscle-cars from Ford and Holden. Production never got off the ground, and only nine cars were ever made.

Steam trains puff around and through Whiteman Park; there are tram and train rides, a hot-metal printing shop, a tractor museum, pottery and art gallery. All these diversions are easily swallowed by Whiteman's 4,200 hectares (16 sq miles) of native bushland and wetlands – an area 10 times larger than Perth's Kings Park.

German brews

Back on the gastronomic trail of West Swan Road, a pair of German-style microbreweries, **Elmar's** in the Valley (No. 8731; tel: 08-9296 6354; Wed–Sun) and **Duckstein** (No. 9720; tel: 08-9296 0620; Wed–Sun) each make their beer according to the "Bavarian Purity Law" of 1516. Only pure water, malt and hops are used. Elmar's, which makes pilsner, wheat beer, draught ale and a non-alcoholic malt beer, has a beer garden. At Duckstein, the beer is accompanied by traditional German food and the strains of a mechanical oompah band.

Organically made pilsner has reaped awards for the **Feral Brewing Co.** (152 Hadrill Road; tel: 08-9296 4657; open daily). Fine food and wine are served in the restaurant and on verandas overlooking the vineyard. Following Feral's success, other wineries are also microbrewing, including **Ironbark Brewery** (55 Benara Road; tel: 08-9377 4400; Wed–Sun), a traditional full-mash brewery producing speciality beers, regular pilsner, iron bock and wheat beer, as well as fruity cherry ale and a ginger beer.

ABOVE: Swan Valley is famous for its wine but it also has a growing number of excellent breweries. **BELOW:** the Motor Museum at Whiteman Park.

Arts and crafts

Several wineries have galleries, but the best selection of paintings, sculpture and souvenirs is sold in specialist galleries such as **Gom-boc Gallery Sculpture Park** in Middle Swan (50 James Road; tel: 08-9274 3996; Wed–Sun; January by appointment only), the southern hemisphere's largest gallery, much of it devoted to outdoor sculpture.

Another is the **Maalinup Aboriginal Gallery** (10070 West Swan Road; tel: 08-9296 0704). Operated by local Nyungar people, it also offers evening entertainments, storytelling, didgeridoo-playing and bush food-tastings.

Australian artists are also foremost at the **Monet Gallery** (85 Great Eastern Highway; tel: 08-9277 3685; Thur–Sun), where originals in watercolour, oils, acrylics and pastels are sold at affordable prices. Metal sculpture is the speciality of **Battistessa Studio** (12 Neuman Road, Herne Hill; 08-9296 4121), where the Swan Valley-born artist Antonio Battistessa accepts commissions and works in forged-iron.

ABOVE: bust of state engineer C.Y. O'Connor, builder of Mundaring Weir and the pipeline that carried water to the goldfields at Kalgoorlie.
BELOW: Mundaring Weir. **BELOW RIGHT:** chimney of the No. 1 Pump Station.

THE HILLS

Driving in WA is easy-going, even in Swan Valley with all its tourist attractions. Driving through the hills of the Darling Range is more leisurely still. You can enjoy speedy access to small towns such as Kalamunda and Jarrahdale, and natural attractions such as Mundaring Weir and John Forrest National Park.

Named after Lord John Forrest (state premier 1890–1901), **John Forrest National Park ❹**, on the crest of the Darling Range, comprises 1,600 hectares (6 sq miles) of jarrah forest abundant in native flora and fauna. Entrances lie along the Great Eastern Highway, about 7km (4 miles) from Guildford. A walk through the trees of the park – marri (red gum), bull banksia, wandoo, balga (grass tree) and paperbark along the creeks – reveals abundant birdlife. The Splendid Wren and Scarlet Robin are common; rarer, but sometimes seen here, are the Golden Whistler, Mountain Duck and even the Wedge-Tailed Eagle.

A recommended heritage trail in the park follows the Eastern Railway line, built in 1894, alongside Jane

Brook. Though closed in 1966, the route is still ballast-covered, and the brook can be heard tumbling along the valley below. At **National Park Falls** (at their best after winter rains between July and September) the water drops 25 metres (82ft) over massive granite rocks. The best picnic area is beyond Deep Creek Bridge, where steps, garden walls and paths were built near the brook by sustenance workers during the 1930s Depression.

Further on is WA's only railway tunnel, 340 metres/yds long. You can see light at the end of this tunnel, but a torch is useful. Covering the whole trail can take several hours. Be careful on very hot days, and observe the usual bush precautions – carry a hat, sunblock and water, and stick to the trail. There's a kiosk, tavern, barbecue facilities and toilets in the park.

Mundaring Weir

A few kilometres along the Great Eastern Highway are **Mundaring** ❺

and the road to **Mundaring Weir**. Gold was the making of Perth, but when the 1890s strikes were made, water was almost as precious as the yellow metal found at Coolgardie and Kalgoorlie. In 1899 the intrepid state engineer C.Y. O'Connor began work on a huge reservoir on the Helena River from where water would be pumped 560km (350 miles) to the semi-arid diggings. The pipeline took four years and cost £2.5 million, but could pump 5 million gallons of water daily to the goldfields and agricultural areas along the way. The "Golden Pipeline" remains the world's longest pipeline, and still carries fresh water to the goldfields.

C.Y. O'Connor is remembered and honoured in WA for this and other remarkable works.

ABOVE: settler's house at Kalamunda History Village.

BELOW: classical music concerts are a feature at the Mundaring Weir Hotel.

BELOW: another quiet day in Jarrahdale, an old logging town.

The starting point in the O'Connor story is the No. 1 Pump Station he built here. Now the O'Connor museum, staffed by dedicated volunteers, the impressive 19th-century building with a 41-metre (135ft)-high chimney contains massive steam engines and boilers. Watch for the clock, permanently fixed at the time C.Y. O'Connor died – almost certainly by his own hand.

A walking trail starting at the Pump Station passes the 1898 **Mundaring Weir Hotel** (www.mundaringweirhotel.com.au), built for pipeline workers and used as an office by O'Connor. The current owners put the establishment back on the map by engaging a soprano to sing in the restaurant. She brought her own pianist – David Helfgott, now made famous by the film *Shine*. He (and others such as James Morrison and Jane Rutter) performs regularly beside the hotel pool.

Bibbulmun Track
Kalamunda History Village
Address: 56 Railway Road
Tel: 08-9293 1371

Opening Hrs: Mon–Thur and Sat 10am–3pm, Sun 1.30–4.30pm
Entrance Fee: charge

At neighbouring **Kalamunda ❻**, early European settlement of the region can be explored at the **Kalamunda History Village**. It has an original post office dating from 1901, the district's first state school, a settler's cottage, workshops and two railway stations, all equipped with original artefacts and furnishings.

Mundaring and Kalamunda are centres in an area rich in natural attractions. As well as local walks – in Fred Jacoby Forest Park, or on the abandoned Jorgensen Park golf course – there is the 1,000km (620-mile) **Bibbulmun Track**, which begins from Kalamunda. Meandering through the wild and picturesque countryside of the southwest, it is one of the world's great long-distance trails. It can take up to eight weeks to reach Albany on the south coast, but sections can be covered in shorter time frames (there are cabins for overnight stops). For options, including single-day walks without a

TIP

Armadale's Visitor Centre (40 Jull Street; Mon–Fri 9.30am–4.30pm, Sat–Sun 10am–3pm) can supply a wide range of local information and maps.

pack, contact the **Bibbulmun Track Foundation** (tel: 08-9481 0551; www.bibbulmuntrack.org.au).

If cycling is more appealing to you than hiking, the Munda Biddi cycle trail, which starts in Mundaring (www.mundabiddi.org.au), will eventually run all the way down to Albany. Again, it has cabins en route.

Kalamunda is the starting point for another round of wineries in the Bickley Valley. Elevated conditions on the Darling Scarp have produced a cluster of award-winning boutique vineyards, such as Piesse Brook and Hainault.

The Scarp is the rocky edge of the Darling Range, itself the edge of a huge plateau. Clear air and distance from the bright lights of Perth were factors when the century-old **Perth Observatory** (tel: 08-9293 8255; www.perthobservatory.wa.gov.au) moved to Bickley. Star-viewing night tours take around 90 minutes and are available (Oct–May) with use of the telescopes. Day tours are available one week each month (Feb–Nov) as well as on the first Sunday of the months June–Sept. Longer viewing nights are available Feb–Mar, but booking is required.

THE DAMS

Life in a city that clings to the warm western shore of the world's driest continent concentrates the mind on water. Visiting the dams is a pleasant day out, especially on the rare days when the water spills over. That hasn't happened for some years, but the dams around **Armadale** ❼, with their parklands and waterfalls, still draw plenty of picnickers. This southern end of the Darling Range is bounded by state forest, worked by loggers for more than a century.

The Kwinana Freeway is a better route to Armadale than the congested (by Perth standards) Albany Highway, or take the railway along the centre strip of the freeway.

Serpentine and **Pipehead** dams are a short drive along Jarrahdale Road (off the South Western Highway out of Armadale) which leads through the old logging town of **Jarrahdale**.

Fine food and wine are less plentiful here than in the northern hills, but **Millbrook Winery** (tel: 08-9525 5796; daily 10am–5pm; www.millbrookwinery.com.au) is well worth seeking out. From Jarrahdale follow the signs through the forest for a couple of kilometres, at which point you will come upon a terraced winery cut into the surrounding hillside and set beside a broad lake. It produces excellent Shiraz (Hermitage) and Viognier, and wine tasting in the cool, lake-level room is very pleasant.

On the way back from Millbrook consider stopping by the churchyard on Chestnut Road, the starting point for short walks through the woods.

Armadale is surrounded by tourist attractions. The **Reptile & Wildlife Centre** (308 SW Highway; tel: 08-9399 6927; daily 10am–4pm; charge) conserves and shows native reptiles, as well as bats, eagles, dingoes and other creatures. The centre rescues and rehabilitates wildlife as well as teaching

ABOVE: wine tasting at Millbrook Winery.
BELOW: Araluen Botanic Park.

ABOVE: taking the boat to Penguin Island.

Mandurah is known as the Peel Region after the pioneer and speculator Thomas Peel (1793–1865), cousin of the British Home Secretary Sir Robert Peel. Thomas planned to settle the Mandurah region with emigrants in return for land. However, a chain of unfortunate events led to the failure of his settlement scheme and his eventual decline and death.

the public to identify venomous and non-venomous snakes.

A little further out, **Tumbulgum Farm** (SW Highway, Mundijong; tel: 08-9525 5888; entry free but charge for shows; only open on days when they have group bookings; www.tumbulgumfarm.com.au), an Aboriginal venture, is the place to come if you want to learn how to crack a stock whip, milk a cow, feed lambs, or try billy tea and damper.

Araluen Botanic Park (Croyden Road, off Brookton Highway; tel: 08-9496 1171; daily 9am–6pm; charge) is one of the area's greatest attractions. Bush walks by flowing streams and picnic spots among spectacular garden displays are boosted with mass plantings of bulbs, annuals and other plants from August through to October. Araluen is an Eastern states Aboriginal word meaning "singing waters" or "place of lilies". The cool, moist climate of this valley inspired J. J. Simons to found a holiday camp for the Young Australia League here in 1929. The "Grove of the Unforgotten" is a tribute to the 88 YAL members killed in World War I.

SOUTH OF MANDURAH

South of Perth, the Cockburn and Kwinana coast is mostly industrial. **Rockingham** has some beach-front attractions, but Safety Bay's **Penguin Island ⑧** is the most appealing destination en route to Mandurah (take the Kwinana Freeway to the end and follow the signs for Safety Bay).

Wildlife – seals, sea lions and whales – are abundant on and around a string of offshore rocky islands, but only Rottnest is developed for tourism. Garden Island is a naval base, and rocks like Carnac are snake-infested and inhospitable. Whale-watching cruises run from Hillary's Marina in October and November, but little Penguin Island, with a colony of around 1,100 birds, is much more accessible. It's so close to shore that people used to wade to it through the warm, shallow water, but sudden tides can be dangerous. Instead, book a ride on the ferry (Mersey Point Jetty, Safety Bay Road, Rockingham; tel: 08-9591 1333; mid-Sept–early June); the moderate cost includes entry to the Discovery Centre where young penguins are fed. Their eyes are sensitive to bright light, so you need to seek them out under walkways and other shelter.

Mandurah

From Safety Bay, Highway 1 is the best route to **Mandurah** ❾, once the fastest-growing city in Australia (trains take 50 minutes from Mandurah to Perth). Mandurah has a permanent holiday atmosphere, partly because so much of the city overlooks canals, the ocean or the Peel Inlet. Many of its restaurants, craft shops, art galleries and cultural buildings are set around **Mandjar Bay**, a lovely location for dining.

Inexpensive estuary and canal cruises are an excellent way to get the feel of this watery city. Several operators can be found on the jetty close to Mandurah Art Centre. Skippers are skilled at finding the dolphins that live in the estuary; just to see them surf and barrel-roll ahead of your cruiser is worth the fare.

Fishing is also popular, as is crabbing. On summer weekends many people hunt for the blue mannas, wading the shallows with scoop nets and stout shoes, while others drop crab pots from their boats. The Mandurah crab festival is a major annual event.

Thrombolites

Mandurah's southern boundary is **Yalgorup National Park** (www.naturebase.net), a sanctuary for water birds and wildlife, though it is its colony of living, rock-like creatures known as thrombolites *(see box below)* that makes Yalgorup's Lake Clifton special. Thrombolites date back 3.5 billion years, and like the stromatolites of Hamelin Pool, in Shark Bay (northwest WA; *see page 193*), are the earliest-known life on earth. Living examples are rare; it is thought that they survive at Yalgorup because Lake Clifton contains springs of fresh groundwater high in calcium carbonate.

The only access point is via the Coast Road, 25km (15 miles) south of Mandurah, indicated by a large brown sign for the Lake Clifton platform, an observation walkway built across the shallows. A right turn leads to the walkway, alongside Cape Bouvard winery. ❏

TIP

Houseboats can be hired for cruises on the estuary or along the Murray River (for details contact the Mandurah Visitor Centre; tel: 08-9550 3999; www. visitmandurah.com).

BELOW: kayaking at Rockingham.

Thrombolites

Dating back 3.5 billion years (or more) to the Pre-Cambrian and Cambrian ages, the thrombolites of Yalgorup are living organisms made by the earliest-known life on Earth. In their time, thrombolites and stromatolites (which can be found at Hamelin Pool, in Shark Bay, Northwest WA), were the dominant lifeform in the clear, shallow seas. Their lifecycle created extensive reef systems.

The existence of these organisms today has helped scientists understand how life on Earth evolved. Similar organisms helped to form the rich iron-ore deposits of the Hamersley Range, in the Pilbara's Karijini National Park, some 2,000 million years ago.

BEST RESTAURANTS, BREWERIES AND BARS

Restaurants

Kalamunda

The Kalamunda Hotel
43 Railway Rd. Tel: 08-9257
1084. Open: L & D daily. **$$**
The Kalamunda Hotel is
an elegant building with
some good food to
match. The menu fea-
tures old favourites,
including a beef-and-
Guinness pie made from
a secret family recipe,
and some new ideas
such as kangaroo fillet,
served with a salad of
sun-dried tomato,
capsicum, feta cheese
and pears atop a
beetroot and potato rosti.

Le Paris Brest
22 Haynes St. Tel: 08-9293
2752. Open: B & L Tue–Sun,
D Tue–Sat. **$$–$$$**
By day Le Paris Brest

serves light meals and
delicious desserts, while
by night it transforms into
a romantic eatery. Gold
Plate Award winners
several times over, it has
created a name for
innovative dishes and
excellent sweets.

Thai on the Hill
2 Haynes St. Tel: 08-9293
4312. Open: D Tue–Sun. **$$**
Literally perched on the
hill on Haynes Street, this
Thai restaurant might be
looking a little tired on
the outside, but don't
worry. The food inside is
fresh and interesting.

Cicerello's
2/73 Mandurah Terrace. Tel:
08-9535 9777. Open: L & D
daily. **$–$$**
The younger sibling of the
well-loved Fremantle
branch, Cicerello's serves

cheerful, family-friendly
fare. Directly on the
water, it's a perfect spot
for a relaxed lunch or
early dinner.

Miami Bakehouse
Shop 6, Falcon Grove Shopping Centre, Old Coast Rd.
Tel: 08-9534 2705. Open:
daily from 6am. **$**
The Miami Bakehouse is
one of Perth's best bake-
ries. Its pies range from
reliable steak and kidney
to the more adventurous
crab and feta. Coffee,
sandwiches and cakes
are also available.

**Stage Door Bar and
Brasserie**
Mandurah Performing Arts
Centre, Ormsby Terrace. Tel:
08-9586 3733. Open: B, L &
D daily. **$$**
Sample dishes include
roast veg and chèvre tart,
quince chicken breast
and couscous salad, Chi-
nese barbecue pork fillet
and spicy Thai beef
salad. The service is
friendly and attentive.

Mundaring

Little Caesar's
7/7125 Great Eastern Hwy.
Tel: 08-9295 6611. Open: D
Wed–Mon. **$**
This pizzeria is considered
to be one of the best in
the region.

The Loose Box
6825 Great Eastern Hwy.
Tel: 08-9295 1787. Open: L
Sun, D Wed–Sat. **$$$$**

Fine award-winning
French cuisine in idyllic
surroundings. Top-quality
ingredients are used,
including organic herbs
and vegetables grown in
their own on-site garden.
The Loose Box also has
several beautiful chalets
where you can stay over-
night, in case you
indulge too much from
the wine list.

Mundaring Weir Hotel
Mundaring Weir Rd.
Tel: 08-9295 1106. Open: L
daily, D Sat. **$**
Serves counter meals –
good honest pub grub –
daily, and the restaurant
opens up on a Saturday
night for dinner. Worth
coming for the location –
a grand old building with
a beautiful courtyard nes-
tling in the bush. Known
for its Sunday session,
complete with afternoon
spit roast from 3pm
onwards.

Swan Valley

**Chester's of Heafod
Glen Winery**
8691 West Swan Rd. Tel:
08-9296 3444. Open: L
Wed–Sun, D Fri and Sat.
$$$
The rustic charm of Ches-
ter's lends itself to a
romantic night out or a
happy family gathering
during the day. There are
wines made on site and
the cuisine is award-win-
ning. The signature dish
is roasted red emperor
wrapped in prosciutto

LEFT: a sound choice in
Guildford, Swan Valley.

and stuffed with a scallop and salmon mousse, topped with charred scallops in organic apple glaze.

Darlington Estate

39 Nelson Rd. Tel: 08-9299 6268. Open: L Wed–Sun, D Fri and Sat. **$$$**

The food at this winery restaurant is sublime. The style is European, with well-balanced flavours. The signature dish is a lamb shank wrapped in pastry. The wines are good and the views are beautiful.

Dear Friends

100 Benara Rd. Tel: 08-9279 2815. Open: L & D Wed–Sun. **$$$**

Dear Friends is an elegant and welcoming restaurant serving modern Australian food with an international influence. The signature dish is a rabbit terrine accompanied by a potato, bacon and caraway salad with a pear purée. They also offer a dégustation menu of eight courses with matched wines. It's popular, so remember to book in advance.

Houghton's Jacaranda Café

Dale Rd, Middle Swan. Tel: 08-9274 9543. Open: L daily, 10am onwards. **$$**

Prices for a three-course dinner per person with a half-bottle of house wine:

$ = under AUS$25
$$ = AUS$25–40
$$$ = AUS$40–70
$$$$ = over AUS$70

Houghton's menu focuses on simple ideas done well, such as smoked salmon and brie baguette, and a cheese platter with three cheeses, antipasto, dried and fresh fruit, nuts, crusty bread and butter.

Lamont's

85 Bisdee Rd. Tel: 08-9296 4485. Open: light meals until 5pm Sat, Sun and public holidays. **$$**

This winery serves an inventive tapas menu alongside wine tasting on Saturdays and Sundays from 11am.

The Mallard Duck Café

Corner of West Swan Rd and John St. Tel: 08-9296 1352. Open: B Sun only, L Wed–Sun, D Fri–Sat. **$$**

The Mallard Duck isn't well known in Perth, but it's well worth a visit. The restaurant provides sensational food, scenic views and great atmosphere. Breakfast is à la carte and lunch options include stuffed mushrooms and open steak sandwiches. The dinner menu is small but satisfying.

Rose & Crown Hotel

105 Swan St. Tel: 08-9347 8100. Open: B Sat–Sun, L & D daily. **$$**

This historic hotel has a beautiful garden area and a majestic interior. The Rose & Crown offers modern Australian food, using excellent local produce. If you feel like something light, share the tasting plate, which changes daily. You'll

Bars and Breweries

Mash Brewing

10250 West Swan Rd. Tel: 08-9296 5588. Open: L Mon–Tue 11am–5pm, L & D Wed–Sun 11am–9pm, bar open on weekends till late. **$$**

Boasting classic and modern-style beers, Mash's ales are handmade; head Brewer Dan Turley's handprint, Mash's signature logo, is a reminder of that.

Tke Kimberley Rum Company

Great Northern Hwy, Middle Swan. www.canefire.net. Tel: 08-9250 5422. Open: daily noon–5pm.

This is Western Australia's leading boutique rum distillery. The liquor is fermented using cane sugar grown and triple distilled on the premises.

Duckstein Brewery

9720 West Swan Rd. Tel: 08-9296 0620. Open: L & D Wed–Sun. **$$**

This German brewery not only makes excellent beer, but has a huge list of German food to accompany it. The Brewer's Pan – a fry packed with pan-fried potatoes, kassler smoked pork cutlets and bratwurst sausage – is recommended.

Elmar's in the Valley

8731 West Swan Rd. Tel:

08-9296 6354. Open L Wed–Sun, D Fri–Sun. **$$**

Elmar and wife Annette have created their own microbrewery and restaurant serving great German food. Every dish is prepared with care, from the pumpernickel bread to the schweinebrated (German-style roast pork), schnitzels and zeribel (onion) sauce.

Ironbark Brewery

55 Benara Rd. www.ironbark brewery.com.au. Tel: 08-9337 4400. Open: Wed–Thur 10.30am–5.30pm, Fri–Sat 10.30am–late, Sun 10.30am–6pm. **$$**

Aussie memorabilia, blacksmith bellows, a mouldboard plough table and 44-gallon drum tables randomly decorate this alfresco-style brewery which offers a range of speciality beers made from malts around the world.

The Feral Brewing Company

152 Haddrill Rd. www.feral brewing.com.au. Tel: 08-9296 4657. Open: Mon–Thur 11am–5pm, Fri–Sat 11am–late, Sun 11am–5pm. **$$**

Feral has the largest range of beers in the Swan, boasting 16 on tap and more on the horizon.

enjoy the great food in a unique environment.

Stewart's at Brookleigh

1235 Great Northern Hwy. Tel: 08-9296 6966. Open: L & D Wed–Sun. **$$**

The rustic villa at Stewart's stands majestically over the property, which

doubles as an equestrian estate. The courtyard area is perfect for relaxing with a bowl of pasta or a gourmet wood-fired pizza, or you can choose from the modern Australian à la carte menu.

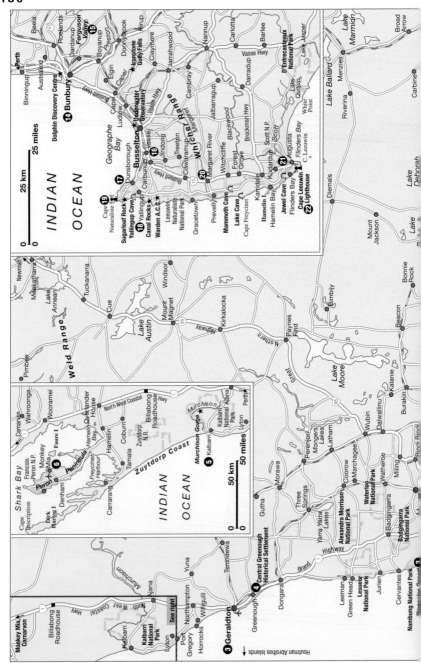

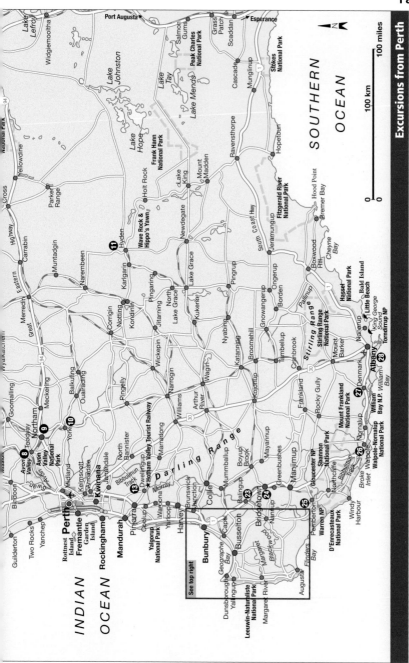

Excursions from Perth

INDIAN OCEAN

SOUTHERN OCEAN

Port Augusta
Esperance

N

100 km
100 miles

See top right

EXCURSIONS FROM PERTH

Dense forests, white beaches, cliffs plummeting
into inky ravines, and carpets of wild flowers
that stretch as far as the eye can see...
Western Australia's captivating landscapes
are as diverse as the state is large

Perth is an attractive city, but to appreciate fully the natural variety and beauty of this corner of Australia you need to venture a little further afield. The destinations included in this chapter range from Kalbarri National Park in the north to Albany in the south and Kalgoorlie in the east. They do not cover the whole of WA, a vast state comprising around a third of Australia, but include all the worthwhile destinations within a two-day drive. Head south and you'll find a wine region revered around the globe; head north for some of the best windsurfing, fishing and snorkelling in the country; and head east to visit Western Australia's most historic towns.

Perthites think nothing of driving for three hours or longer to reach places considered close to the city. Visitors can choose to self-drive (there are numerous hire-car and campervan companies based in Perth; *see page 224*) or join an organised tour. Alternatively, bus services operate daily to many destinations.

Several places that may seem too far to visit when time is short can be readily accessed by air. Qantas, Virgin Blue, Skywest, Jetstar and Skippers

Aviation offer air services to some of WA's larger towns, such as Kalgoorlie and Albany.

Rail travel is more limited, but eastbound travellers can climb aboard the Prospector, a fast train that travels to Kalgoorlie.

HEADING NORTH

The coastal area stretching north from Lancelin to Kalbarri is known for its perfect beaches, met by rugged gorges and wild flower plains. This area is excellent for fishing, windsurfing,

PRECEDING PAGES: Murchison Gorge, Kalbarri National Park. **LEFT:** Busselton Jetty. **RIGHT:** forest near Karridale.

ABOVE: just off Waterloo Road, look out for signs for Yanchep National Park (50km/30 miles north of Perth). It offers wetlands, woodlands, bush walks and displays of Aboriginal culture.
BELOW: the Pinnacles Desert.

snorkelling and adventure opportunities such as sand-boarding.

Lancelin and the Pinnacles

The coastal town of **Lancelin** lies 127km (79 miles) north of Perth, protected by two large rock islands and surrounded by towering sand dunes. It is easily reached from the city by heading north along Wanneroo Road, which becomes Lancelin Road.

Gusty winds off the Indian Ocean make this one of the top destinations for windsurfing and surfing, attracting top sportsmen and women from around the world. But it also caters to novices, who can join one of a number of learn-to-surf tours available from Perth. Adrift Surf Tours offers day experiences that include basic tuition, equipment and lunch. Extended tours, including accommodation at the Lancelin Lodge YHA, are also available (tel: 1800 094 480).

For a real adrenalin rush, you may want to give sand-boarding a go. Go West Tours (tel: 08-9226 3348) runs day tours from Perth that include sand-boarding, exploration of the

Nambung National Park and a walk through the Pinnacles.

Another exhilarating way to experience the sand dunes is to journey over them in a 4WD. Desert Storm Adventures (based in Lancelin; tel: 08-9655 2550) operates the world's largest 4WD vehicle, taking passengers on an adrenalin-pumping ride over dunes that are ordinarily too large to negotiate. Sand-boarding is also included in these tours.

From Lancelin, one of the most popular excursions is to the eerie **Pinnacles Desert** ❷, in the heart of the Nambung National Park, about 245km (152 miles) north of Perth. Considered one of WA's most distinctive attractions, the Pinnacles Desert is an extensive area of stone monuments that rise up from the desert floor, some reaching up to 3 metres (15ft) high. Most major coach tours include a stop at the Pinnacles on their northbound itineraries. If you're self-driving, take Nambung National Park Pinnacles Drive off the Brand Highway. From the car park (charges AUS$10 per vehicle), it's a short walk to the Pinnacles area,

The Pinnacles

The strange limestone formations known as the Pinnacles were formed around 30,000 years ago by winter rain leaching into the sand dunes and turning the lower levels of the lime-rich sand into a soft limestone. Plants then grew upon the surface of the dunes, accelerating the leaching process and causing a hard cap to form on the top of the dune. Wind erosion eventually removed the surrounding sand, leaving the hard rock that was underneath exposed to the elements; the wind and rain then moulded the rock into weird and wonderful shapes. The process continues to this day: the submerged sections of the Pinnacles are thought to be as deep as the exposed sections are high.

although if weather conditions are poor, a 4WD might be necessary to enter the park. A circular track leads around the park, with a lookout at the northern end.

Located between Lancelin and the rock-lobster-fishing community of Cervantes, **Nambung National Park** features beautiful beaches, coastal dune systems, shady groves of tuart trees and low heathlands. The vegetation bursts into flower from August to October. To get there, take the Brand Highway and turn west towards Cervantes, then south into the park.

Geraldton
Western Australian Museum
Address: 1 Museum Place
Tel: 08-9921 5080
Opening Hrs: daily 9.30am–4pm
Entrance fee: by donation

From the Pinnacles, continue north along Brand Highway to **Geraldton** ❸, approximately five hours' drive from Perth. Considered the gateway

to the north, Geraldton is a bustling coastal city and a good place to base yourself for a couple of days of fishing, diving and wild flower-viewing during spring. For an in-depth insight into WA's history visit Geraldton's branch of the **Western Australian Museum**, which has displays on the farming history and geology of the area, an aquarium showcasing its marine life, and a shipwrecks gallery. Many Dutch explorers met their watery fate on the reefs surrounding the Abrolhos Islands. The most famous casualty was the *Batavia*, whose reconstructed stern is in the Shipwreck Galleries in Fremantle *(see page 135)*.

Central Greenough Historical Settlement
Address: Brand Highway, Greenough
Tel: 08-9926 1084
Opening Hrs: daily 9am–5pm, museum 10am–4pm
Entrance Fee: charge

ABOVE: view over Geraldton.

TIP

Skywest flies to Geraldton daily, departing from Perth domestic terminal. In Geraldton, hire a car from Avis, Budget or Hertz, which all have offices at the airport, and self-drive to Greenough and surrounding areas.

ABOVE: the 19th-century schoolhouse at Central Greenough Historical Settlement.
BELOW: drive carefully at dusk and at night, when wildlife is most active.

To discover more about the history and heritage of WA, visit the **Central Greenough Historical Settlement** ❹, a 20-minute drive south of Geraldton. Its collection of 19th-century colonial buildings, restored by the National Trust, includes a church and a schoolhouse.

The 57km (35-mile) **Heritage Trail and Drive** is a great way to experience the hamlet and other historical sites around Greenough. Maps are available from local tourist offices for a small fee. Alternatively, contact Yamatji Cultural Trails (08-9956 1110) for a guided tour of the area.

For a spectacular wildlife experience, book a tour to the idyllic **Houtman Abrolhos Islands**. Sixty km (37 miles) west of Geraldton, the Abrolhos is an archipelago of 112 islands clustered into three main groups – Wallabi, Easter and Pelsaert. Home to temperate and tropical marine life and large colonies of marine birds, the islands offer superb snorkelling,

birdwatching and fishing. For an eco-adventure call Odyssey Expeditions (tel: 08-9192 5230).

Kalbarri National Park

From Geraldton, continue 160km (100 miles) north along Brand Highway to reach **Kalbarri** ❺. Alternatively, Greyhounds Australia (www.greyhound.com. au) and Transwa (www.transwa.wa.gov. au) operate direct bus services between Perth and Kalbarri. Once in Kalbarri, you can rent a vehicle from Kalbarri Cars 4U2 Hire (tel: 08-9937 1290).

Kalbarri has long been a favourite holiday destination for West Australians, with Perthites regularly making the six-hour drive, equipped with snorkel, fishing, surfing and windsurfing gear for the outdoor opportunities on offer. However, the summer months can be scorching in Kalbarri, so for a milder experience, visit the area during winter.

Kalbarri offers a wealth of outdoor and adventure activities. It is renowned for deep-sea fishing, with snapper, groper, dhufish, Spanish mackerel and tuna all likely catches. Even if you've never fished before, the spectacular coastal cliffs, plus the chance to see dolphins, make it a worthwhile trip. Whale-watching cruises are popular from June to December when humpback whales gather in the sheltered waters to give birth to their calves.

Kalbarri is surrounded by the rugged **Kalbarri National Park**, sliced by the 80km (50-mile) **Murchison Gorge**. Myriad adventure activities are offered in the park, including canoeing along the Murchison River, abseiling, bushwalking and 4WD tours *(see below for activity tour companies)*.

Kalbarri Wild Flower Centre

Address: Ajana Road, Kalbarri
Tel: 08-9937 1229
Opening Hrs: June–Oct Wed–Mon 9am onwards
Entrance Fee: charge

Kalbarri is one of the best places in WA to witness displays of wild flowers (in bloom from late July through spring and into early summer). Twenty-one plant species are found, including banksia, grevillia, kangaroo paw, featherflower, smokebush, starflower and several orchids that are unique to the area. You can learn more about Kalbarri's wild flowers by taking a trip to the Kalbarri Wild Flower Centre. Here you can take a stroll along an interpretive nature trail or join a guided walk through Kalbarri's Native Botanic Garden.

To venture north of Kalbarri to **Monkey Mia ⑥** and Shark Bay is not easy in the space of a couple of days, unless you fly to Monkey Mia. But the opportunity to wade into shallow seas and interact with wild dolphins makes this a very popular excursion. Coach tours tend to make it a three-day trip, taking in Kalbarri, the Pinnacles Desert and New Norcia on the return leg. **Shark Bay**, of which Monkey Mia is just a small part, is a World Heritage site, comprising a series of cliff-lined peninsulas and islands. The high salinity of the southern parts of Shark Bay has allowed the growth of stromatolites at Hamelin Pool – giant

TIP

Travelling by bus can be a relaxing, air-conditioned way to travel. Call the Transwa information line, tel: 1300 662 205, or visit www.transwa.wa.gov.au for timetables.

BELOW: Kalbarri National Park.

Exploring Kalbarri

To get the most out of Kalbarri National Park and the multitude of adventure activities on offer, especially when time is limited, you may want to sign up with a specialist tour operator. We've listed some of the prominent companies, but be sure to ask around. **Kalbarri Safari Tours**, tel: 08-9937 1011. **Kalbarri Boat Hire**. For a canoe safari, tel: 08-9937 1245. **Kalbarri Abseil**, tel: 08-9937 1618. **Kalbarri Sand-Boarding**, tel: 1800 886 141.

For deep-sea fishing or whale-watching tours, contact **Kalbarri Explorer Ocean Charters**, tel: 08-9937 2027, or **Kalbarri Reefwalker Adventure Tours Coastal Cruises**, tel: 08-9937 1356.

masses of algae that are considered the oldest form of life on earth.

The whole area is rich in wildlife such as dugongs, humpback whales and green and loggerhead turtles. Several wildlife-cruise operators are based in **Denham**.

New Norcia

An easy and popular excursion from Perth (often combined with a trip to the Pinnacles) is to the Benedictine community of **New Norcia** ❼, situated in the middle of the bush 132km (82 miles) north of Perth, a two-hour journey by car along the Great Northern Highway (alternatively, Transwa runs a return service from Perth to New Norcia on Tuesday and Thursday and a one-way service on Friday and Sunday).

WA's only monastic town, comprising 64 buildings laid out in a cross formation, the community was founded by Dom Rosendo Salvado in 1846 (see page 35), a missionary. Visitors who want to explore at their own pace can take the New Norcia Heritage Trail, an easy 2km (1½-mile) walk linking most of the

ABOVE: a pair of pelicans at Monkey Mia.
BELOW: wildlife-spotting cruises operate from Monkey Mia.

major sites (details from the Museum and Art Gallery, *see below*). Alternatively, a two-hour guided walking tour departs daily from the Museum and Art Gallery entrance at 11am and 1.30pm (tel: 08-9654 8056). This includes entrance to the monks' private chapel, and concludes with the opportunity to sample tasty treats from the New Norcia bakery, such as New Norcia nut cake and Dom Salvado Pan Chocolatti.

The main areas of interest are the chapel of **St Gertrude's College**, the first boarding school for girls in WA, which is adorned with Art Deco frescos, and the **Abbey Church**, decorated with locally inspired *sgraffito* and an image of Our Lady of Good Counsel, said to have been held up by Dom Salvado to repel a bush fire in 1847. The Abbey Church also contains the tomb of the founder.

As well as telling the story of the monastery's founding, the **Museum and Art Gallery** (daily 9am–4.30pm) is stuffed with artefacts and photographs that provide fascinating insights into pioneer life in the mid-19th century. It also has a

fine set of paintings collected by the monks over the years. The art display changes regularly.

EAST OF PERTH

Head east from Perth and within an hour you'll find yourself in Western Australia's lush **Avon Valley**, home of the historic town of York and kilometre after kilometre of farming country.

Self-driving is an excellent option if you're heading to destinations close to the city, such as Toodyay and York, but for those looking to travel further east to Kalgoorlie or Hyden, home of the iconic Wave Rock, Transwa and Greyhounds service the main towns two to three times a week.

Toodyay

If you're heading out of Perth along Toodyay Road, you'll reach the pretty, historic town of **Toodyay** ❽ after a one-hour drive, making it an attractive option for an easy day trip with

a picnic lunch. Built in 1861, the town was originally known as Newcastle, but following opposition to the name by townsfolk in Newcastle, New South Wales, it was rechristened Toodyay in 1911. Its many old buildings have been carefully restored.

Connor's Mill

Address: 7 Piesse Street, Toodyay
Tel: 08-9574 2435
Opening Hrs: Sat–Sun 10am–4pm, Mon–Fri 10am–3pm
Entrance Fee: charge

Begin a tour at **Connor's Mill** on Stirling Terrace, Toodyay's main street. Built in 1870 to grind the local wheat, it is now a tourist centre that pays homage to Moondyne Joe, a notorious bushranger, and the son of a Welsh blacksmith who was transported to Australia for stealing bread.

Those who have planned ahead and packed a picnic lunch should head for **Duidgee Park**, on Harper Road off Stirling Terrace. Situated on the banks of the Avon River, it is an ideal spot for an afternoon picnic or barbecue.

ABOVE: although traffic is scarce in rural areas, you are bound to encounter the massive "road trains" which can be several trailors long.
LEFT: statue of New Norcia's founder, Rosendo Salvado.
BELOW: St Gertrude's, New Norcia.

ABOVE: Wave Rock.

To the southeast of Toodyay, along the Toodyay–Northham Road, is **Northam** ❾ (98km/61 miles east of Perth along the Great Eastern Highway). A hub for the surrounding farming area, Northam has more historic buildings than anywhere else in the state. To see the most interesting, pop into the Visitor Centre at 2 Grey Street (tel: 08-9622 2100) and pick up a brochure on the Historic Town Walk – a 2km (1-mile) walk and 4km (2½-mile) drive linking the main locations.

The old railway station on Fitzgerald Street in the centre of town was a hive of activity in the 19th and 20th centuries. Now listed with the Australian National Trust, it has been converted into a **Museum** (Sun 10am–4pm) full of railway memorabilia.

While on Fitzgerald Street, wander down to the Fitzgerald Street Bridge. Just near here is the Suspension Bridge, which is said to be the longest pedestrian suspension bridge in Australia. Surrounding the bridge, on the banks of the Avon, are some lovely picnic spots.

York

York Motor Museum

Address: Avon Terrace, York
Tel: 08-9641 1288
Opening Hrs: daily 9.30am–3pm
Entrance Fee: charge

Another historic town is **York** ❿, 35km (22 miles) south of Northam along Northam Road (from Perth, York is best accessed by taking Great Eastern Highway, then turning right onto Great Southern Highway, which leads directly into town). This tiny town is easy to explore on foot: many of the most impressive buildings are located on Avon Terrace, the main street. One of the main attractions here is the **York Motor Museum**, which has a sister museum on Victoria Quay in Fremantle. Home to more than 100 classic and vintage cars and motorcycles, it is one of the finest collections in Australia.

Just off Avon Terrace, at 7–13 Broome Street, is **Jah Roc Gallery** (10am–5pm; tel: 08-9758 7200), makers of fine furniture. Making everything from wine racks to beds, Jah Roc has won many awards for its pieces, and has an impressive international clientele. There's also a great little café here.

Hyden and Wave Rock

From York, it's a two-hour drive to **Hyden** – home of the iconic Wave Rock. Self-drivers should continue south along Great Southern Highway and turn left at the T-junction onto Brookton Corrigin Road. Passing through the towns of Corrigin and Kondinin, you'll eventually reach Hyden.

Alternatively, a number of light-aircraft charter services fly to Hyden from Perth's Jandakot airport (tel: 08-9417 0900); flights take approximately an hour. Regular coach services also pass through Hyden, stopping at Wave Rock, and Transwa (www.transwa.wa.gov.au) operates a twice-weekly bus service.

Once in Hyden, **Wave Rock** ⓫ is a quick 4km (2½-mile) journey east. At 15 metres (50ft) high and 100 metres/yds long, this unique rock represents a perfect surfer's wave that appears frozen in time, though it is actually one wall of a huge granite dome, underscored by erosion. Making the rock even more unusual are the vertical bands of colour, caused by water run-off containing carbonates and iron oxide.

While you're at the rock, you might like to take the time to visit other interesting rock formations in the immediate area. **Hippo's Yawn** is a 20-minute walk away, and the **Humps** and the **Breakers** are also nearby. For details on how to get to these rocks, pop into the tourist office at the Wave Rock Wild Flower Shop and Visitor Centre (tel: 08-9880 5182).

Kalgoorlie

Beyond the expanse of wheat and sheep-farming country that stretches four hours east from Perth is the main goldfields town of **Kalgoorlie** ⓬ – a town made famous during the goldrush era of the late 1800s. Kalgoorlie isn't considered close to Perth, but a 1½-hour flight on either Skywest or Virgin Blue makes this legendary destination accessible to travellers with a day or two up their sleeve. At Kalgoorlie airport, cars or 4WDs can be hired from the major car-rental companies – Avis, Budget, Hertz – as well as a selection of smaller operators.

An alternative means of transport is the Prospector, a fast train service that replaces a much older service.

TIP

The best time to view Wave Rock is from August to December when the wild flowers are in bloom and the field of wheat behind is golden.

BELOW: emus are a fairly common sight in the road-side bush.

The Gold Rush

WA has the nation's most prosperous primary industry, with enormous reserves of gas, oil and mineral wealth

Western Australia is the nation's treasure house. "We've golden soil and wealth for toil", a line from Australia's national anthem, is especially true here.

Surveyors had suspected the existence of gold since the 1850s. By 1890 it proved true at places such as Yuin, Yilgarn, the Pilbara and the Murchison. Digs in 1891 produced gold worth £226,284. Within a year, fresh finds had made Australia one of the world's greatest gold-producers, and in 1900 WA mines produced £6 million worth of metal.

Paddy Hannan, the man who discovered Kalgoorlie, is generally celebrated as the man who made WA's future glitter. There's some truth to the tale, but two earlier explorer-miners really paved the way.

Arthur Bayley and John Ford were both experienced miners familiar with the dangers of the bush. After several setbacks, the two men passed through boggy country to the place known to the natives as Coolgardie. Bayley and Ford prospected the surrounding flats. In minutes Ford picked up a ¼ ounce nugget; before dinner they found 20 ounces of gold. On this lucky spot, which they named Fly Flat, they uncovered a reef of gold which would become famous throughout the mining world.

The rush was on. Two other prospectors, Foster and Baker, tracked them from Southern Cross, and staked a claim close by: within three days they had found 200 ounces of gold. The excitement soon spread. In Perth and Fremantle everyone seemed to be carrying tents, picks and shovels. Until the Coolgardie railway opened, 100-strong camel trains loaded with provisions were a common sight.

Coolgardie became a small town, but with thousands of men searching for gold, scarce food and water and poor sanitation became major problems and accounted for the loss of many lives.

It was the abortive Mount Youle rush that led Paddy Hannan to WA's most important gold-bearing find of all – Kalgoorlie. Once more, luck played its part. Hannan's party ran out of water en route to Mount Youle and camped at Mount Charlotte. When rain fell the party pushed on, but without Hannan and another man, Flannigan. It seems that Flannigan had found a couple of nuggets and persuaded Hannan to stay behind. In a few days they had over 100 ounces. They went back to Coolgardie, posting their claim at 9pm on a Saturday night. Within hours Coolgardie was almost deserted and in a week more than 750 men were fossicking round Hannan's find. The legend was born and WA's future was secure. ❑

ABOVE: gold nuggets and bar from Kalgoorlie.
LEFT: a lucky strike outside Perth Mint.

The must-see in "Kal" is undoubtedly the Super Pit. This working gold mine runs day tours on the third Sunday of every month as part of the Kalgoorlie-Boulder Market Days, which are held in Burt Street. The one-hour tours depart from the Super Pit Shop (on the corner of Burt and Hamilton streets) at 10am, 10.30am, 11am and 11.30am. To book ahead, tel: 08-9093 3488. For those whose visit does not coincide with the tours, there is a Super Pit lookout (7am–9pm daily; free), just off the Goldfields Highway. Night viewing is highly recommended – the pit is lit up by blinding high-voltage lights. A locally operated tour company, Finders Keepers, also runs two-and-a-half-hour tours Tuesday to Sunday (for details email: finderskeeperswa@bigpond.com).

Australian Prospectors' and Miners' Hall of Fame

Address: Goldfields Highway, Kalgoorlie, www.mininghall.com

Tel: 08-9026 2700
Opening Hrs: daily 9am–4.30pm
Entrance fee: charge

To discover more about Kalgoorlie's mining history, visit the **Australian Prospectors' and Miners' Hall of Fame**, on the Hannans North Reserve on the Goldfields Highway. Here you can pan for gold, tour interactive galleries, take an underground tour, watch gold-pouring demonstrations and enjoy a twilight tour with a barbecue meal.

Infamous for its working-girl history (an industry that still thrives today), Kalgoorlie also offers a tour of a working brothel. While this might not be for everyone, the guided tour through **Langtrees 181** (tel: 08-9026 2181), at 181 Hay Street, gives curious visitors a sneak peek at the rooms and the amazing memorabilia collected over the years. The tour includes a running commentary on the history of the industry in the town.

ABOVE: the Super Pit at Kalgoorlie.

Most bars in Kalgoorlie have a "back bar" or sports bar, and a "front bar", which is more family-friendly. The back bar of many Kalgoorlie pubs is where you'll find the famous Kalgoorlie skimpy, or topless waitress, as they're more commonly known in most parts of the world.

TIP

Due to the risk of bush fires, the Hotham Valley Forest Ranger train only operates during winter months. During the warmer season, the Hotham Valley Tourist Railway runs a diesel train between Pinjarra and Dwellingup.

There's almost a pub on every corner in Kalgoorlie. In its heyday, the town boasted 93 hotels, while today there are 25 – not bad for a city that's only 67 sq km (26 sq miles) in area. There are three types of pubs in Kalgoorlie – those aimed at the miners, those that cater for families, and those that keep the young crowd entertained. For something unique, the Metropole Hotel on Burt Street in Boulder features a mineshaft that leads to the Super Pit (tel: 08-9093 1281). For a high-energy night out, try Judd's Pub at the Kalgoorlie Hotel (tel: 08-9021 3046) and Paddy's Ale House at the Exchange Hotel (tel: 08-9021 2833). Pubs and hotels close at midnight.

The Goldfields Pipeline, a 557km (346-mile) pipeline from Perth to Kalgoorlie, supplies the city with water. Controversial in its day, the pipeline proved a huge success, and its creator, C.Y. O'Connor (see page 142), is considered one of Australia's engineering greats.

SOUTH OF PERTH

Head south of Perth for the region's top wineries, gourmet produce (cheese, chocolate and olive oil), and dense karri and jarrah forests.

If you're catching the bus from Perth, Transwa has a daily service that stops at all major towns on the South Western and Bussell Highways (tel: 1300 662 205). South West Coach Lines also runs a regular service between Perth and the major southwest towns (tel: 08-9324 2333 for timetables and fares).

Dwellingup

The timber town of **Dwellingup** ⓭, 97km (60 miles) south of Perth, is a popular barbecue and picnic destination for Perthites. To get there, travel south along South Western Highway through Serpentine, then turn left at North Dandalup towards Dwellingup.

Hotham Valley Tourist Railway

Address: 86A Barrack Street, Perth, www.hothamvalleyrailway.com.au
Tel: 08-9221 4444

The main attraction here is the **Hotham Valley Tourist Railway**. From May to October, the railway

BELOW: Bunbury, WA's fastest-growing city.

operates the Pinjarra Steam Ranger – a traditional steam train which takes passengers from Pinjarra to Dwellingup.

The Dwellingup Forest Train runs from Dwellingup, through the forest and back again, every weekend and on public holidays.

The railway also operates the **Etmilyn Forest Heritage Trail** (tel: 08-9221 4444 for information). Departing from Dwellingup railway station every Saturday and Sunday, it makes the 8km (5-mile) ride through the town of Holyoake to Etmilyn, where passengers can disembark for a 30-minute walk through blackbutt, jarrah, red gum and banksia. This is particularly worth doing during the wild flower season in spring.

The **Forest Heritage Centre** (daily 10am–5pm; tel: 08-9538 1395), on Acacia Street, Dwellingup, is home to the Australian School of Fine Wood. Built in the shape of three giant jarrah leaves, it has a gallery where the students' work is displayed and offers educational tours.

Hiking and biking

Dwellingup is one of five southwestern towns on WA's **Bibbulmun Track** – a 1,000km (620-mile) hiking trail running south from Kalamunda in the Perth Hills to Albany, with track camps at regular intervals. The Bibbulmun Track Foundation hosts regular group walks. Alternatively, you can buy a walking guide from Mountain Designs in Perth (862 Hay Street, tel: 08-9322 4774).

Like the Bib Track, the Munda Biddi Trail will (once completed) also run from the Perth Hills to Albany. Designed for mountain bikers, it is an extension of the trail that currently runs from Mundaring to Collie (www.mundabiddi.org.au).

Bunbury

From Dwellingup, it's a 1½-hour drive to the southern city of Bunbury

ABOVE: statues soak up the sun. **BELOW:** keen hikers may want to sample the Bibbulmun Track, a 1,000km (620-mile) path between Kalamunda and Albany.

TIP

The new Underwater Observatory has quickly become Busselton's star attraction. During the summer months, it pays to book in advance, otherwise there's a good chance you'll miss out.

– WA's third-largest population centre. If you're self-driving, head west from Dwellingup towards Pinjarra and turn left onto South Western Highway, which leads straight to Bunbury, passing through **Harvey** on the way. A lush farming community, Harvey is home to the popular Harvey Fresh Juices.

Dolphin Discover Centre

Address: Koombana Beach, Koombana Drive
Tel: 08-9791 3088
Opening Hrs: daily 9am–3pm in winter and from 8am–4pm Nov–Apr
Entrance fee: charge

One of the main attractions at **Bunbury** ⑭ is the Dolphin Discovery Centre. A community of bottlenose dolphins visits the beach daily to feed, and visitors can stand on the beach within an arm's reach of the mammals. Dolphin cruises depart daily from November to April, and the centre offers popular "Swim with the Dolphins" tours.

Another worthwhile attraction, this time to see birdlife, is **Big Swamp Reserve** (free) on Prince Phillip Drive, a couple of minutes from the CBD. This man-made wetland, home to more than 70 species of water birds, is crossed by a 2.5km (1-mile) boardwalk with secluded bird hides.

You can pick up an information brochure to the wetlands at the **Big Swamp Wildlife Park** (daily 10am–5pm; small charge; tel: 08-9721 8380), just across the road. Among its abundance of native animals look out for the white kangaroo – one of only a small number in Australia.

The hippest new location in Bunbury is the recently developed Marlston Hill, home to a host of restaurants and bars, including Vat 2, Barbados Tavern and Nightclub, Jivin J's and local celebrity Aristos's fish-and-chip joint. Most restaurants open early and close late, serving lunch from around noon–2pm and dinner from around 6pm.

The Ferguson Valley

If you head east from Bunbury towards Balingup along South Western Highway, you'll pass through the lovely and underrated **Ferguson Valley** ⑮, home to a growing wine region. You can stop in at a handful of cellar doors for tastings; visit Wellington Dam for a spot of birdwatching, bushwalking and picnicking, and meander through undulating hills. On your way through, you may want to take a quick look at **Gnomesville** (on the intersection of Wellington Mill and Ferguson roads), which is home to more than 1,000 garden gnomes placed in the village by locals and passers-by.

Busselton

The gateway to the Margaret River Wine Region, **Busselton** ⑯ is one of the top destinations for locals and visitors alike. Its location on **Geographe Bay** – one of only two north-facing and therefore protected bays in WA – also makes it perfect for

BELOW: friendly face at the Dolphin Discovery Centre, Bunbury.

families and swimmers. From Bunbury, Busselton is an easy half-hour's drive south along Bussell Highway (if you're coming from Perth, take South Western Highway to Busselton, 232km/144 miles south).

One of Busselton's most photographed features is **Busselton Jetty**. At over 1,800 metres/yds in length, this is the longest wooden pier in the southern hemisphere. It is packed with a range of family-friendly attractions.

Underwater Observatory

Address: Busselton Jetty, Busselton
Tel: 08-9754 0900
Opening Hrs: Dec–Apr 8am–5pm, May–Sept 10am–4pm, Oct–Nov 9am–5pm
Entrance Fee: charge

The jetty's **Underwater Observatory**, which is under renovation and due for completion in 2011, allows visitors to descend 8 metres (26ft) below sea level for amazing views

of tropical and temperate fish and tropical coral.

The boatshed-style **Interpretive Centre** (summer 8am–6pm, winter 9am–5pm), 50 metres/yds offshore from the jetty, relates the history of the jetty. You can also watch the underwater world beneath the jetty via a marine cam, browse through the arts and crafts on display, and purchase tickets for the Red Jetty Train that ferries passengers up and down the pier.

Dunsborough and Yallingup

Located just west of Busselton, along Caves Road, are the towns of **Dunsborough** ⑰ (26km/16 miles from Busselton) and **Yallingup** ⑱ (32km/20 miles). Surrounded by vineyards, this booming area is one of the most popular weekend getaways for Perthites. Half- and full-day winery tours are especially popular. For organised tours, contact Milesaway

ABOVE: explore the many attractions of Busselton Jetty.
BELOW: tasting may be required to test the veractiy of the claim.

ABOVE: Sugarloaf Rock.
BELOW: ornamental detail, Margaret River.

area include **Yallingup Galleries** (tel: 08-9755 2372) and **John Miller Design** (tel: 08-9756 6336), both on Marrinup Drive, Yallingup.

Six kilometres (4 miles) south of Yallingup, and 1.5km (1 mile) west of Caves Road, on Injidup Springs Road, is **Wardan Aboriginal Cultural Centre** (Wed–Mon 10am–4pm; charge; tel: 08-9756 6566; www.warden.com.au), where you can discover more about the culture of the Wardani, the local indigenous people. In addition to an interpretive gallery, it offers a 1km (½-mile) bush story trail, tool-making and spear-throwing workshops, and music and dance performances.

Best beaches

Dunsborough boasts excellent beaches, perfect for families. For more secluded beaches follow Naturalist Road, northeast of Dunsborough, to **Meelup**, **Eagle Bay** and **Bunker Bay**. **Smith's Beach**, off Caves Road and Canal Rocks Road south of Yallingup, is one of the area's best spots for surfing.

Naturaliste Road will also take you to the tip of **Cape Naturaliste** ⓳ with its old lighthouse (daily 9.30am–4pm last entry; charge), built in 1903, and hiking trails. The 135km (84-mile) Cape to Cape Walk leads from here to the Cape Leeuwin Lighthouse. It is not as developed as the Bibbulmun Track, but it winds through the Leeuwin–Naturaliste National Park, passing many natural attractions, such as Sugarloaf Rock and Three Bears, the area's best surf break. A guide to the trail is available from the Margaret River Visitor Centre.

Margaret River

From Dunsborough and Yallingup, continue south along Caves Road, turning left at Carters Road to **Margaret River** ⓴. Alternatively, if you are driving from Perth (279km/173

Tours (tel: 08-9754 2929) or Taste the South Winery Tours (tel: 0438 210 373). If you prefer to visit the wineries independently, many of the best ones are on Caves Road and the roads leading off it between Yallingup and Gracetown. All the wineries are well signposted.

Galleries also abound in the area. Heading south along Caves Road from Dunsborough and Yallingup, turn left onto Gunyulgup Valley to reach **Gunyulgup Galleries** (daily 10am–5pm, tel: 08-9755 2177), which sits alongside Lamont's Cellar Door and Restaurant, overlooking an idyllic lake. Gunyulgup shows the work of many of WA and Australia's best artists in a wide range of media, from glass through to woodcarvings and painting. Neighbouring Lamont's *(see page 212)*, owned by celebrity WA chef Kate Lamont, who also has a restaurant in East Perth *(see page 111)*, is open for wine tastings from 11am to 5pm Saturday to Sunday.

Other interesting galleries in the

miles), take the Busselton Bypass and head south to Margaret River along Bussell Highway.

Margaret River is home to some of WA's top wineries, including Vasse Felix (tel: 08-9756 5014) and Voyager (tel: 08-9757 6354), both just a 10-minute drive from the town of Margaret River. Begin a wine tour at the Margaret River Regional Wine Centre, in the Margaret River Visitor Centre on Bussell Highway in the heart of town. It holds regular free varietal wine tastings and can supply maps to all the wineries in the area.

Another popular attraction in Margaret River is the **Eagles Heritage Wildlife Centre** (Boodjidup Road; flight displays at 11am and 1.30pm; charge).

Bikes, hikes and caves

The surrounding karri forest makes the Margaret River area a popular hiking and mountain-biking destination. For mountain-biking tours contact Dirty Detours (tel: 0417 998 816), and for information on walks in the area, pop into the Visitor Centre.

Stretching from Busselton down to Augusta, the **Leeuwin-Naturaliste Ridge** is dotted with limestone caves (charges for the more spectacular). If you would like to tour the caves, stop off at **Caveworks** (tel: 08-9757 7411), on Caves Road, 25km (15 miles) south of Margaret River, which manages the caves.

Located at the entrance to **Lake Cave** (tours every half-hour from 10.30am–2.30pm plus a final tour at 3.30pm; charge), it has explanatory displays about the caves and friendly staff who can direct you to other caves in the area, including **Jewel Cave** (tours every hour 9.30am–11.30am, every half-hour from 11.30am–1.30pm, final tour 3.30pm; charge), the most spectacular, 8km (5 miles) north of Augusta, and **Mammoth Cave** (self-guiding 9am–6pm, last entry 5pm; charge), the largest chamber, located 21km (13 miles) south of Margaret River.

Augusta

Nestled on Flinders Bay at the mouth of the Blackwood River at the southernmost end of the Margaret River

ABOVE: choice fish for sale in Augusta.
BELOW: Vasse Felix vineyard.

ABOVE: view from Balingup Heights.
BELOW: the spectacularly sited Cape Leeuwin Lighthouse.

Wine Region, **Augusta** ㉑ is a wonderful place to unwind. On Bussell Highway, 65km (40 miles) south of Margaret River (Caves Road also leads straight here from Yallingup), it is the ideal place to fish, swim or go on a leisurely cruise up the river.

There is also no better place in WA to go whale-watching. Southern rights and occasionally even the rare blue whale visit during their yearly migration up the coast. The whales stay from May through to August, with up to 200 whales playing in Flinders Bay during the season's peak. The best way to experience the mammals is to join one of Naturaliste Charter's daily tours (tel: 08-9755 2276).

Cape Leeuwin Lighthouse ㉒ (tours available at 30-minute intervals daily; charge), on Leeuwin Road south of Augusta, is a famous landmark and also a wonderful place to watch the whales during the season.

Balingup

If it's the great forests of the south that interest you, head back to Bunbury and take South Western High-

way 65km (40 miles) southeast to the tiny town of Balingup. On the way, you will pass through other small towns, including **Donnybrook**, in the midst of a lush fruit-growing area, where you will find roadside vendors selling apples in season.

Reminiscent of the English countryside with rolling green hills, **Balingup** ㉓ is located in the Blackwood River Valley, a lovely spot to bushwalk along part of the Bibbulmun Track (see page 178), birdwatch and browse through the town's quaint galleries.

The Old Cheese Factory Craft Centre on Balingup–Nannup Road (tel: 08-9764 1018) houses the largest collection of antiques in WA (contrary to its name, cheese is not produced here). Tourist information is also available, and there is a café for those looking to refuel. Other galleries include Jalbrook Alpaca Knitwear in the centre of town on South Western Highway (tel: 08-9764 1190), and, just next door, the Balingup Bronze Gallery and Organic Fair Trade Coffee and Teahouse (tel: 08-9764 1843).

Just before you reach the Old Cheese Factory is the Balingup

Lavender Farm (Sept–Apr daily 10am–4pm; small charge to view the garden), idyllically set in rolling hills. Here some 35 varieties of lavender are turned into the farm's own lavender oil.

Just 2km (1 mile) south on the South Western Highway is the **Golden Valley Tree Park**. This 60-hectare (150-acre) park comprises native and exotic trees from around the world. It's well signposted and the perfect setting for a picnic.

Bridgetown

In the centre of the Blackwood River Valley, **Bridgetown ㉔**, a 20-minute drive from Balingup along South Western Highway (or 272km/170 miles southeast of Perth), is an attractive and vibrant town with several old buildings and a packed calendar of events *(see below)*.

Just before you get to Bridgetown you'll pass through **Greenbushes**. To stretch your legs, stop at the Heritage Park here (opposite the Discovery Centre), where you can follow signposted walking trails ranging from 3km (1½ miles) to 15km (9 miles).

The Discovery Centre (Sat and Sun 10am–2pm; tel: 08-9764 3883) displays aspects of the local mining industry, including a mock shaft and a prospector's hut.

Bridgetown lies in the midst of apple orchards. At the **Cidery** (Wed–Mon 11am–4pm, Fri 11am–2pm; tel: 08-9761 2204), at 43 Gifford Road on the east side of Bridgetown, you can sample cider and juices, traditionally crushed and pressed.

Pemberton

From Bridgetown, continue south down South Western Highway, through the timber town of **Manjimup**, to **Pemberton ㉕**, 33km (20 miles) southeast of Bridgetown. Arguably the Southwest's most popular inland getaway, Pemberton is an ideal springboard for exploring the forest.

Fishing for trout and marron (freshwater crayfish) is a popular activity here. Information on places to fish and how to obtain permits are available from Pemberton Visitor Centre. Novice fishermen can get a helping hand at the King Trout

While travelling around the Perth region you will come across many place names ending in "up", an Aboriginal word meaning "place of". Manjimup, for example, means place of Manjim, an edible weed used by the Aborigines.

BELOW: getting the measure of a tingle tree in Walpole.

Bridgetown Festivals

The small town of Bridgetown has gained something of a reputation for its various festivals, which draw locals and visitors throughout the year. These range from the Bridgetown Blues, WA's largest blues festival, attracting international blues and root musicians, held in November, to the Festival of Country Gardens, featuring more than 50 private gardens that are opened to the public, held from October to November. Other events include the Blackwood Marathon, held every October, and a powerboat race, the Blackwood Classic, held along the Blackwood River in March. For a month-by-month listing of the town's festivals log on to www.bridgetown.com.au.

Restaurant & Marron Farm (daily 9.30am–5pm, closed Thur during the school term; tel: 08-9776 1352) on Northcliffe Road. You'll be given a rod and bucket and left to fish in the farm's dam, which is well stocked with trout and marron.

Alternatively, visit Karri Valley Resort, which offers all manner of outdoor activities, from horse riding to canoeing and trout-fishing. You don't have to be a guest at the resort, and activities are surprisingly inexpensive. There's also equipment for hire for those who'd rather go it alone.

Tree-climbing

During the 1930s and 1940s, a series of fire lookouts was constructed in the top of gigantic karri trees surrounding Pemberton. While the trees are no longer being used for this purpose, visitors are permitted to climb three of the trees, including the magnificent Gloucester Tree, rising 65 metres (200ft), situated 3km (1½ miles) east of Pemberton in the **Gloucester National Park**; the Dave Evans Bicentennial Tree, in **Warren National Park**, a 15-minute drive from Pemberton on Vasse Highway; and the Diamond Tree, also a 15-minute drive north of Pemberton, on South Western Highway. An entry fee to the National Parks applies.

The Great Southern

Home to some of the country's most picturesque beaches, dense forest, magnificent rugged coastal scenery, and boutique wineries, the **Great Southern** is a clean, refreshing part of the state with a good tourism infrastrucutre.

Head southeast of Pemberton on South Western Highway to **Walpole** ㉖. Located in the middle of the Walpole–Nornalup National Park, 420km (260 miles) south of Perth, Walpole combines thick forests, beaches and rugged coastline, making it an ideal holiday destination.

The thrilling **Valley of the Giants Treetop Walk** (daily 9am–5pm, and 8am–5.15pm in Christmas school holidays; small charge; wheelchair access) lies 13km (8 miles) east of Walpole along South Coast Highway. Here, a 600-metre-long boardwalk passes through the canopy of the surrounding tingle forest, allowing you to walk through the trees. During Christmas school holidays a wonderful night tour is available at scheduled times (tel: 08-9840 8263 for more information).

On ground level, a boardwalk called the **Ancient Empire Walk** (free) winds through the base of the wide-girth trees, some of which are 16 metres (52ft) in circumference.

Denmark

At Walpole, South Western Highway becomes South Coast Highway and continues east to **Denmark** ㉗ (412km/256 miles south of Perth), a peaceful and pretty town along the Denmark River.

There are a number of scenic drives around the town. One of the best is the **Scotsdale Tourist Drive**, a 34km (21-mile) route east along Scottsdale Road, then left onto McLeod Road, which eventually leads onto South Coast Highway. It passes many of the region's best wineries, art galleries and local producers. Some to watch out for are Howard Park Winery (tel: 08-9848 2345), Denmark Farmhouse Cheese and Ducketts Mill Winery (tel: 08-9840 9844), and Matilda Estate (tel: 08-9848 1951). At the end of the drive is the famous **Greens Pool** in the William Bay National Park.

The **Mount Shadforth Scenic Drive** is also worth taking. Starting in Denmark, on North Street, it also passes wineries and galleries on the way to Mount Shadforth Lookout, where you are greeted by spectacular views over Wilson Inlet, the Nullaki Peninsula and the Southern Ocean.

Albany

The city of **Albany** ㉘ (409km/254 miles southeast of Perth, or if you're coming from Denmark, 50km/30 miles east on Lower Denmark Road) is one of Western Australia's leading holiday centres with rushing rivers, a

TIP

On your way to Denmark from Walpole, make sure you stop in at the Nornalup Teahouse (08-9840 1422). This little spot is of the "blink and you'll miss it" variety, but it's worth the journey stop. It is open for breakfast, lunch and dinner Wednesday to Monday.

BELOW: the Natural Bridge, Torndirrup National Park.

In 1914, in the spectacular King George Sound, off Albany, 39 ships assembled to carry the Australian and New Zealand Army Corps to Gallipoli in Turkey. Prominent among the Anzacs who sailed to Gallipoli were WA's 10th Light Horse Regiment, whose memorial overlooks King George Sound.

spectacular coastline, wineries, and nearby National Parks.

The drive from Perth to Albany along Albany Highway takes approximately 4½ hours, but for those who are short of time, Skywest (www.skywest.com.au) offers a daily air service from Perth domestic airport to Albany, where there are a number of hire-car companies.

The city is situated on King George Sound, where southern right and humpback whales visit from June to October on their yearly migration north. The whales can be viewed from the Sound's shore, or, for close-ups, take a whale-watching cruise (possibilities include Silver Star Cruises, tel: 0428-429 876, or Albany Whale Tours, tel: 0408-451 068).

Whale World

Address: Whaling Station Road, Frenchman Bay
Tel: 08-9844 4021
Opening Hrs: daily 9am–5pm with guided tours every hour, final tour 4pm
Entrance Fee: charge

Albany was once a whaling town, with a whaling station located on Cheynes Beach, just past Torndirrup National Park on Frenchman Bay Road. Whaling operations ceased in 1978, but **Whale World** (at the old site) documents the town's whaling past. A steam-powered whaler, *Cheynes IV*, built in 1948, is open for inspection.

While you are visiting Torndirrup National Park, take in the dramatic coastal scenery. Situated along the rugged coastline, the Gap is an awe-inspiring 24-metre (78ft) chasm, which visitors can view from the safety of a steel cage on the cliff's edge. The Natural Bridge is a large granite rock that's been eroded over time to create a large arch. No admission charges apply.

On the way back from the park, turn left onto Princess Road, which turns into Sandpatch Road, to the **Verve Energy Wind Farm**, Australia's largest wind farm, with 12 eerie turbines, 65 metres (over 200ft) high, perched on a hill overlooking the coast. Viewing platforms and boardwalks offer views of both the turbines and West Cape Howe, WA's most southern tip. Entry is free and there is 24-hour access.

Back in town, the former HMAS *Perth* is visible floating in the shallows of King George Sound, the mast rising out of the water. Scuttled in 2001, the vessel is a popular dive site for snorkellers and divers. For a guided tour, call Albany Dive and Whale Charters, tel: 08-9842 6886.

Some of WA's most beautiful beaches lie close to Albany, among them **Nanarup Beach** (off the Lower Kalgan Road 25km/15 miles east of town), popular with surfers.

Little Beach

Located in Two People's Bay National Park (30km/18 miles east of Albany), Little Beach is a sheltered cove ideal for swimming; and Two People's Bay, Manypeaks, is a sheltered swathe, where a one-hour trail leads over the headland and along the beach. ❑

BELOW: looking down on Whale World.

BEST RESTAURANTS AND BARS

North of Perth

Geraldton

Skeeta's Restaurant and Café
101 Foreshore Drive.
Tel: 08-9964 1619. Open: B, L & D daily. **$$**
Skeeta's specialises in seafood, yet they've got the non-fish eaters covered, too, with pasta, steak and chicken dishes. The whiting fillets served with crispy potatoes and salad are a favourite, as is the seafood platter for two.

Tanti's Restaurant
174 Marine Terrace.
Tel: 08-9964 2311. Open: L Wed–Fri, D Mon–Sat. **$$**
Tanti's fresh Thai cuisine incorporates many different aspects of Thai cooking. Signature dishes are chicken and cashew, thai beef salad and tom yum soup.

Kalbarri

Black Rock Café
80 Grey St. Tel: 08-9937 1062. Open: B & L Tue–Sun, D Tue–Sat. **$$**
Black Rock serves generous, interesting food ranging from strawberry pancakes at breakfast to

their signature surf-and-turf dinner options – lobster mornay, grilled prawns, fillet steak, potato rosti and salad. The view of the Murchison River as it meets the ocean is spectacular.

Restaurant Upstairs
Porter St. Tel: 08-9937 1033. Open: L & D daily in school holidays, Fri–Wed outside school holidays. **$**
The food and ambience are great, with a beautiful view of the river mouth and ocean. The interior is fresh and modern, with changing artworks from all around Australia.

The Grass Tree Café and Restaurant
94–96 Grey St. Tel: 08-9937 2288. Open: L & D Thur–Tue. **$$–$$$**
With its sweeping view across to the ocean, the Grass Tree brings a touch of sophistication to this relaxed town. The food is modern Australian.

East of Perth

Kalgoorlie

Saltimbocca
90 Egan St. Tel: 08-9022 8028. Open: D Tue–Sun. **$$$**
The house speciality here is the veal saltimbocca, in a creamy prosciutto, sage and white-wine sauce. Known for its home-made pastas.

South of Perth

Albany Area

Lavender Cottage
55 Peels Place. Tel: 08-9842 2073. Open: Mon–Fri morning tea and lunch, Fri night dinner only. **$$**
This delightful French restaurant is cosy and friendly. Order a Lavender gourmet platter for lunch or try the duck confit followed by the crème brûlée at dinner.

Maleeya's Thai Café
Porongurup Rd. Tel: 08-9853 1123. Open: L & D Fri–Sun. **$$–$$$**
This is recognised as one of the best dining options in the southwest. The food is fresh and fantastic. Many of the vegetables are grown in the gardens. Booking essential.

Wild Duck
Shop 5, 112 York Terrace.
Tel: 08-9842 2554. Open: D Wed–Sun. **$$$$**
This restaurant offers a sophisticated alternative to takeaway fish 'n' chips. Wild Duck offers a quietly sensible yet stylish, old-school dining experience. Start off your night with the tasty home-made bread, then move on to such dishes as the veal fillet on truffled polenta, paired with beef cheek, Persian feta mash and red wine jus. To top off the night, the desserts are scrumptiously creative and hard to refuse.

Prices for a three-course dinner per person with a half-bottle of house wine:
$ = under AUS$25
$$ = AUS$25–40
$$$ = AUS$40–70
$$$$ = over AUS$70

RIGHT: Vasse Felix winery in the Margaret River area.

Bunbury

Aristos Waterfront
15 Bonnefoi Boulevard. Tel: 08-9791 6477. Open: L & D daily. $–$$
Situated over the water at the Marlston Hill development, Aristos serves fresh seafood along with regular fish and chips. Coffee, cakes and wine as well.

Vat 2
2 Jetty Rd. Tel: 08-9791 8833. Open: B, L & D daily. $$–$$$
Vat 2 in Bunbury serves great food and wine. Located near the water in the Marlston Hill development, it caters for those looking for a light seafood snack or a more substantial meal (grilled meats and pastas). The interior is modern and bright and the service is efficient.

Bunker Bay

Other Side of the Moon
Bunker Bay Rd. Tel: 08-9756 9159. Open: B, L & D daily. $$$$
Located in the up-market Quay West resort, with views over olive trees and the swimming pool to the ocean. The food is modern Australian and uses the freshest local produce, such as marron and lamb. The desserts are especially recommended, and they have an excellent buffet breakfast too.

Busselton and Vasse

Equinox Café
343 Queen Sreet. Tel: 08-9752 4641. Open: B, L & D daily. $$

This waterfront restaurant is surrounded by lovely Moreton Bay fig trees and has a beautiful view of the ocean. Its interesting Australian and international cuisine is as popular with locals as it is with visitors.

The Old Post Office Tearooms
4 Queen St. Tel: 0458 224 661. Open: Tue–Sun 10am–4pm. $$
Situated in a heritage building that was Busselton's old courthouse, jail and post office (now an arts precinct), this hidden gem serves home-made morning and afternoon tea, light lunches and high tea.

The Goose
Geographe Bay Rd. Tel: 08-9754 7700. Open: B, L & D daily. $$
Overlooking the ocean, right next to the Busselton Jetty, The Goose is a light and airy restaurant serving quality food. The modern menu changes regularly. Sample dishes include tapas and seared tuna steaks with olives and roast veg. Gorgeous views whatever the weather.

Blackwood River

Blackwood River Tavern
Lot 201 Brockman St. Tel: 08-9764 1830. Open: L & D Tue–Sun. $$
This tavern has introduced a dining option that Balingup desperately needed: the atmosphere is friendly and the food satisfying. The portions are large, especially the

fish 'n' chips and the steak dishes. Those who prefer lighter meals will find options such as seafood and salad.

Newtown House
737 Bussell Highway. www.newtownhouse.com.au. Tel: 08-9755 4485. Open: L & D Tue–Sat. $$$
Newtown House serves sophisticated fare in a house built in 1851. Sample dishes include Margaret River venison, celeriac and roast garlic, baked quince, shiraz jus, and, for dessert, hot caramel soufflé, lavender ice cream, hot caramel sauce.

Margaret River Region

Cape Lavender
Lot 4 Carter Rd, off Metricup Rd, Wilyabrup. www.capelavender.com.au. Tel: 08-9755 7552. Open: L daily. $$–$$$
Cape Lavender has won several Gold Plate awards for its food. The menu includes items such as nachos, antipasto, ploughman's platters, pie and soup of the day. The farm also grows lavender which is made into a variety of products, including lavender scones and lavender sparkling wine.

Clairault
Caves Rd, Wilyabrup. www.clairaultwines.com.au. Tel: 08-9755 6655. Open: L daily. $$–$$$
This is a stylish restaurant which epitomises what dining in the Margaret River region is all about. The food is modern Australian and includes such

dishes as home-made gnocchi with roast tomato, Spanish onion confit, goat's cheese and pine nuts, followed by grilled figs with pistachio honeycomb and rose water syrup. In winter it is nice to snuggle up next to one of their fires with a large glass of red wine.

Flutes Restaurant
Caves Rd. www.flutes.com.au. Tel: 08-9755 6250. Open: L daily. $$$
Flutes is located in the beautiful Brookland Valley Winery, overlooking a dam. Expect French-Australian cuisine using lots of local produce including game, yabbies, ostrich, lamb, duck, chicken, barramundi and prawns. This restaurant has been on the scene for many years and continues to please.

Voyager Estate
Stevens Rd, Margaret River. www.voyagerestate.com.au. Tel: 08-9757 6354. Open: L daily. $$$
Voyager Estate offers the best in local produce and award-winning wines. Great attention is paid to creating dishes that will work well with the wine – from the seared scallops on cauliflower purée, to the wonderfully aromatic lamb rack with spring vegetables, pink verjuice butter and nutty tarator sauce.

Lamont's
Gunyulgup Valley Drive, Yallingup. www.lamonts.com.au. Tel: 08-9755 2434. Open: L daily, tapas Fri–Sun 5–7pm. $$$

The elegant food at this popular eatery is matched by its wonderful setting – perched over a lake in the middle of the bush. The menu includes exquisite combinations such as sugar-cured Margaret River Venison, black pepper shortbread and tapenade, and Pemberton marron, roasted baby potatoes, lime and chive beurre blanc.

Wills Domain

Corner Brash and Abbey Farm roads, Yallingup. Tel: 08-9755 2327. Open: L daily. **$$$**

The Haunold Family has a wine-making past that is steeped in 15th-century European history and tradition.

Wino's

85 Bussell Highway, Margaret River. www.winos.com.au. Tel: 08-9758 7155. Open: tapas 3pm onwards, D daily. **$$**

Located in the heart of Margaret River, this is a chilled restaurant serving excellent food. The dark wood floors and chalkboards are reminiscent of a European bar, and the extensive tapas menu is European in character. There is an extensive wine selection, as you would expect.

Prices for a three-course dinner per person with a half-bottle of house wine:
$ = under AUS$25
$$ = AUS$25–40
$$$ = AUS$40–70
$$$$ = over AUS$70

Wise Vineyards

Eagle Bay Rd, Dunsborough. www.wisewine.com.au. Tel: 08-9755 3331. Open: B & L daily, D Fri and Sat. **$$$**

Wise is a beautiful winery, and the restaurant has been situated to take full visual advantage of the rolling vineyards and bush. The menu here changes to reflect the seasons, and whether it's beer-battered fish with hand-cut fries or a delicate crab pasta, you'll be pleased with your choice.

Vasse Felix

Corner of Caves and Harman's South roads, Cowaramup. www.vassefelix.com.au. Tel: 08-9756 5000. Open: L daily. **$$$**

Vasse Felix is one of the top wineries, and this is a top restaurant serving high-quality modern Australian food. The timber and stone building is a great place to sit and relax while you look out over the vineyards.

Nornalup Teahouse Restaurant

South Coast Highway, Nornalup. www.nornalup teahouse.com.au. Tel: 08-9840 1422. Open: B, L & D Wed–Mon. **$$**

This beautifully converted cottage has an idyllic setting. The food is also extremely good. Call ahead because the opening times change from time to time, and booking on weekend evenings is highly recommended. Nornalup is definitely a hidden treasure.

Bars

Bootleg Brewery

Puzey Rd, Wilyabrup. www.bootlegbrewery.com.au Tel: 08-9755 6300.

When the sun is shining there is nothing better than sitting in Bootleg's garden sipping on one of their local brews overlooking the lake. Enjoy some pub grub or just a drink. There is live music on most weekends in the warmer months.

Blackwood Valley Brewing Company

43 Gifford Rd, Bridgetown. www.thecidery.com.au. Tel: 08-9761 2204.

This southwest cidery recognises the contribution of the early pioneer families to establishing a world-renowned apple industry. Choose from a range of refreshing ciders such as apple kiss, sweet rosie or spider cider.

Cider works

Wattle Bird Court, Capel. www.ciderworks.mysouthwest. com.au. Tel: 08-9727 1000.

This Capel cidery captures the romance, nostalgia and chivalry of medieval times in its brews. They can be enjoyed not only because of that strong tradition, but also for their complexity and delicate flavours.

Duckstein Brewery Margaret River

3517 Caves Rd, Wilyabrup. www.duckstein.com.au. Tel: 08-9755 6500.

These beers are made through the tradition of Reinheitsgebot – The Purity Law of 1516 – where only water, malt and hops are used to produce the beer, making the final brew an excellent taste.

Jarrah Jacks

Kemp Rd, Pemberton. www.jarrahjacks.com.au. Tel: 08-9776 1333.

This brewery is surprisingly kid-friendly, and comes complete with a playground as well as a café and cellar door. With regional cuisine to complement the brews, Jarrah Jacks is a good place to enjoy the views of this picturesque valley.

Old Coast Brewery

West Break Rd, Myalup. www.ocrb.com.au. Tel: 1300 792 106.

Drive through a 1,000-tree olive grove and find your way to this scenic 24-hectare (60-acre) rural property and enjoy a substantial meal to complement your choice of wine or beer.

The Real River Factory

75 Goldfields Rd, Donnybrook. www.therealriverfactory.com. Tel: 08-9731 0311.

Set within about 12 hectares (30 acres) of fruit trees, The Real River Company is the perfect venue to enjoy a nice refreshing apple cider, apple juice or enjoy a spot of lunch.

Wild Bull Brewery

Pile Rd, Ferguson. www.wildbull brewery.com.au. Tel: 08-9728 0737.

Situated in the heart of the Ferguson Valley, this boutique brewing house also offers local wines, organic/preservative-free wines, cider and light meals.

WILDFLOWERS OF WA

In spring, the bush is ablaze with wild flowers, from bold and brilliant banksias to delicate ice daisies

Western Australia is known for its wild flowers. The display is most spectacular during spring (August through to November), though at almost any time of the year you will find some flowers brightening the olive- and sage-greens of the bush. Banksias, for example, often bloom in autumn or winter.

The state has some 10,000 species of wild flowers; 6,000 of them are native to the state, and journeys in spring will be rewarded by stunning roadside displays. But some areas are particularly well endowed: Kalbarri National Park, the karri forests around Pemberton, and the Stirling ranges north of Albany are known to the locals as being particularly colourful. The southwest part of the state is known for more delicate flowers such as the orchid, kangaroo paw and mountain bell.

Closer to Perth, John Forrest National Park is another rich area for botanical exploration, or you could simply spend a day visiting Kings Park Botanic Garden, especially during its Wild Flower Festival in September, when colours run riot through central Perth and everyone becomes a bit of an expert gardener.

ABOVE: Albany bottlebrush is more commonly associated with the eastern states (it was one of the plants the naturalist Joseph Banks collected on Cook's voyage of 1770), but you will also find it in WA, especially in damp habitats.

LEFT: in spring, daisies of many types and colours carpet forest clearings and fields.

ABOVE: a typical roadside display near Kalbarri in spring. If you have a special interest in wild flowers it can be worth taking an escorted wild flower tour, an option offered by most of the day-tour operators in Perth.

RIGHT: succulents, such as these in a forest near Karridale, also flourish, especially in the south.

GRASS TREES

Even if you are not in Western Australia during the wild flower season, the bush is a fascinating landscape with a rich biodiversity that is at last being championed by conservationists after well over a century of indiscriminate land clearance for agriculture.

Among the many types of eucalyptus (gum trees), paper bark and banksias, the tree that perhaps stands out above all others is the grass tree (Xanthorrhoea). With a distinctive fire-blackened trunk surmounted by a mop of spiky grass and spear-like flower shaft, the trees are known as *balga* (black boys) to the Aborigines, who traditionally used a waterproof resin produced from the base of the plant to make glue and rubbed the dried flower shafts together to create fire. The nectar from the flowers of the plant was also used to make a sweet fermented drink.

Grass trees are very slow-growing (about 1 metre/3ft every 100 years) but can live for hundreds of years. Like many other bush plants, they have evolved to withstand bush fires, and germination is actually assisted by fire. The distinctive flower shaft will often shoot up in the year following a bush fire.

BELOW: there are 12 species of the delightfully named kangaroo paw (the flower resembles a paw tipped with small white claws). The distinctive red and green kangaroo paw *(Anigozanthos manglesii)* is Western Australia's floral emblem.

LEFT: Banksias have large cone-shaped flowers comprising hundreds of tiny individual flowers. The temperate southwest corner of WA supports some 60 different species, many of which flower in winter. Banksias are named after Joseph Banks, the botanist on board Captain Cook's famous voyage along the eastern seaboard in 1770.

INSIGHT GUIDES TRAVEL TIPS
PERTH & SURROUNDINGS

TRANSPORT

GETTING THERE AND GETTING AROUND

By Air

Airlines are virtually the only way into Perth from abroad. Occasional cruise ships dock at Fremantle, but unless you have lots of time to spare on the journey, you'll have to travel by plane. Most direct flights are routed via Singapore, and overnight stops there are a popular way to break the 20-hour haul from Europe. Another popular route is via Dubai, often with Emirates, which divides the trip into two more equal legs. Fortunately there are plenty of airlines (listed below) serving Perth, and the runways are ready for the next generation of supersize jets.

Air New Zealand
Tel: 13 24 76
www.airnewzealand.com.au
British Airways
Tel: 1300 767 177
www.britishairways.com
Cathay Pacific
Tel: 13 17 47
www.cathaypacific.com.au
Emirates
Tel: 08-9322 6786
www.emirates.com/au
Garuda Indonesia
Tel: 08-041 807 807 or

08-9214 5100
www.garuda-indonesia.com
Qantas
Tel: 13 13 13
www.qantas.com.au
Royal Brunei
Tel: 08-9321 8757
www.bruneiair.com/australia
Singapore Airlines
Tel: 13 10 11
www.singaporeair.com.au
South African Airways
Tel: 1300 435 972
www.flysaa.com
Thai Airways
Tel: 1300 651 960
www.thaiairways.com.au

Domestic Airlines

If you're already in Australia, there are direct flights from all other major cities with Qantas (see above), Jetstar and Virgin Blue. New airlines make occasional forays into this tough market but none has stayed the course.

Jetstar
Tel: 131 538
www.jetstar.com
Flights all around Australia and also to a host of Asian destinations.
Virgin Blue
Tel: 13 67 89
www.virginblue.com.au
Flights to and around the north of Western Australia are regular and reliable because of the stream of

fly-in/fly-out workers at the mines in WA.
Skywest
Tel: 1300 660 088
www.skywest.com.au
Golden Eagle Airlines
Tel: 08-9140 1181
www.goldeneagleairlines.com.au
Based in Port Hedland and covering the Pilbara and Kimberley regions.
Northwest Regional Airlines
Tel: 9192 1369
www.northwestregional.com.au
Based in Broome.

Airports

Perth airport (www.perthairport.com) has separate terminals, about 5km (3 miles) apart, for domestic and international flights. If you are connecting with a flight, your airline will arrange shuttle transport. Otherwise taxis are the only link between the two locations.

The domestic terminal is about 10km (6 miles) from the city centre (AUS$26 by taxi), the international terminal is 13km (AUS$33) from the centre.

By Rail

Railway buffs consider the Indian Pacific railroad one of the world's great rides. Great Southern Railway (tel: 13 21 47; www.gsr.com.au) operates the twice-weekly service into Perth from Sydney, via

Adelaide and Kalgoorlie. The full journey of 4,352km (2,704-miles), much of it through the Nullarbor desert, takes 64 hours and can be done in varying degrees of comfort from sit-up-and-ache to private sleeper compartment.

By Bus

Coach services across the Nullarbor from the eastern states have been abandoned but one quirky option remains. You could arrive from the north. Greyhound (tel: 1300 473 946; www.greyhound.com.au) runs long-haul buses from Adelaide to all major cities east and north, so travellers could take the scenic route, north to Darwin, thence to Kununurra, Broome, Exmouth and down to Perth. The Ghan train also runs from Adelaide to Darwin, via Alice Springs.

By Road

Driving to Perth from the eastern states is considered a rite-of-passage for many West Australians. Perth to Adelaide is 2,642km (1,642 miles); to Melbourne 3,375km (2,097 miles); to Sydney 3,902km (2,425 miles).

Although there's a lot of feature-less desert on the Nullarbor, you can make occasional diversions to the southern coast. Before considering the driving option take full safety advice from motoring organisations, and compare hire/fuel costs with internal flight deals.

GETTING AROUND

Flying

From the International Airport

The only way of getting to and from the International Airport to the city centre is by taxi from just outside the terminal (beware: you may have to queue a long time) or by the City Shuttle, a 24-hour mini-bus service

Perth City Shuttle (tel: 08-9277 7958; www.perthshuttle.com.au; AUS$15 from domestic, AUS$20 international) meets all flights, and runs to and from city hotels and the main train station. Booking advised, especially if arriving after 9pm (it is essential to book return rides to the airport).

Fremantle Shuttle (tel: 08-9457 7150; www.fremantleairport shuttle.com.au) runs to and from the port city's hotels and backpackers' lodges (AUS$30) and private addresses (AUS$35). Services run Monday to Saturday at 9am, 11.30am, 2pm and 5.30pm.

From the domestic terminal

In addition to the shuttle service, public buses make the 20-minute run into central Perth bus station from the domestic terminal. Departures run from 5.30am–11pm (from 7am on Sat, 9am–7pm on Sun), and from the bus station to the airport 6.25am–11.17pm.

Walking

Perth is small, the weather is usually fine and walking is more viable (and safe) here than in many cities. Designed on a grid-like system, the city centre is easy to get around and is well signposted. The main bordering streets of St George's Terrace, Milligan Street, Wellington Street and Barrack Street literally form a box around the city with everything else in between. Equipped with sun hat, dark glasses, sunblock and a bottle of water, you're fit for anything.

Buses

Transperth (InfoLine; tel: 13 62 13) runs city buses, trains and the ferry.

Central city bus travel is free in the inner zone, which includes most parts visitors will want to see. Traffic jams are few, and buses are plentiful, so this is a quick way around town. The free service applies to all regular buses while they're in the central zone, as well as CATS (Central Area Transit).

The free CATS are distinctive buses – red, blue or yellow, depending on the route – linking the main tourist sights and running from early morning until early evening. Computer readouts and audio messages at their dedi-

ACCOMMODATION

ACTIVITIES

A – Z

BELOW: empty roads make driving outside the city a pleasure.

cated bus stops tell you when the next CAT is due (generally within five minutes).

Most other bus routes head out of Perth in a radial pattern, which is fine for visitors heading for the beaches, Fremantle etc. There are fewer services circling the city from suburb to suburb.

Disabilities

Transperth helps passengers with disabilities to access trains. Call 1800 800 022 an hour in advance and a Customer Service officer will meet you at the station. Transperth Hearing Impaired line is 08-9428 1999. Prams and wheelchairs are easily accommo-dated on trains, ferries, CAT buses and the new green and silver Mercedes fleet of buses. How-ever, some older buses don't have extendable ramps; Infoline will give information on which routes do.

Tickets

Bus ticket prices depend on how many zones your journey covers. Pay the driver as you board the bus. Train and ferry tickets are bought at self-service machines.

DayRider tickets are good value for unlimited, day-long travel on all Transperth services after 9am weekdays and all day on weekends and public holidays. Family Riders provide all-day travel for up to 7 people. Smart-Rider electronic ticketing is a quick, cash-free system for use on any Transperth bus, train or ferry service system: it is available to students and the elderly.

Ferry

Perth's only regular ferry is also operated by Transperth, between Barrack St Jetty on the north side of the Swan and Mends St Jetty in South Perth. The ferry is a pleasant approach to the restaurants, bars, pubs and shops on the South Perth Esplanade and Perth Zoo.

In the 1820s settlers travelled by ferry – converted whale boats – all the way upriver from Fremantle to Guildford. The regular trans-Perth service started in 1898, after a channel was dredged between Barrack and Mends streets.

Taxis

Hail taxis on the street, find them on a rank, or phone Black and White (tel: 13 10 08) and Swan (tel: 13 13 30). Most are large Ford or Holden sedans for up to four passengers. Maxi taxis from Black and White take up to 10; they also have service for the disabled (call the special number tel: 1300 658 222 for these). General rates are reasonable, a small flagfall charge followed by a rate per kilometre.

Trains

Wellington Street is the central station, with an underground terminal planned for the nearby Mandurah line. Modern air-conditioned trains run south through Perth to Fremantle; north to Joondalup; and also down the coast to Mandurah and through Guildford to Midland. It's a comfortable and efficient way to travel, especially during the day. Night security has been a problem in the past and more guards and video surveillance have greatly improved the situation. Even so, avoid quiet, out-of-town stations late at night.

Long-distance buses

For longer country trips coach lines are a good alternative to driving yourself. Greyhound Australia (tel: 1300 473 946; www.greyhound.com.au) is based at the East Perth Terminal at the Public Transport Centre. Check the site for details of special passes for unlimited travel on the Greyhound network which covers most of Australia. From Perth buses run north to many pleasant spots such as Kalbarri, Monkey Mia and Broome.

South West Coach Lines (tel: 08-9324 2333) leave the city busport on Mounts Bay Rd at least once a day for Busselton, Dunsborough, Margaret River, Bunbury and Augusta. Booking is required. Integrity Coach Lines (tel: 08-9226 1339 or 1800 226 339; www.integritycoachlines.com.au) runs luxury coaches from Welling-ton Street bus station every

BELOW: taxis can be hired on the street or from a rank.

ABOVE: things have moved on a little bit since this 1930s garage in Kalamunda History Village.

Thursday, returning Saturday, on a 21-hour haul to Port Hedland. Stops include Mount Magnet, Cue, Meekatharra and Newman.

Driving

Australians drive on the left, as in the UK. Cars are usually the best options for visitors as they provide flexibility and convenience. If your driving licence is written in English you can most likely use it in Australia for up to three months. An international driving permit will always be acceptable.

RAC (Royal Automobile Club: tel: 13 11 11 for breakdown help; www.rac.com.au) is the only motoring club, with separate branches in all states. Membership is advised, especially if you are travelling out of town. Vehicle rental companies usually arrange a breakdown service.

Remember there will be variations in road rules in Australia, and they can vary between states. WA's rules can be checked on the government website www.wa.gov.au.

A few pointers: seat belts must be worn by driver and passengers;

drivers must indicate lane-changing and never change lane in the immediate vicinity of traffic lights or junctions. Perth's speed limit is 50km/h (about 30mph) unless otherwise signed. Local streets will have 50km/h (30mph) signs; school zones are 40km/h (25mph). The top speed in the country is 110km/h (about 70mph). On the freeway it's only 100km/h (about 60mph). On freeways, vehicles can overtake on the left or right.

Vehicle hire

Major car hire firms in Perth are Avis (tel: 08-9325 7677; www.avis.com.au), Budget (tel: 13 27 27; www.budget.com.au) and Hertz (tel: 08-9321 7777; www.hertz.com.au). Others include Thrifty (tel: 08-9464 7715; www.thrifty.com.au/wa), Budget (tel: 13 27 27; www.budget.com.au) and Europcar (tel: 1300 13 13 90; www.deltaeuropcar.com.au).

Northside Rentals (tel: 08-9345 5855; www.northsiderentals.com.au) have everything from cars to motorhomes and trucks. Executive (tel: 08-9421 1550; www.executive.com.au) will entrust you with sports and luxury

vehicles as well as more mundane cars.

Campervan and motorhome specialists include Britz (tel: 08-9478 3488; www.britz.com.au), CampaboutOz (tel: 1800 210 877; www.campaboutoz.com.au) and Wicked Campers (tel: 1800 246 869; www.wickedcampers.com.au) whose vans come multicoloured, with graffiti, for the young at heart.

Cycling

Cycling paths have been developed all around Perth, alongside the freeway, coast and even into the hills. One path leads around the Swan in central Perth and all the way down to Fremantle. The Perth Bicycle Network (www.dpi.wa.gov.au/cycling) is a useful source of information. Maps are available from bike shops, or the Bicycle Transportation Alliance (2 Delhi St, West Perth; tel 08-9420 7210). About Bike Hire (cnr Riverside Drive/Plain St; tel: 08-9221 2665; email: lhoffman@aboutbikehire.com.au; daily 9am–5pm) rents bikes, double bikes, quadcycles with trailers, baby seats etc, as well as in-line skates.

ACCOMMODATION

SOME THINGS TO CONSIDER
BEFORE YOU BOOK THE ROOM

Choosing a Hotel

Perth is a small city where you can stay in the very centre at moderate cost, and walk to theatres, entertainments, park and river. But easy travel on fast trains, clean, air-conditioned buses (free in the city) and relatively inexpensive taxis means you can stay at the beaches or in leafy suburbs and quickly get to Perth and Fremantle. Thirty minutes takes you just about anywhere. Driving yourself to and from the centre is not a nightmare, either.

If you crave full-service, luxury hotel accommodation there's little choice but Adelaide Terrace, city riverside and Burswood. However, high-quality, clean accommodation is available in all price ranges, at moderately priced hotels, bed-and-breakfast houses, and even backpackers' hostels all across the metropolitan area.

Great value and lavish comfort can also be experienced at some inner-city bed-and-breakfast establishments, and in genteel western suburbs such as Nedlands and Mosman Park. The B&B accommodation here matches the area.

Even rural locations in Swan Valley or the Darling Ranges are only 30 minutes from the city, and staying outside Perth, even for a short time, is a fast way to get the feel of the real Australia.

Even though tourism in Western Australia has grown steadily over the last decade or so, the Holiday Inn at Burswood is the first hotel to open in Perth since 1993. If the developers are correct, increasing numbers of travellers are looking for both independence and self-catering, leading to the growth of apartment hotels, especially in the entertainment areas of Northbridge, Subiaco and the CBD.

There appears to be no shortage of places to stay in Perth, and out of the December–February high summer season all hotels, including those that are rated "luxury" in the following listing, will offer special rates. It's worth spending the time to place a call to check out any special deals, at any time of the year, even if a hotel is above your own usual price range.

Self-catering

Once you leave Perth and go out of town it's a different story regarding hotels, as there are few large towns or hotels. Caravan and campsites are the most common accommodation in much of the countryside, because so many Australians and overseas visitors go bush. Indeed this is the only practical way to see the immense countryside. To this end, we have also included a selection of caravan sites in the listings. Most have cabins, so you don't have to have a tent or van to use them.

Other accommodation is mostly clustered in and around country towns. Call ahead rather than just showing up, and don't forget to consult local visitor centres – listed here – for unique alternatives, such as farmstays and B&B locations.

Long-term holiday rentals are available on properties in many areas, especially close to Perth, and these can be a good money-saving option. Almost all will be let by local estate agents, and REIWA (Real Estate Institute of WA) lists most of them. A useful website is www.reiwa.com.au.

HOTEL OR PUB?

Be aware that in Australia a sign saying hotel can simply mean a pub and is not necessarily an indication of accommodation, especially where grand old properties are concerned. This dates from the days when all pubs had rooms for rent and were often the only accommodation to be found in a small town.

PERTH

ACCOMMODATION

Luxury

Duxton
1 St George's Terrace
Tel: 08-9261 8000
Toll free: 1800 681 118
www.duxton.com
 p254, B4
Beautifully renovated
hotel in a heritage
building, formerly
Perth's old tax office.
Close to concert hall,
state governor's
residence, Swan River
and shops.
Hyatt Regency Perth
99 Adelaide Terrace
Tel: 08-9225 1234
www.perth.regency.hyatt.com
p255, C4
Pool, tennis court,
fitness centre, sauna –
everything expected of a
5-star hotel. Elegant
dining or café-style,
several bars. Close
to the central
business district.

BELOW: the Duxton Hotel was once a tax office.

**Intercontinental
Burswood Resort**
Gt Eastern Highway
Tel: 08-9362 8888
Toll free: 1800 999 667
www.burswood.com.au/hotels
p255, D2
Riverside location 3km
(2 miles) east of town
centre. Spectacular
buildings with luxurious
accommodation.
Facilities include
18-hole golf course,
theatre, state tennis
centre and the only
casino in WA.
Sheraton Perth
207 Adelaide Terrace
Tel: 08-9224 7777
www.starwoodhotels.com/
sheraton/perth
p254, C4
Close to CBD, main shop-
ping areas, Cultural Cen-
tre and entertainments.
Heated pool, gym and
steam room. All rooms
have views of Swan River.

Expensive

**Darby Park Quest
Subiaco**
222 Hay Street
Tel: 08-9380 0800
www.darbypark.com.au
p252, C2
In cosmopolitan area
west of Perth centre, with
boutique shops, restau-
rants and bars, cinema
and Regal Theatre
nearby. A/C apartments
have full kitchen and
laundry; outdoor pool,
spa and BBQs. The Vic
specialises in seafood.
Eight Nicholson
8 Nicholson Road
Tel: 08-9382 1881
www.8nicholson.com.au
p252, B3
Exclusive, chic and pri-
vate are three words to
describe this boutique
hotel which is within
walking distance to all
that Subiaco has to offer.
The Outram
32 Outram Street
Tel: 08-9322 4888
www.wyndhamvrap.com/resorts/
theoutram
p253, D2
This is Parisian-style
chic in downtown Perth
and is only a few kilome-
tres to the city and Kings
Park. Surrounded by
many restaurants, this
boutique hotel is a
fabulous option.
The Richardson Opus
32 Richardson Street
Tel: 08-9217 8888
www.therichardson.com.au
p253, D2
This new and luxurious
hotel boasts 74 guest
rooms and suites, on
eight floors, most with

private balconies. All
have been carefully
designed with the mod-
ern traveller in mind.
There is a first-class
restaurant and day spa .

Moderate

Aarons Hotel
70 Pier Street
Tel: 08-9325 2133
Toll free: 1800 998 133
www.aaronsperth.com.au
p254, B3
Centrally placed, on free
CAT bus route around
Perth. Modern and
comfortable rooms, and
a bright bar and grill;
good, friendly service.
Beaufort House
237 Beaufort Street
Tel: 08-9227 8316
Email: dmitchell@eftel.com.au
p254, B2
Fine house in quiet area

PRICE CATEGORIES

Prices are for a standard
double room, without
breakfast unless stated
– including 10 percent
GST (VAT).
Luxury: over AUS$300
Expensive:
AUS$200–300
Moderate:
AUS$100–200
Budget:
under AUS$100

for entertainment and restaurants, and bus route for central Perth, 1km (½ mile). A/C, private bathroom, fridge in rooms.

Criterion Hotel Perth
560 Hay Street
Tel: 08-9325 5155
Toll free: 1800 245 155
www.criterion-hotel-perth.com.au
⑪ p254, B3
Central, opposite historic Perth Town Hall, beautifully restored Art Deco building in main shopping area, with pub in basement.

Durham Lodge
165 Shepperton Road, Victoria Park
Tel: 08-9361 8000
www.durhamlodge.com
⑫ p259, E3
South of the river, close to southern attractions. Elegant old home with baby grand piano, comfortable furnishings. Private guest wing; spa bath or showers, A/C, TV, DVD, phone, bar, fridge.

Holiday Inn Burswood
Great Eastern Highway
Tel: 08-9362 8888
www.burswood.com.au/hotels
⑬ p255, D2

A less expensive option on the same riverside site as the Interconti-nental Burswood hotel. Holiday Inn patrons have access to all Intercontinental restau-rants and facilities.

Metro Hotel
61 Canning Highway
Tel: 08-9367 6122
Toll free: 1800 00 4321
www.metrohotels.com.au
⑭ p259, D3
South of the city with views across Canning River; swimming pool, restaurant, bar and BBQ to cook your own food or barbecue pack from the restaurant. Some rooms have a fully equipped kitchen. 15-minute walk to Perth Zoo and ferry across Swan to Barrack Street Jetty. Five minutes' drive to Burswood, WACA or town centre.

Miss Maud Swedish Hotel and Restaurant
97 Murray Street
Tel: 08-9325 3900
Toll free: 1800 998 022
www.missmaud.com.au
⑮ p254, B3
With a quaint and quirky

auberge-styled exterior, this hotel is close to the inner city and shops. Features smorgasbord and alfresco dining area with popular coffee shop. Miss Maud does exist and runs a popular café/ patisserie chain.

New Esplanade Hotel
18 The Esplanade
Tel: 08-9325 2000
www.newesplanade.com.au
⑯ p254, A3
Close to river and Barrack Street Jetty and within easy reach of city shopping, CBD, Cultural Centre. No restaurant, but breakfast served in the Esplanade Café. Some suites have full kitchen.

Pension of Perth
3 Throssell Street
Tel: 08-9228 9049
www.pensionperth.com.au
⑰ p254, A1
Quiet Federation-style home near Hyde Park; 4 master bedrooms with en suite (spa or bath), fine furnishings and French antiques. Silver-service breakfast can be had in the lounge or by the pool.

Quest on James
228 James Street
Tel: 08-9227 2888
⑱ p254, A2
Offers one-, two- and three-bedroom fully furnished modern apartments in a good location in Northbridge. All guests have access to an outdoor area that includes a pool, spa and BBQ. It does not have a restaurant facility but is within walking distance of a number of eateries and nightlife hotspots.

Sullivans Hotel
166 Mounts Bay Road
Tel: 08-9321 8022
⑲ p252, E4
www.sullivans.com.au
Small, family-owned hotel on the river below Kings Park escarpment. Near Convention Centre, and Jacobs Ladder up to park. Free Blue CAT bus runs into town from outside the hotel. Free internet access.

Wentworth Plaza Comfort Inn
300 Murray Street
Tel: 08-9338 5000
Toll free: 1800 355 109
www.wentworthplazahotel.com.au
⑳ p254, A3
In lively shopping and entertainment area. Rooms or family apartments with A/C, TV and internet. Three restaur-ants and two bars including a pub.

Budget

Bailey's Hotel-Motel
150 Bennett Street
Tel: 08-9220 9555
Toll free: 1800 199 477
www.baileysmotel.com.au
㉑ p255, C3
Homely hotel opposite park – walking distance from centre or 5 minutes on free city buses.

BELOW: Pension of Perth.

Comfortable units with A/C, swimming pool and BBQ. Restaurant serves "home-style" cooking, and room tariff includes continental breakfast.

Billabong Backpackers Resort
381 Beaufort Street
Tel: 08-9328 7720
www.billabongresort.com.au
㉒ p254, B1
Adjacent to Northbridge entertainment/restaurant area; A/C and modern facilities, with pool and gym; free breakfast.

Kings Park Motel
255 Thomas Street
Tel: 08-9381 0000
Toll free: 1800 655 362
www.kingsparkmotel.com.au
㉓ p252, B4
Facing Kings Park on road leading to University of WA, single, double, triple or family rooms, some with cooking facilities. All are en suite and have fridge, A/C, TV; pool and BBQ area. Expensive.

The Old Swan Barracks
6 Francis Street
Tel: 08-9428 0000
www.theoldswanbarracks.com
㉔ p254, B2
Close to Cultural Centre, art gallery and museum, and Northbridge entertainment/restaurant area. Many facilities including pool/snooker, kitchen, internet.

The Witch's Hat
148 Palmerston Street
Tel: 08-9228 4228
Toll free: 1800 818 358
㉕ p254, A1
Off Russell Square, Northbridge, in historic 1897 town house. Very pleasant and popular.

Apartments

Aarons All Suites Hotel
12 Victoria Avenue
Tel: 08-9318 4444
Toll free: 1800 000 675
www.aaronssuites.com.au
㉖ p254, B3
A range of modern, fully equipped A/C apartments, with rooftop spa and BBQ area very near CBD/Adelaide Terrace.

Broadwater Resort Apartments
137 Melville Parade, Como
Tel: 08-8474 4222
www.broadwateres.com.au
㉗ p258, A4
South of the river, minutes away from shopping, Perth Zoo and restaurants. Heated swimming pool, spa and tennis court, and North Indian cuisine restaurant with alfresco courtyard. Apartments have full kitchen.

City Stay Apartment Hotel
875 Wellington Street
Tel: 08-9215 1515
Toll free: 1800 819 191
www.citystay.com.au
㉘ p253, E2
Comfortable apartments with cooking facilities, pool, spa, BBQ and gym. 1.5km (1 mile) from centre with free buses passing the door. Located opposite Harbour Town.

Mont Clare Boutique Apartments
190 Hay Street
Tel: 08-9224 4300
www.montclareapartments.com
㉙ p255, C4
Near Claisebrook inlet of the Swan, with restaurants nearby and the free red CAT bus for easy 5-minute trips to the city centre (1.5km/1 mile away). Well-furnished 1-, 2- or 3-bed apartments with A/C, full kitchen and laundry.

The Peninsula Riverside Serviced Apartments
53 South Perth Esplanade

ABOVE: the Witch's Hat.

Tel: 08-9368 6688
www.thepeninsula.net
㉚ p257, E2
Offers one-, two- and three-bedroom self-contained apartments, all serviced three times a week. All Riverview, Standard and Courtyard apartments are situated in lush landscaped gardens.

Quest West End
Corner of Milligan and Murray streets
Tel: 08-9480 3888
www.westend.property.questwa.com.au
㉛ p253, E3
At the border of CBD and the main shopping areas, with easy access to the restaurants and entertainments of Hay Street, Murray Street and Northbridge. Modern A/C apartments with full kitchen; gym.

Regal Apartments
11 Regal Place
Tel: 08-9221 8614
Toll free: 1800 778 614
www.regalapartments.com.au
㉜ p255, D3
A/C apartments sleep up to 7; fully equipped kitchen and laundry.

The Sebel Residence East Perth
60 Royal Street
Tel: 08-9223 2500
㉝ p255, D3
Offers stylish studio, one- or two-bedroom self-contained apartments.

Caravan Park

Central Caravan Park
34 Central Avenue, Ascot
Tel: 08-9277 1704
Toll free: 1300 760 060
www.perthcentral.com.au
㉞ p255, D1
Just 7km (4 miles) from the city centre with fully powered sites and tent sites, in addition to 1-bed cabins and 2-bed park homes. They also have a heated pool, BBQs, and a campers' kitchen. Linen is included in the price.

PRICE CATEGORIES

Prices are for a standard double room, without breakfast unless stated – including 10 percent GST (VAT).
Luxury: over AUS$300
Expensive: AUS$200–300
Moderate: AUS$100–200
Budget: under AUS$100

FREMANTLE

ABOVE: Perth's near neighbour is a good place to stay.

Luxury

Esplanade
Corner of Marine Terrace and Essex Street
Tel: 08-9432 4000
Toll free: 1800 998 201
www.esplanadehotelfremantle.com.au
Elegant gold rush-era building with atrium, 2 pools, 3 spas, fitness centre, bar and 2 restaurants. Most rooms have private balconies with views overlooking popular parklands, tropical gardens and pools. Across Marine Terrace lawns is Fishing Boat Harbour, with restaurants and entertainment.

Moderate

Freo Mews
111 South Terrace
Tel: 08-9336 6379

www.members.iinet.net.au/~freomews
Elegant apartments for 1 to 6 people in 2-storey mews houses; rooms are comfortable, with good amenities, and the location is central for all attractions.

Kilkelly's B&B
82 Marine Terrace
Tel: 08-9336 1744
Renovated 1883 mariner's cottage opposite Fishing Boat Harbour. Stroll to tourist attractions, restaurants, markets and shops. Rooms open onto upper veranda.

Pier 21 Apartment Hotel
7–9 John Street
Tel: 08-9336 2555
www.pier21.com.au
On the banks of the Swan, with river views, fully serviced 1- and

2-bed A/C apartments with kitchen, TV, VCR and DVD. Indoor and outdoor pools overlooking the river marina, 2 spas, tennis and squash courts, BBQ area.

Port Mill
3/17 Essex Street
Tel: 08-9433 3832
www.babs.com.au/portmill
Heritage building in the heart of Fremantle – shares Essex Street mews with cottages around courtyard. Three luxury rooms with balcony.

SUNSET COAST

Cottesloe

Moderate

Cottesloe Beach Chalets
6 John Street
Tel: 08-9383 5000
www.cottesloebeachchalets.com.au
Just off oceanfront Marine Parade, Cotteslow Beach Chalets has self-contained A/C andsleep up to 5, with full cooking facilities and laundry. There is also a pool and BBQ. The nearby pub is a favourite for younger patrons.

Mosman Beach Apartments
3 Fairlight Street
Tel: 08-9285 6400

www.mosmanbeach.com
Between Perth and Fremantle, 300 metres/yds from the beach with 1-, 2- and 3-bed apartments in a tropical garden setting. There is a heated pool, BBQ area and gym.

Ocean Beach Hotel/Motel
Corner of Eric Street/Marine Parade
Tel: 08-9384 2555
www.obh.com.au
Overlooking the Indian Ocean, Ocean Beach is a refurbished, modern and lively location with seafront restaurant, café, pizza-bar and 2 bars heavily used by younger clientele.

Rosemoore Cottage
2 Winifred Street, Mosman Park
Tel: 08-9384 8214
www.rosemoore.com.au
Mosman is an up-market western suburbs peninsula between the river and ocean. This is a renovated house with country-style furnishings, walking distance from railway station and bus services, and 2 minutes' drive to river or Cottesloe Beach. Hearty breakfasts.

Hillary's Boat Harbour

Moderate

Sundowner Ocean View Motel

10 Lawley Street
Tel: 08-9246 4699
www.oceanviewmotel.com.au
Just 70 metres/yds from the beach and midway between Scarborough and Hillary's. Self-contained A/C units with cooking facilities and BBQ.

Hillary's Harbour Resort Apartments
68 Southside Drive

Tel: 08-9262 7888
Toll free: 1800 240 078
www.hillarysresort.com.au
Harbourside 1-, 2- and
3-bed modern units on
Sorrento Quay board-
walk (restaurants,
shops, bars and
entertainments), with
views across the
marina; all with full
kitchen and laundry,
TV, DVD. There is a
pool, spa and sauna,
and BBQ area.

**Quality Resort
Sorrento Beach**
1 Padbury Circle
Tel: 08-9246 8100
www.sorrentobeach.com.au
Metres from the beach,
facing Hillary's Boat Harbour with its restau-
rants, bars, shops, ferry
to Rottnest and AQWA
aquarium experience.
The resort has an out-
door pool, spa, sauna
and BBQ; along with
hotel-style 2- and 3-bed
studio apartments with

kitchen, and 1-bed
luxury spa-apartments.

Scarborough
Expensive
**Rendezvous
Observation City Hotel**
The Esplanade
Tel: 08-9245 1000
Toll free: 1800 067 680
www.rendezvoushotels.com
A luxury hotel on the
beach, Rendezvous
is a rare example of a
high-rise building on the
coast. Wide-ranging
facilities include several
restaurants and bars,
as well as a nightclub,
pool, spa, tennis courts
and a gym.

Moderate
The Dunes
15 Filburn Street
Tel: 08-9245 2797
www.interleaf.ie/dunes
Email: dunes@swiftdsl.com.au
Set back from the West
Coast Highway, but close

to beach and facilities,
the Dunes is only 20
minutes from Fremantle.
Modern, well-appointed
2-bed A/C units, full
kitchen, laundry, TV,
VCR; private courtyard
with BBQ.

Sunmoon Resort
200 West Coast Highway
Tel: 08-9245 8000
Toll free: 1800 090 054

www.sunmoon.com.au
Close to beach,
restaur-ants and
entertainment. Hotel
rooms, studio apart-
ments and 2- or 3-bed
units in distinctly Asian
style. Tropical gardens
with pool, and Café
Eclipse, a licensed
restaurant serving
Australasian cuisine.

BELOW: Rendezvous Observation City in Scarborough.

AROUND PERTH

Carmel
Luxury
Fawkes House
84 Union Road
Tel: 08-9293 5549
www.fawkeshouse.com.au
Fawkes House Country

PRICE CATEGORIES
Prices are for a standard
double room, without
breakfast unless stated
– including 10 percent
GST (VAT).
Luxury: over AUS$300
Expensive:
AUS$200–300
Moderate:
AUS$100–200
Budget:
under AUS$100

Spa Retreat offers peace
and relaxation and is
surrounded by beautiful
vineyards. There is a
selection of both
accommodation and day
spa packages.

Kalamunda
Budget
**Carmelot Bed and
Breakfast**
145 Carmel Road
Tel: 08-9293 5150
www.members.westnet.com.au/
smithers/carmelot
A particular sense of
humour pervades this
Bed and Breakfast, with
3 medieval-themed
rooms – King Arthur,
Lancelot and Guinevere

(with a 4-poster, cano-
pied bed, of course).
There's a sword set in a
stone in the gardens of
Carmelot, which is sur-
rounded by orchards and
just 5 minutes' drive from
Kalamunda History Vil-
lage. Carmelot also has a
swimming pool, spa and
BBQ. All rooms are en
suite; the tariff includes a
fullly cooked breakfast,
afternoon tea and a
morning newspaper.

Mandurah
Moderate
Atrium Hotel
65 Ormsby Terrace
Tel: 08-9535 6633
www.atriumhotel.com.au

Within walking distance
of the beach, this hotel
is centred on an impres-
sive atrium with palm-
fringed, heated indoor
pool and spa, cocktail
bar and Seasons Res-
taurant (7am until late).
Accommodation
comprises studios,
1-, 2- and 3-bed apart-
ments with full cooking
facilities. There's also

a sauna, tennis, and games room.

Mandurah Foreshore Motel
2 Gibson Street
Tel: 08-9535 5577
www.mandurahwa.com.au/ foreshoremotel
Situated in the centre of Mandurah, close to restaurants and shops, and facing the foreshore, with 18 doubles, a selection of family rooms, all en suite, A/C, fridge, TV, tea/coffee. Facilities include a swimming pool, spa and BBQ area.

Mandurah Holiday Village
124 Mandurah Terrace
Tel: 08-9535 4633
www.mandurahholidayvillage. com.au
Located near the centre of town and 100 metres/ yds from the beach; 2-bed self-contained villas sleep 6–8 people; plus spa apartments, with a private courtyard or balcony. The complex includes a swimming pool, spa, tennis courts, playground, BBQ area.

Budget
Port Mandurah Canal B&B
3 Reverie Mews

Tel: 08-9535 2252
www.babs.com.au/portmandurah
This is a boutique waterside B&B in the redeveloped canal area. Two comfortable en suite double rooms, with lounge and balcony, overlook the water. Watch out for the dolphins frolicking in the waves while you have your breakfast. It's a nice situation, and just a five-minute walk from the town centre.

Perth Hills
Budget
Mundaring Weir Hotel
Mundaring Weir Road
Tel: 08-9295 1106
www.mundaringweirhotel.com.au
Historic Weir Hotel is surrounded by jarrah forest, and is very popular as a centre for walkers using the many local trails. Eleven modern units overlook the forest, or pool/amphitheatre area, where open-air concerts are held in the summer months and kangaroos roam around in the evenings. Rooms have open wood fires and good facilities.

Swan Valley
Expensive
Novotel Vines Resort
Verdelho Drive, The Vines
Tel: 08-9297 3000
www.novotelvines.com.au
A luxury resort and country club noted for its 36-hole championship golf course. A range of accommodation includes family rooms with 2 double beds, bedroom/lounge suites, self-contained 2- or 3-bedroom apartments. Novotel also offers restaurants and bars, swimming pool, spa, gym, tennis and squash courts.

BELOW: Port Mandurah Canal B&B.

Moderate
Swan Valley Oasis Resort
10250 West Swan Road
Tel: 08-9296 5555
www.swanvalleyoa m
This resort-style hotel is set in tropical gardens on 22 hectares (55 acres) of land adjacent to the Swan River. Facilities include A/C, spa rooms, fridge, TV and wireless internet. A luxury, self-contained double apartment with kitchen and laundry is also available. Resort has heated pool and spa, gym, sauna and laundry, and fully licensed restaurant.

FURTHER AFIELD

Albany
Moderate
Albany Harbourside
8 Festing Street
Tel: 08-9842 1769
www.albanyharbourside.com.au
This group has a wide selection of accommodation, mostly in the town centre opposite the *Brig Amity* replica ship, old jail and museum. Modern apartments

sleep 4–6; equipped with kitchen and laundry, each with private courtyard. Overlooking the garden, children's playground and BBQ area is a bungalow with wide verandas and 3 bedrooms. Nearby is a 100-year-old restored cottage with 3 bedrooms, and a 1924 town house; all well furnished, modernised, fully

equipped.
Comfort Inn
191 Albany Highway
Tel: 08-9841 4144
www.comfortinnalbany.com.au
Well-furnished and comfortable hotel with all facilities, including A/C, cable TV and room service; plus Seashells licensed restaurant.
Memories of Albany B&B
118 Brunswick Road

Tel: 08-9842 9787
www.members.westnet.com.au/

ABOVE: Lakeside Country Resort in Armadale.

memoriesofalbany
Historic home with views over harbour, near centre. Three suites are decorated with period furniture and furnishings: Heritage Suite has 4-poster bed and private lounge; Courtyard Suite has a dressing room, private courtyard with outdoor table and chairs onto lawns and shady garden; Harbour Room has French doors to balcony and views across park to harbour. All rooms with usual amenities plus complimentary chocolates, port and home-made biscuits. Elegant dining room. Price includes breakfast.

Budget
Bayview Backpackers
49 Duke Street
Tel: 08-9842 3388
www.yha.com.au
In a quiet street 300 metres/yds from centre, this popular backpackers' has large kitchen, dining and social areas, together with the log-fired "dungeon" lounge for TV and VCR. Laundry,

internet kiosk, bicycle hire, linen (except towels) supplied; free BBQ every Wed night.
Middleton Beach Holiday Park
28 Flinders Parade
Tel: 08-9841 3593
Toll free: 1800 644 674
www.holidayalbany.com.au
On white sandy beach of Ellen Cove, 3km (2 miles) from town, with café, restaurant and hotel nearby. Chalets and cabins in garden setting, with patio; all have full kitchen, electric blankets and TV. Also caravan sites, some with en suite. Undercover camp kitchen and BBQs make home cooking easy. The site's recreation centre has table tennis, movies, heated pool and spa; kids' club in summer.

Armadale
Moderate
Lakeside Country Resort
50 Canns Road, Bedfordale
Tel: 08-9399 7455
www.lakesidecountryresort.com.au

High in the Darling Range with views to Perth and ocean, fully self-contained English country-style cabins are set around a lake. Each has a deck onto the water, and a dinghy moored there for paddling around and fishing. All have A/C, TV, kitchen and gas BBQ. Elizabethan Village pub and restaurant is only 200 metres/yds away.

Budget
Jarrahdale Holiday Carriages
324 Jarrahdale Road
Tel: 08-9525 5780
www.jarrahdaleholidaycarriages.com
Something different – a night or two in a converted vintage railway carriage on a 10.5 hectare (26-acre) rural property in a National Park. Four carriages, 3 doubles, 1 family-size, are set well apart for privacy and equipped for cooking, with A/C, heaters, electric blankets and outdoor BBQ. A 5th carriage has 2 toilets and 2 showers.

Balingup
Moderate
Kirup Kabins Farmstay
Mailman Road, Kirup
Tel: 08-9731 6272
www.kirupkabins.com.au
Kirip Kabins is a working farm with cows, sheep, chickens, geese and an emu. You can feed the animals and collect eggs for breakfast. There are 2- and 3-bed cabins and cottages, with log fires and verandas overlooking rolling hills. Kirup is about 10km (6 miles) from Balingup.
Balingup Rose B&B
Lot 1, 109 Jayes Road
Tel: 08-9764 1205
www.balinguprose.com.au
Rural setting in Blackwood River Valley with wonderful views; very close to Bibbulmun Track (Perth to southern coast trail). Country-style decor, antique furniture and jarrah floors, open log fire in lounge. Three rooms, all en suite, 2 with wide veranda. Full breakfast included .

Busselton
Moderate
Abbey Beach Resort
595 Bussell Highway
Tel: 08-9755 4600
www.abbeybeach.com.au

PRICE CATEGORIES
Prices are for a standard double room, without breakfast unless stated – including 10 percent GST (VAT).
Luxury: over AUS$300
Expensive:
AUS$200–300
Moderate:
AUS$100–200
Budget:
under AUS$100

Luxury beachside resort 7km (4 miles) from Busselton; 1-, 2- and 3-bed A/C apartments and studios with views over ocean or pool from large balcony. Each has full kitchen, laundry, spa, TV, VCR, CD. Three pools, gym, squash, tennis, playground, bars and restaurant.

Busselton Jetty Chalets
94 Marine Terrace
Tel: 08-9752 3893
Toll free: 1800 628 688
www.busseltonjettychalets.com
Short walk across a park to beach and jetty, comfortable 2-bed chalets with A/C, full kitchen, BBQ area and playground.

Budget

Kookaburra Caravan Park
66 Marine Terrace
Tel: 08-9752 1516
Email: kookpark@compwest.net.au
Central – 2-minute walk from town centre, jetty and beaches. Park has 150 powered caravan sites, camping area with camp kitchen and BBQ, and on-site cabins. Linen can be hired.

Observatory Guest House
7 Brown Street
Tel: 08-9751 3336
www.observatory-guesthouse.com
New guesthouse a short walk from centre, beach and restaurants. All 4 rooms have en suite, tea/coffee, fridge, TV, DVD. Tariff includes full breakfast.

Denmark
Luxury–Budget

Denmark Observatory Resort
Mount Shadforth Road
Tel: 08-9848 2233

www.karrimia.com.au
High on Mount Shadforth in 24 hectares (60 acres) of rolling hills, with accommodation from luxury spa studios to en suite caravan sites. 1- or 2-bed bungalows ($$) have full kitchen, TV, DVD, VCR, CD, fans, heating and large private deck with outdoor seating and BBQ. Split-level spa studios ($$$): kitchenette, balcony with BBQ. Motel rooms have similar set-up, without lounge. Uncluttered decor with mainly handcrafted teak furniture. Caravan/motor-home sites ($) in garden setting with en suite, large communal laundry and BBQ area, games room, pool table, computer and pinball games, table tennis. Southern End Restaurant with spectacular views makes good use of local produce and wines (open all day Sat–Sun, D daily).

Moderate

Denmark Waters B&B
9 Inlet Drive
Tel: 08-9848 1043
www.denmarkwaters.com.au
Just 2km (1 mile) from town, with views across Wilson Inlet. Two apartments, each with en suite and lounge, TV, DVD, fridge, tea/coffee. Cooked breakfast is served in your suite or on veranda overlooking waters of the inlet.

Budget

Blue Wren Travellers Rest YHA
17 Price Street
Tel: 08-9848 3300
www.denmarkbluewren.com.au
Backpackers' purpose-

built in 2001 in town centre. Kitchen and laundry are bright, modern and well equipped. Internet access, bicycles; single, double or family rooms, and gender-specific dorms. Produce and wines.

Koorabup Motel
South Coast Highway
Tel: 08-9848 1044
Toll free: 1800 131 044
www.koorabup.com.au
Built of rammed earth, Koorabup ("place of the black swan") is in rural bushland but only 5 minutes from the centre of Denmark. Motel units have limited cooking facilities, TV, heating and a private balcony with bushland views. 1- and 2-bed apartments have full kitchen and laundry.

Dunsborough
Moderate

Dunsborough Central Motel
50 Dunn Bay Road
Tel: 08-9756 7711
www.dunsboroughmotel.com.au
Dunsborough Central is a town-centre motel in a garden setting with outdoor pool, spa and BBQ area. 1-bed spa rooms and 2-bed superior rooms, all with A/C, TV, tea/coffee and kitchenette. Spa rooms have a dining area.

Dunsborough Beach Cottages
95 Gifford Road
Tel: 08-9756 8885
Toll free: 1800 816 885
www.dunsborough-beach.com.au
Modern 2- or 3-bed, resort-style cottages on white-sand beach of Geographe Bay; short walk to shops and restaurants. Good facilities, including a full kitchen, TV, DVD, log fires and

outdoor area with BBQ; swimming pool and playground.

Dunsborough Rail Carriages and Farm Cottages
123 Commonage Road
Tel: 08-9755 3865
www.dunsborough.com
Historic, fully restored and beautifully presented, 1-bed jarrah railway carriages – set in 40 hectares (100 acres) of farm and bushland 2km (1 mile) from town centre. All have en suite, TV, fans, veranda and a limited kitchen, and there's a shared BBQ. Or you could choose the 2-bedroom cedar cottages with full kitchen, laundry facilities, electric fans, TV, DVD and wood-fired heaters. Can sleep up to 8 people. Farm animals – as well as plenty of kangaroos!

Budget

Dunsborough Inn
50 Dunn Bay Road
Tel: 08-9756 7277
www.dunsboroughinn.com
Recently built budget accommodation attached to the Dunsborough Central Motel; has self-contained units and backpacker facilities. Communal kitchen and dining room, with recreation areas.

Geraldton and Greenough
Moderate

African Reef Resort and Tarcoola Beach Caravan Park
5 Broadhead Avenue
Tel: 08-9964 5566
www.africanreef.com.au
Overlooking Tarcoola Beach, this resort has hotel, villa or apartment

ACCOMMODATION ◆ 231

accommodation; swimming pool and award-winning restaurant with cocktail bar. Motel units: A/C, ocean views, tea/coffee, fridge, TV. Some apartments have kitchen facilities. Resort tariff includes continental breakfast. Tarcoola Beach Caravan Park has 26 private and exclusive en suite sites, 10 general sites, all shady and a short walk to the beach. Park adjoins the resort and shares facilities.

Best Western Hospitality Inn
169 Cathedral Avenue
Tel: 08-9921 1422
www.geraldton.wa.hospitalityinns.com.au
In the centre of town, with standard and de luxe hotel rooms, or 2–3-bed A/C apartments with full kitchen and laundry. Inn has swimming pool and BBQ facilities. Emerald Room restaurant with cocktail bar specialises in seafood, especially lobster in season.

Ocean Centre Hotel
Foreshore Drive/Cathedral Avenue
Tel: 08-9921 7777
www.oceancentrehotel.com.au
This hotel benefits from being in the centre of town while also offering amazing ocean and harbour views. Modern well-appointed standard or de luxe rooms, some with private courtyard, others with balcony. Sirocco's bar/restaurant has ocean views, and is a good place to watch the sunset.

Budget

Hampton Arms Inn
Company Road, Greenough
Tel: 08-9926 1057
www.hamptonarms.com.au
Fascinating 1863 historic inn which claims to be haunted; standing in the mist-shrouded courtyard in the early morning, it seems credible. Country-pub atmosphere in the small, timbered bar and elegant dining in the original ballroom. Inn has 5 rooms with 2 shared

bathrooms, a bookshop holding more than 20,000 out-of-print volumes, and a bric-a-brac shop. The tariff includes continental breakfast; a full cooked breakfast is also available on request.

Ferguson Valley
Moderate
Kingtree Lodge
111 Kingtree Road,
Wellington Mills, Dardanup
Tel: 08-9728 3050
www.kingtreelodge.com.au
B&B in two-storey federation-style home and vineyard, 35km (22 miles) from Bunbury, set in 40 hectares (100 acres) of jarrah forest. Luxury accommodation in 4 double, self-contained suites. Cellar-door lunch area with wine-tasting room, and fully licensed, elegant dining room.

Swallow Valley B&B
Henty Road, Burekup
Tel: 08-9726 3960
www.fergusonvalley.net.au
Swallow Valley is in a

country garden with its own billabong (stream) and forest. Two A/C rooms have fridge, microwave, tea/coffee, BBQ, and wood fire for winter. Cooked or continental breakfast; lunch or dinner available. Burekup Hills are 20 minutes from Bunbury in Ferguson Valley wine area.

Kalbarri
Moderate
Kalbarri Palm Resort
8 Porter Street
Tel: 08-9937 2333
www.palmresort.com.au
Situated two minutes' walk from harbour, beach, shops and restaurants, this is Kalbarri's earliest large-scale modern resort, with hotel-style rooms and 2-bed family apartments with full cooking facilities. Resort has 2 swimming pools, tennis courts, bowls, cricket, a playground and BBQ area.

Pelican Shore Villas
Grey Street/Kaiber Street
Tel: 08-9937 1708
Toll free: 1800 671 708
www.members.westnet.com.au/pelicanshores
Very high standard A/C villas, each with full kitchen and laundry, and

BELOW: the harbour at Kalbarri.

located on the harbour road close to beaches and restaurants. The front villas overlook spectacular coastline and breaking surf, and crayfishing boats navigating the approach into Murchison River.

Budget
Kalbarri Backpackers YHA
51 Mortimer Street
Tel: 08-9937 1430
www.yha.com.au/hostel
Centrally located with BBQ, swimming pool, cooking facilities, laundry, food-and-drink vending machine, and bicycles for hire.

Kalgoorlie
Moderate
Best Western Hospitality Inn
560 Hannan Street
Tel: 08-9021 2888
www.hinnkalgoorlie.bestwestern.com.au
Well-appointed A/C motel rooms, fridge,

tea/coffee-making. Swimming pool and BBQ area, licensed restaurant and cocktail bar. Continental breakfast included.

Rydges Hotel and Resort
21 Davidson Street
Tel: 08-9080 0800
Toll free: 1800 198 001
www.rydges.com
The only "5-star" establishment in the Goldfields; luxurious rooms with spa, some with full cooking facilities. Large heated pool, and award-winning Larcombe's Bar and Grill.

Quality Inn Railway Motel
51 Forrest Street
Tel: 08-9088 0000
Toll free: 1800 355 209
www.railwaymotel.com.au
Central, facing historic railway buildings, with hotel rooms and self-contained A/C units, fridge, tea/coffee. Pool, spa; dinner and breakfast served in Carriages restaurant.

Margaret River
Moderate
The Grange on Farrelly
18 Farrelly Street
Tel: 08-9757 3177
Toll free: 1800 650 100
www.grangeonfarrelly.com.au
Small, stylish motel set in gardens; short stroll to the main street, restaurants and shops. Some room have spas, while some have 4-poster beds; all have en suite, A/C, TV, tea/coffee. The restaurant is in a historic building serving good Asian-influenced food.

Margaret's Forest
96 Bussell Highway
Tel: 08-9758 7188
www.assured.net.au
Located at the edge of the forest but just 100 metres/yds from the town centre, shops and restaurants. Choice of studio, 1- or 2-bed apartments, all with forest views, A/C, kitchen, internet, TV. Most have a spa, courtyard, balcony

or deck with BBQ.

Budget
Margaret River Lodge
220 Railway Terrace
Tel: 08-9757 9532
www.mrlodge.com.au
Set in a quiet 1ha bush-land setting, offering a total of 100 single and double beds in 26 dormitory, en suite and family rooms.

Expensive
Merribrook
Armstrong Roadd, off Cowaramup Bay Road
Tel: 08-9755 5599
www.merribrook.com.au
Small and relaxing luxury resort comprising ten private chalets. Treatments such as aromatherapy massage and reflexology are complemented by superb food. Prides itself on providing an eco-friendly experience.

Budget
Riverview Tourist Park
8–10 Willmott Avenue
Tel: 1300 666 105

BELOW: the heated pool at Rydges Hotel and Resort, Kalgoorlie.

www.riverviewtouristpark.com
On the river, 500 metres/yds from centre for supermarket, shops, restaurants; 20 powered sites, some with en suite; 30 cabins, most with en suite, all with full kitchen, A/C and TV. Cycle and walk trails nearby, canoes for hire.

Mount Barker

Budget

Hayrocks B&B
St Werburghs Road
Tel: 08-9851 2196
www.interbed.com.au/listings/hay-rocks.htm
In a delightful rural setting, with views across vineyards and the Hay River Valley; 2 rooms with en suite, a private entrance, and outdoor tables under the veranda. Guest dining/sitting room has TV, VCR, CD, coffee/tea, BBQ. Cooked breakfast included, and dinner available. On the Mount Barker Heritage Trail, 11km (7 miles) from the centre of town.
Mount Barker Valley Views
Albany Highway
Tel: 08-9851 3899
www.valley-views.com.au
In-town motel in garden setting; 20 units with fridge, A/C, cable TV, electric blankets; plus 5 chalets with full cooking facilities.

New Norcia

Moderate

Benedictine Monastery Guest House
Gt Northern Highway
Tel: 08-9654 8002
www.newnorcia.wa.edu.au/guesthouse
People feeling the need

for some peace and contemplation will appreciate a stay in this monastery. Simple double and single bedrooms, some with en suite facilities. Quiet ambience, and guests are encouraged to pray and eat with the monks. Food is excellent, and tariff ($75 per person) includes 3 meals per day.

Budget

New Norcia Hotel
Great Northern Highway
Tel: 08-9654 8034
www.newnorcia.wa.edu.au/hotel.htm
Classic Australian country hotel built in 1927 for parents visiting children at the monastery school. Simple but comfortable, with shared bathroom and toilet facilities. Rooms have electric blankets (it does get cold in winter), ceiling fans, fridge, tea/coffee. Breakfast and dinner served in the dining room, usually including famous New Norcia breads. Tariff includes continental breakfast.

Pemberton

Luxury–Moderate

Forest Lodge Resort
Vasse Highway
Tel: 08-9776 1113
www.forestlodgeresort.com.au
Historic lodge in Karri forest, 2km (1 mile) from town centre, with a range of accommodation: B&B guest rooms ($$) are in the original lodge; 2-bed chalets or studio motel units have full kitchen ($$$), and the 3-bed Homestead House suits large groups or families. Resort has extensive gardens, and a private lake where les-

sons in fly fishing are given by Brendan Elliott (tel: 08-9772 4386).

Moderate

Old Picture Theatre
Cnr Ellis and Guppy streets
Tel: 08-9776 1513
www.oldpicturetheatre.com.au
Restored heritage timber building in town centre, built as a cinema in 1929. Original features include jarrah floorboards and stained-glass doors, but the modernisation is 21st-century. Choice of self-contained 1-, 2- or 3-bed apartments – called The Projection Room, the Dress Circle etc, according to location. The Stage is for romantics, with a spa, bonus champagne and chocolates, and late checkout. Original owners' cottage is also available. All units have full kitchen, A/C, TV, VCR, internet access. Shared spa, BBQ area and laundry.
Pump Hill Farm Cottages
Pump Hill Road
Tel: 08-9776 1379
www.pumphill.com.au
Pump Hill Farm suits families with children particularly; play area with cubby house and sandpit, and every morning a hay ride to help feed cows, donkeys, sheep and goats – and collect fresh eggs for breakfast. Country-style rammed-earth and mud-brick cottages (1-, 2- and 3-bed) are furnished, with full kitchens, TV, DVD and BBQ; guest laundry.
The Warren Vineyard
Conte Road
Tel: 08-9776 1115
www.warrenvineyard.com.au

Boutique vineyard bed and breakfast 3km (2 miles) from town, beside National Park with valley and vine views. Warren specialises in aged red wines, Merlot and Cabernet Sauvignon; sundowner wine tastings in the rammed-earth tasting room. Just 2 double bedrooms with bathroom, and living area with TV, VCR, DVD, cooking facilities. Rooms are let as a unit, even if only one is occupied.

Porongurup

Moderate

The Sleeping Lady
2658 Porongurup Road
Tel: 08-9853 1113
Country house in an orchard of fruit and avocado trees with views to the Stirling Range. Fully self-catering, self-contained 2-bed cottage, veranda to enjoy sunset, birds and kangaroos.

Budget

Bolganup Homestead
Porongurup Road, nr Porongurup Shop
Tel: 08-9853 1049
www.bolganup.iinet.net.au
Century-old sheep farm homestead run by founding family, now with 3 self-contained suites in house, and

PRICE CATEGORIES

Prices are for a standard double room, without breakfast unless stated – including 10 percent GST (VAT).
Luxury: over AUS$300
Expensive: AUS$200–300
Moderate: AUS$100–200
Budget: under AUS$100

ABOVE: the New Norcia Hotel, ideal for those on a budget.

cottage. 1-, 2- or 3-bed, polished jarrah floors, cooking facilities, TV, VCR, log fire and BBQ on wide veranda with views to Porongurup Range. Birds and kangaroos all around, and boutique wineries in the nearby hills.

Thorns Mountain Retreats

1280 Porongurup Road
Tel: 08-9853 1105
A cricket pitch on a hilltop, in Millinup Winery, makes this place unique. Accommodation is in a self-contained cottage, and a B&B homestead studio. Hillside Cottage adjoins the tasting room and wine store (connecting door kept firmly locked!) with 1 bedroom, plus sofa bed, kitchen, en suite, TV, VCR, laundry and veranda views. B&B Homestead Studio has 2 rooms, for up to 4. The cricket ground, created by owner/cricket fanatic Peter Thorn, is ringed by peaks and stunning views. Guests' matches are welcome – provided spin bowler Peter is included.

Walpole

Moderate

Tree Top Walk Motel

Nockolds Street
Tel: 08-9840 1444
www.treetopwalkmotel.com.au
Modern motel 200 metres/yds from centre, with 6 twin-share rooms, 1 spa room and 3-bed family units; all en suite, with electric blankets, Foxtel TV, tea/coffee, fridge. Room service is available from the Tree Top restaurant, which uses fresh produce; lounge for pre-dinner drinks.

Budget

Coalmine Beach Holiday Park

Coalmine Beach Road
Tel: 08-9840 1026
Toll free: 1800 670 026
www.coalminebeach.com.au
A caravan park on the shore of Nornalup Inlet, 3km (2 miles) from town in Walpole-Nornalup National Park. Near the beach with boat ramp and fishing. En suite duplex and 4-berth cabins, standard cabins, park homes; kitchen, TV,

A/C; most with inlet or bush views, and linen supplied. Caravan sites served by camp kitchen, BBQ area.

Tingle All Over Budget Accommodation

60 Nockolds Street
Tel: 08-9840 1041
YHA-affiliated backpackers' near town centre; 10 rooms for up to 25 people, 2 gender-specific dorms. All standard services; kitchen, laundry, TV, VCR, pool/snooker, BBQ and open fire.

Yallingup

Budget

Caves Caravan Park

Yallingup Beach Road
Tel: 08-9755 2196
www.cavescaravanpark.com
Surrounded by National Park, an easy walk to swimming, surfing and fishing beaches. The choice here is between 2-bed self-contained chalets, private en suite vans, private en suite tent sites and unpowered tent sites. Chalets have full kitchen, heaters, fans, TV and DVD.

Site includes games room, playground, laundry, camp kitchen; nearby beach volleyball, tennis and BBQs.

Moderate

Chandlers Smiths Beach Villas

Smiths Beach Road
Tel: 08-9755 2062
www.chandlerssmithsbeach.com.au
On a hillside surrounded by National Park, 15 comfortable villas, all with beach and ocean views. They are 4km (2½ miles) south of Yallingup and 5 minutes from Smiths Beach for swimming and surfing; 2-bed villas have full kitchen facilities, TV and DVD. Laundry and BBQ on site.

Expensive–Moderate

Wildwood Valley

Wildwood Road
Tel: 08-9755 2120
www.wildwoodvalley.com.au
Wildwood Valley is 8km (5 miles) from town centre, one of the oldest properties in the area. Accommodation ranges from bed and breakfast in main house ($$) to a 2-bed apartment or 1- or 3-bed cottages. Apartment and cottages ($$$) are fully equipped.

PRICE CATEGORIES

Prices are for a standard double room, without breakfast unless stated – including 10 percent GST (VAT).
Luxury: over AUS$300
Expensive: AUS$200–300
Moderate: AUS$100–200
Budget: under AUS$100

A CTIVITIES

THE ARTS, NIGHTLIFE, FESTIVALS, SPORTS, SIGHTSEEING TOURS AND CHILDREN'S ACTIVITIES

THE ARTS

Music and Dance

Classical music

Perth Concert Hall
5 St George's Terrace
Tel: 08-9231 9900
Perth's principal classical music auditorium is home to WASO, the West Australian Symphony Orchestra.

His Majesty's Theatre
825 Hay Street
Tel: 08-9265 0900
A beautiful, ornate Victorian theatre used for all types of musical concerts and productions.

Supreme Court Gardens
Riverside Drive.
Beautiful riverside venue for outdoor summer concerts.

Music Auditorium
WA Academy of Performing Arts, Edith Cowan University
2 Bradford Street, Mount Lawley
Tel: 08-9370 6636

Jazz

Perth has nurtured an outstanding line-up of talented local jazz musicians, and the pool spreads every year because of the internationally respected Conservatorium at WAAPA (Western Australian Academy of Performing Arts). Graduates form many of the groups playing in venues across Perth. Also, Australian and international musos make regular visits to the west, often at the invitation of the PJS (Perth Jazz Society).

JAZZWA: www.jazzwa.com – have a complete rundown of current venues and events.

Charles Hotel
509 Charles Street, North Perth
Tel: 08-9444 1051
Modern jazz on Mon – Perth Jazz Society: www.perthjazzsociety.com.

The Jazz Cellar
Cnr Scarborough Beach and Buxton roads, Mount Hawthorn
Tel: 08-9447 8111
Through the quirky entrance, which is a red phone box, and down the stairs for the most intimate of jazz venues; Fri night only.

The Navy Club
64 High Street, Fremantle
Tel: 08-9336 3752
Traditional and mainstream jazz; Sun afternoons 4 – 7pm.

Universal Bar
221 William Street, Northbridge
Tel: 08-9227 6771

Yokine Bowling Club
Cnr Wordsworth and Latrobe Streets, Yokine
Tel: 08-9377 7003
Trad jazz, for dancing, on Tuesdays Jazz Club of WA; www.jazzclubof wa.asn.au.

Jabe Dodd Park, Mosman
Free open-air jazz picnic on the third Sunday of every summer month, noon – 4pm.

Rigby's Bar and Bistro
Rear of 221 St George's Terrace
Tel: 08-9324 1196
Plays live modern jazz every Friday night.

The Ellington Jazz Club
191 Beaufort Street, Perth
Tel: 08-9228 1088
New York-style jazz club offering food and live music seven nights a week.

Contemporary music

WA produces even more exponents of rock and pop than jazz; you'll find live sounds somewhere in the city almost every night of the week.

Fly By Night Musicians Club
Parry Street, Fremantle
Tel: 08-9430 5976

The Flying Scotsman
639 Beaufort Street, Mount Lawley
Tel: 08-9328 6200

Indi Bar
23 Hastings Street, Scarborough
Tel: 08-9341 1122

Kulcha
1st floor, 13 South Terrace, Fremantle
Tel: 08-9336 4544

Llama Bar
464 Hay Street, Subiaco
Tel: 08-9388 0222

Metro City
146 Roe Street, Northbridge

TRANSPORT
ACCOMMODATION
ACTIVITIES
A – Z

ABOVE: His Majesty's Theatre on Hay Street.

Tel: 08-9228 0500
Metropolis Fremantle
58 South Terrace
Tel: 08-9336 1880
Mustang Bar
46 Lake Street, Northbridge
Tel: 08-9328 2350
The Bird
181 William Street, Northbridge
Tel: 08-6142 3513
www.williamstreetbird.com.

Funk/blues
The Funk Club
Upstairs at The Leederville Hotel,
742 Newcastle Street
Tel: 08-9286 0150
www.funkclub.com.au
Every Friday night from 8pm –
midnight.
The Manor
Rear of Hip-E Club, 663 Newcastle Street, Leederville
Tel: 08-9227 8899
Funk and Hip Hop Friday nights
from 9pm till late.

Contemporary dance
The Irish Club
61 Townshend Road, Subiaco
Tel: 08-9381 5213
Music lessons and set dancing
from 8pm, Mon.

Theatre
Diverse productions go on all year,

with a strong avant-garde scene
supported by small companies
and semi-pro groups.
Astor Theatre
Corner Beaufort and Walcott
streets
This refurbished Art Deco theatre
now plays more than just movies
on original 35mm film, it also
shows theatre productions and
holds live music from local and
international artists.
Barking Gecko
180 Hamersley Road, Subiaco
Tel: 08-9380 3080
Belvoir Amphitheatre
1155 Great Northern Highway,
Upper Swan
Tel: 08-9296 1817
Open-air venue in Swan Valley.
Black Swan Theatre Company
6 Broadway, Nedlands
Western Australia's flagship theatre company which showcases
highly distinctive reinterpretations of international theatre
classics.
The Blue Room Theatre
53 James Street, Northbridge
Tel: 08-9227 7005
Deck Chair Theatre
179 High Street, Fremantle
Tel: 08-9430 4771
**Dolphin, Octagon and New
Fortune Theatres**
On the University of WA campus.
Tel: 08-6488 2691.

His Majesty's Theatre
825 Hay Street, Perth
Tel: 08-9265 0900
Playhouse Theatre
3 Pier Street, Perth
Tel: 08-9325 3344
Quarry Amphitheatre
Waldron Drive, off Oceanic Drive,
City Beach
Tel: 08-9385 7144.
On the slopes of Reabold Hill.
The Regal
Cnr Hay Street/Rokeby Road
Tel: 1300 795 012
Spare Parts Puppet Theatre
1 Short Street, Fremantle
Tel: 08-9335 5044
Yirra Yaakin Aboriginal Theatre
65 Murray Street, Perth
Tel: 08-9202 1966

Cinema
Two major chains, Greater Union
and Hoyts, carry the big-distribution films, but there are many
small, some very small, interesting cinemas located all over
Perth. Programme details can be
found via these hotlines below –
but it's much cheaper to buy *The
West Australian* newspaper for
general listings.
The Astor
659 Beaufort Street, Mt Lawley
Tel: 08-9370 1777
www.liveattheastor.com.au
Heritage-listed Art Deco building
showing modern and classic
films. It is also holds live music
and performances.
Camelot Outdoor Cinema
16 Lochee Street, Mosman
Tel: 08-9385 4793
A charming Art Deco building
with theatre space. Cinema
is in a garden, with deckchairs,
a bar, and food available.
You may BYO food, not alcohol.
Cinema Paradiso
164 James Street, Northbridge
Tel: 08-9227 1771
Galaxy Drive-in Theatre
26 Goollelal Drive, Kingsley
Tel: 08-9409 9664
The very last of the drive-in cinemas that were once all around the
suburbs; featuring up-to-date
films in a nostalgic setting.

Greater Union
Galleria Shopping Centre, Morley
Tel: 08-9275 9255
Hoyts
Tel: 1900 946 987
Luna Cinemas
155 Oxford Street, Leederville
Tel: 08-9444 4056
Luna has one large and many small studio cinemas, as well as an outdoor screen for summer, where there's a bar and you can bring a picnic.
Somerville Auditorium
University of WA, Nedlands
Tel: 08-6488 2440
This is the main screen venue for Perth Festival's Film Season in February; there's another at the Joondalup campus of Edith Cowan University. The Somerville location is very atmospheric, with deckchairs for a comfy viewing experience, and the lawn is lined with tall pine trees providing shade and a wind break; Joondalup is beside an illuminated lake.

Art Galleries

Art Gallery of Western Australia
47 James Street, Perth
Tel: 08-9492 6600
Exhibition Centre
Perth Convention Centre,
21 Mounts Bay Road, Perth
Tel: 08-9338 0300
Perth Institute of Contemporary Art
51 James Street, Perth
Tel: 08-9228 6300

NIGHTLIFE

Wine bars

The Grapeskin, part of Brass Monkey pub. Wide range of quality wine by the glass, and live jazz early on Wed evening.
Must Wine Bar, 519 Beaufort Street, Highgate. A large selection of drinks and good French cuisine.

Whisper Wine Bar, 1/15 Essex Street, Fremantle. This teeny tiny bar is the hottest spot for drinking a cool glass of Chardy or Pinot Noir.

Late-night bars

Andaluz, 21 Howard Street, Perth Late-night bar and tapas with a cutting-edge cocktail list.
East End Bar and Lounge, 189 High St, Fremantle, www.eastendbar. com.au. Inspired by the decadent bars of 1920s old New York, The East End Bar and Lounge offers a warm, stylish environment in which to sip cocktails, listen to live music and mingle with friends, and is located away from the hustle and bustle of Fremantle.
Helvetica, Rear 101 St George's Terrace, Perth. Perth's first whiskey bar is a hidden gem with a swanky outfit and comfortable chairs where you can enjoy a glass of the brown stuff, and they have a good wine selection.
Hula Bula Bar, 12 Victoria Ave-

FESTIVALS

Summer weather is so reliable that there will be competing events most weekends from November through to March.
Perth Cup, New Year's Day. A horse-racing carnival and Perth's premier fashion event. Lots of champagne, posh frocks and outrageous hats.
Fremantle Sardine Festival, Jan. A celebration of the freshly caught sardine, staged on the Esplanade, with loads of cooked fish and other delicacies.
Australia Day Skyworks, 26 Jan. Huge display of fireworks exploding off barges on the Swan River, and the tops of the city's skyscrapers.
Festival of Perth, Feb. Longest-established annual arts festival in the southern hemisphere, with artists from all cultural fields. Includes cinema.
Eat Drink Perth, Mar. Each March the city celebrates its favourite eateries and new din-

ing experiences with this annual festival. Cooking, dining, competitions, chefs and mouth-watering experiences feature during the month-long programme.
Rottnest Festival, Mar. A family occasion with concerts, clowns, buskers and markets.
Fremantle Street Arts Festival, Easter. Entertainment with the skills and outrageous behaviour of the world's best buskers.
Kids in the City, Apr, July and Oct. This provides free family entertainment in Forrest Place. Themes and activities change each school holidays.
Kings Park Wild Flower Festival, Sept. Shows off a huge range of WA native flowers.
Spring in The Valley, Sept and Oct. Celebrates the people and produce of the Swan Valley with fine wines, food, art and music.
Royal Show, early Oct. Showcases vast WA resources, agriculture and industry, plus all the

fun of the fair in Sideshow Alley.
Northbridge Festival, Oct or Nov. City of Perth and Artrage combine to bring alternative arts, theatre, dance, music, visual arts and street performance.
Gay Pride March, Oct. Colourful gay and lesbian parade through the streets of Northbridge.
Fremantle Festival, Nov. Week-long celebration with street parades, parties, concerts, kites and kids' events.
Red Bull Air Race and Festival, Nov. Pilots compete against each other, demonstrating spectacular aerial manoeuvres above the Swan.
City of Perth Festival of Christmas, Nov–Dec
Christmas is officially launched with the Turning on the Christmas Lights event (Nov) and is followed by a string of activities including pageants, the city's Santa train, Carols by Candlelight and the Christmas Nativity.

TRANSPORT

ACCOMMODATION

ACTIVITIES

A – Z

ABOVE: Goldfields Golf Club's course in Kalgoorlie.

nue, Perth. First tiki bar in Perth, specialising in rum-based drinks and cocktails. Wed–Sat from 4pm.
Llama Bar, 464 Hay Street, Subiaco. Voted Perth's best contemporary bar in 2006; very fashionable.
Luxe Bar, 446 Beaufort Street, Highgate. Popular cocktail bar. Wed–Sun from 8pm.
Mrs Brown, 241 Queen Victoria Street, North Fremantle. Small and intimate with mismatched furniture, this bar heaves on a Friday and Saturday night. With an extensive wine and beer list presented in an old-school children's storybook cover, it is an ideal place to start out a night, or have a cheeky one during the day. One of the perks is you can enjoy a burger from Flipside, next door, with your Chardy or imported brew.
Mustang Bar, 46 Lake Street, Northbridge. American-style sports bar with large screens.
Universal Bar, 221 William Street, Northbridge. Live jazz and blues. Wed–Sun.

Nightclubs

Metro City, 146 Roe Street, Northbridge. Spectacular modern building with 10 theme bars set at different levels. Sat from 9pm.
Metropolis Fremantle, 58 South Terrace, Fremantle. Large club with 10 bars, live bands, etc. Fri–Sun.
The Red Sea, 83 Rokeby Road, Subiaco. Popular nightclub with several bars and dance floors. Open Fri and Sat.
The Ruby Room, Burswood Entertainment Complex. Elegant nightclub with four bars and a range of music styles. Wed–Sun.

Casino

Burswood Casino, Great Eastern Highway, Burswood. WA's only casino is open 24 hours in the Burswood Resort complex, with seven restaurants and eight bars.

Gay Scene

For reasonably priced accommodation try **Hotel Northbridge**, 210 Lake Street, tel: 08-9328 5254, or the gay-owned and operated **Pension of Perth** at 3 Throssell Street, tel: 08-9228 9049. For nightlife, try **The Court Hotel**, 50 Beaufort Street; or **Connections Nightclub**, 81 James Street, Northbridge. For more information, contact the Gay and Lesbian Community Services office, tel: 08-9420 7201.

SPORT

Participant Sports

Cycling

(See: Getting Around)
Bicycles can be hired from **About Bike Hire**, Cnr Plain Street and Riverside Drive, tel: 08-9221 2665; or **The Cycle Centre Perth**, 282 Hay Street, East Perth, tel: 08-9325 1176.

Diving

Dive sites are located all around the coast, with many near Perth. Perth Diving Academy, tel: 08-9344 1562; www.perthdiving.com.au, will assist with all diving needs. Local dives include Rottnest and Carnac islands, and extend as far as Dunsborough and Rockingham. You can also dive in the big tank at AQWA (Hillary's) and in the Swan at night. Around Perth the season is Oct–May; further north, at Coral Bay, Broome, etc, it is shorter.

Golf

Visitors are welcome at most private clubs on proof of home-club membership; there may be a fee. There are also public courses of a high standard, such as:

Wembley Golf Complex

The Boulevard, Wembley Downs, Floreat
Tel: 08-9387 7272
A 36-hole course with day/night driving range. Open daily from first light to 8.30pm Sat – Sun, until 9.30pm Mon – Thurs; more expensive at weekends and holidays.

Horse riding

Various horse-riding schools are located around Perth; to hire a horse for a good long ride you'll probably have to go out of town.

Kayaking

Wildlife sea kayaking among seals, sea lions and penguins around Seal and Penguin islands just south of Perth is a one-day excursion with Rivergods Paddle Adventures (tel: 08-9259 0749; www.rivergods.com.au). Double sea kayaks are used, and no experience is necessary on the supervised trip, including transport, lunch, equipment, etc. Rivergods also have a five-day trip to World Heritage-listed Monkey Mia (a chance to paddle among dolphins, turtles, dugongs) as well as whitewater rafting and canoeing.

Running and jogging

Running is popular in Perth, and the 10km (6-mile) circuit around the bridges is well used. **WA Masters Athletics Club** (tel: 08-9390 2056; www.mastersathleticswa.org) welcomes visitors of any age and ability to events, every Sunday morning, at different locations around the city. They also have mid-week track-and-field meetings and training groups.

Sailing

Experienced crew are always welcomed at the various clubs on the Swan. Royal Perth Yacht Club (Australia II Drive; tel: 08-9389 1555) is nearest to the city centre, by the University at Crawley. Many races and events are organised around the river, including the regular Wednesday afternoon twilight sail that's well supported.

Swimming

Australian waters can be hazardous. In Perth, use a beach that's guarded by life savers and swim between the red-and-yellow flags that mark their surveillance area. Well-maintained public pools are located in most parts of Perth. The main one, used for championship events with indoor and outdoor pools, is at **Challenge Stadium**, Stephenson Avenue, Mount Claremont; tel: 08-9441 8222.

Tennis

Many tennis clubs in Perth will welcome visitor players; courts can also be hired for a fee. The **State Tennis Centre**, Victoria Park Drive, Burswood (tel: 08-6462 8300), is open for day and evening court hire, seven days a week.

Tenpin bowling

There is a wide choice of bowling centres, mostly licensed and with food available.

Spectator Sport

Baseball

Baseball isn't widely played, but has a long history here. Representative state team is Perth Heat, playing at Baseball Park, Cnr Nicholson/Wilfred roads, Thornlie.

Basketball

Perth Wildcats are WA's team in the National Basketball League. Their home base is at **Challenge Stadium**, Stephenson Ave, Mount Claremont; tel: 08-9441 8222.

Cricket

The **WACA ground** (Western Australian Cricket Association; Nelson Crescent, East Perth; tel: 08-9265 7222) is HQ of state cricket and venue for all important matches – state, championships, international one-day, the new 20 – 20 format and Test matches. But high-standard matches featuring state players in their local club teams can be seen on ovals across Perth on summer weekends. The Lilac Hill ground in

SURFING

Reliable conditions mean you can catch a wave all year in WA, though would-be surfers would be wise to check in first with the experts at Surfing WA (tel: 08-9448 0004; www.surfingaustralia.com). Courses (for ages 8 – 70) are held at Trigg Beach, which with Scarborough has Perth's best surf. South of Perth, Yallingup and Lancelin are noted for bigger waves, and Margaret River is on the international circuit.

Indian Ocean temperature doesn't vary much in WA, but the wind chill does, and many surfers use wetsuits here. Surfing Australia will advise on shops that rent out suits and boards.

Commercial operators offering tours and training include Surfschool.com (tel: 08-9444 5399; www.surfschool.com), which runs very reasonably priced surf tours and camps – one, two, three or four days – including transport to Lancelin, accommodation and meals as well as five hours of lessons every day. Check with Surfing WA for other recommended operators.

Guildford is one of the finest, worth a visit for its lovely rural setting by the river. Another is in the grounds of the University of WA.

Football

Australian Rules Football is the most popular spectator sport. WA has two national teams, West Coast Eagles and the Fremantle Dockers, vying for local support. Each plays home games at Subiaco Oval, and local club games (WAFL – WA Football League) are played all around Perth.

Greyhound racing

Greyhounds WA holds two meetings every week at **Cannington Stadium** (Cnr Albany Highway/ Station Street; tel: 08-9458

ABOVE: kite-sailing offers a new twist on surfing.

4600). Buffet meals and bar service available; entry cost low on Saturday, free on Wednesday.

Harness racing

Gloucester Park (Nelson Crescent, East Perth; tel: 08-9323 3555) is a major Australian harness-racing centre with lots of meetings: every Friday (except Good Friday) plus afternoon or twilight meets on Mon, Tue and Sat. There are open areas, bars and three on-course restaurants, and a stunning entry (reminiscent of the last days of the Raj). The track is near the river, opposite the WACA; entry cost low.

Horse racing

Perth has two racetracks, each just a short ride from the city centre. **Ascot**, tel: 08-9277 0777, with its outdoor bars and restaurants, is used for summer meetings. **Belmont Park**, tel: 08-9470 8222, is on the river with enclosed facilities to keep punters warm and dry in the winter. Entry is generally free midweek, unless there is a special meeting, and cheap (around AUS$10) at weekends. Ascot's Perth Cup, on 1 Jan every year, is the racing and fashion highlight of the season.

Soccer

Soccer is slowly gaining ground in WA. The state team is Perth Glory, based at the **Members Equity Stadium**, 310 Pier Street, East Perth. Local teams play on grounds across the city.

Tennis

The Hopman Cup is Perth's big international tennis tournament, played by mixed doubles in Dec/ Jan at the Burswood Dome, at the **Burswood Entertainment Centre**, tel: 08-9362 7777. The Davis Cup is also played there. **Royal Kings Park Tennis Club**, tel: 08-9217 6300, is part of the newly developed Next Generation fitness club.

SIGHTSEEING TOURS

Boat trips

Cruising down the river is an excellent way to get to Fremantle, taking in views of Kings Park, Melville Water and the coves and beaches on both sides of the Swan. Both **Oceanic Cruises** (tel: 08-9325 1191; www.oceaniccruises. com.au) and **Captain Cook Cruises** (tel: 08-9325 3341; www. captaincookcruises.com.au) offer one-way or return trips, including tea/ coffee and commentary. They take around an hour each way; Captain Cook throws in a free winetasting on the return leg.

Walking

In the city free tours are available with City Perth volunteers. Meet them at the information kiosk in Murray Street Mall, near Forrest Chase, 11am for a city orientation Monday to Saturday, and 2pm for tours on attractions, history, arts and culture Monday to Friday, 12pm Sunday.

Bus

The **City Sightseeing and Kings Park Tour Group** (tel: 08-9203 8882) is a hop-on-hop-off double-decker bus that visits 10 Perth City destinations.

Helicopter

A slightly different way to see Perth is by helicopter. Choose from a range of tours from across the city and Kings Park to Fremantle, Perth's beaches and the Swan River. Go to www.helitraining.com.au, tel:08-9499 7755.

Pub Crawl

One way to see Perth by night is via a pub crawl. It may sound like it's for the youngsters but getting around Perth in the evening and trying to find taxis can be a hassle. **Aussie Pub Crawl** (www. aussiepubcrawls.com.au; tel: 08-9221

2400) will pick you up and drop you off door-to-door and take you to either your own desired itinerary or one of their recommended ones.

CHILDREN'S ACTIVITIES

Extra events and projects are put on at venues during school holidays: details from the **Perth Visitor Centre**, tel: 1300 361 351.

Western Australian Museum
Perth Cultural Centre, James Street
Tel: 08-9212 3700
Apart from being a genuinely interesting visit any time of the year, the museum organises special children's activities during school holidays.

Maritime Museum
Victoria Quay, Fremantle
Tel: 08-9431 8444
Following clues to find hidden rats was a recent special topic for school-holiday visitors.

Perth Zoo
20 Labouchere Road, South Perth
Tel: 08-9474 3551
Great collections of native and exotic animals in natural enclosures; children's activities include an overnight stay in the summer months. Open 9am–5pm daily.

AQWA (Aquarium of Western Australia)
Hillary's Boat Harbour
Tel: 08-9447 7500
Fascinating insight into WA's sometimes bizarre marine life, including a spectacular underwater tunnel for close encounters with large sharks and rays.

Hillary's Boat Harbour
About 25 minutes' drive north of the city, this is a lively venue for children of all ages. There's a gentle, shallow-water beach, a water-slides complex, lots of shops, restaurants, yachts and motor launches, and an aquarium.

Scitech
City West, Sutherland Street
Tel: 08-9215 0700
Mon–Fri 9.30am–4pm, weekends and school holidays 10am–5pm.

A science discovery centre with fascinating hands-on experiments, and child-oriented (sometimes, to an adult mind, revolting) special topics! Puppet shows are aimed at 3–7-year-olds; and there's a theatre performance on varying topics. Entry price includes Planetarium.

Horizon Planetarium
Tel: 08-9215 0700
High-tech multimedia shows like Launch Pad, Search for Life, Astronaut, and "all about the night sky".

Kings Park
Follow in the footprints of dinosaurs in the Western Power Parkland, or play on the fort, swings and rides at Hale Oval (lots of shady areas for summer). Walk through treetops on the Federation Walkway, and enjoy the views across the Swan River.

Adventure World
179 Progress Drive, Bibra Lake
Tel: 08-9417 9666
Oct–Apr, 10am–5pm daily during school holidays; closed Tue and Wed out of holiday times. There's unlimited use of all the rides and attractions once you have paid the entry fee – quite high – to enter this big adventure park. "The Rampage" is the

scariest ride of all, not for the faint-hearted.

Whiteman Park
Lord Street, Whiteman
Tel: 08-9209 6000
Only 30 minutes' drive from central Perth, the 4,050-hectare (10,000-acre) park is open every day of the year, 8.30am–5.30pm, and a great place for children. A variety of steam and diesel locomotives can take you around the park, or there's an electric tram to a picnic area. Bike hire, children's pool and mini electric cars are among the other attractions. Within Whiteman is Caversham Wildlife Park – worth visiting to see native animals and birds close up, and Molly's Farm animals. You can even have a camel ride.

Tumbulgum Farm
1475 South Western Highway, Mundijong
Tel: 08-9525 5888
www.tumbulgumfarm.com.au
The show, involving sheep mustering on horseback, sheep-shearing, working sheepdogs, learning how to crack a stock whip and milk a cow, is based in Caversham Wildlife Park, within Whiteman Park. Show times are 10am, 1pm and 3pm daily and shows last approximately 45 minutes.

BELOW: out and about in Fremantle.

TRANSPORT

ACCOMMODATION

ACTIVITIES

A – Z

AN ALPHABETICAL SUMMARY OF PRACTICAL INFORMATION

A dmission Charges

Compared with the UK and USA, admission charges to sights and attractions are fairly low, and often free for museums. The Museum and the Art Gallery of WA, for example, are free except for special exhibitions, and Fremantle's museums all accept voluntary entry donations, except for the new Maritime Museum and Fremantle Prison.

Concession rates are available in many places on production of a senior or student card.

B udgeting for Your Trip

Perth's economy is stable, and property prices have rocketed in recent years. But this hasn't been reflected in rising prices for visitors. In general, costs compare favourably with the UK, and are probably on a par with the US, although you won't find so much in the way of cheap hotel/motel chains. Public transport is very cheap (free buses in Perth city centre, for example) and petrol is considerably cheaper than in the UK. The cost of flights, hotels, etc can be brought down considerably by booking well in advance and using the internet to search for good deals. Prices in rural areas are likely to be lower than in Perth itself.

As a very rough guide, expect to pay the following :
Double room per night in a medium-level hotel: AUS$125.
Simple lunch per person: AUS$20.
Two-course dinner per person with house wine: AUS$40–50.
Car hire per week: medium-level car from AUS$400.
Miscellaneous (drinks, admission charges, etc) per person per day: AUS$30.

If you buy goods to take home to the value of AUS$300 or more, remember that you can claim back GST (sales tax) at the airport upon presentation of your receipt (see opposite).

C hildren

Most establishments recognise that children are a fact of life and

CLIMATE CHART

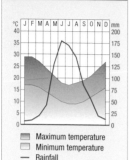

Maximum temperature
Minimum temperature
— Rainfall

therefore cater for them. Many wineries in the southwest of Western Australia and the Swan Valley go so far as to have playgrounds so adults can enjoy a glass of wine while keeping an eye on their kids (Clairault; tel: 08-9755 6655, and Wills Domain; tel: 08-9755 2327 are two). Almost all restaurants, with the exception of fine dining and those with degustation-style menus, have highchairs and meals specifically for children. Students and children under 14 years are generally allowed concessions when entering museums etc, and children under four years of age are almost always free. Many of the larger hotels across Perth have reputable babysitting services, which incur a fee.

Climate

Perth's Mediterranean-style climate has four distinctive seasons, although the sun shines most days, all year. Rainfall has decreased alarmingly in recent years, but the long-term pattern is for most of the year's rain to fall during the winter months – June–Aug, easing off in spring. The city is often dry for months on end, and summer can be very hot, with temperatures in the high 30s Celsius (95–102°F).

Average temperatures are: winter 18°C (65°F), spring (Sept–Nov) 22°C (72°F), summer (Dec–

Feb) 32°C (86°F), autumn (Mar–May) 24°C (75°F). If these temperatures sound high, remember that WA's low humidity makes them much more bearable than similar temperatures in London, for instance. A perfect day in Perth would have a top temperature of 26–9°C.

What to wear

Lightweight clothing is best most of the year, a few layers that will mix and match, plus cool, comfortable shoes or sandals. Even in winter one good sweater will be sufficient, plus a folding umbrella. Top coats are rarely seen in Perth. Informality is the general rule, and you'll be comfortable in casual clothes, even shorts, just about everywhere. Hats, sunglasses and sunblock are advisable; the sun is fierce.

Ties and jackets are hardly ever worn except in business situations. In top hotels and restaurants you might feel more comfortable with one or the other, so the staff don't outdo you.

When to visit

If you don't enjoy hot weather, autumn (Mar–May) is the best time of year to be in Perth. Temperatures moderate, the Freman-

tle Doctor (WA vernacular for the local sea breeze) calms down, and gardens recover from summer heat. In spring the weather is warming up, so there will still be showers, and it is the windy season, although the blue jacaranda trees start to bloom, and across WA thousands of varieties of wild flowers appear. Summer can get very hot, with daytime temperatures over 37°C (100°F) for several days at a stretch, but the evenings are wonderful. Winter rains usually fall in short, heavy bursts, often with sunny breaks. It can be warm in the sun, cool in the shade, with overnight temperatures as low as 1°C (33°F).

Crime and Safety

In a life-threatening or time-critical emergency, dial 000 for fire, police or ambulance. For non-emergency police attendance, dial 131 444.

Perth is a relatively safe place, with no unusual risks or problems, but in any big city a certain level of care must be taken. Be extra vigilant late at night, especially in the vicinity of bars and clubs. At this time a taxi is probably the best way to move around, unless you're just walking a short

CUSTOMS REGULATIONS

You must declare all food, plant material and animal products on arrival. The regulations are prominently displayed on arrival, and failure to comply can result in very large penalties.

Duty free allowance is: AUS$900 worth of goods (not including tobacco or alcohol, and reduced to AUS$450 for under 18s); 2.25 litres of alcohol in total, including wine, beer and spirits; 250 cigarettes, or 250g of tobacco/cigars.

Under a Tourist Refund Scheme the GST (general sales tax) on goods bought in Australia can be refunded on departure at the airport. Conditions are: this

applies only to goods carried as hand luggage, or worn to travel; value must be a minimum of AUS$300, spent in one store, shown on a single invoice; goods must be bought within 30 days of departure. Items like clothing and cameras can have been used prior to departure, but partly consumed alcohol and perfume cannot be claimed. To claim the tax refund, wear or carry the goods to the Tourist Refund Scheme office (beyond customs and immigration desks), together with the invoice, your passport and boarding pass.

ABOVE: beware of the very strong sun, especially on the beach.

way on busier, well-lit streets. Lock car doors and don't leave valuables or bags on display in parked cars. Don't carry more cash than you need; use hotel deposit boxes.

Security at quiet railway stations has been a problem, and it's being dealt with by extra police and security guards, plus wide use of video surveillance. Even so, the quieter stations should be avoided late at night.

A network of 135 CCTV cameras in the central area and Northbridge is manned 24 hours a day, 7 days a week. Some car parks also have security-camera surveillance. At the push of a button, emergency communication poles in the shopping malls and Northbridge communicate directly with the Citywatch Police Post. Two late-night supervised taxi ranks operate in Northbridge on Fridays and Saturdays from midnight–4am.

At the beach

Parked cars – especially those emblazoned with hire-company stickers – are a target for petty thieves. If possible, leave nothing in the car; your belongings are all much safer with you on the sands.

Beach safety extends to the ocean, too. Swim only where there are lifeguards, or the water is very placid. Don't swim in grey or overcast conditions, and stay in the shallows. Take extra care on rocks where waves are pounding; occasionally, freak massive waves, known as "king waves", have washed people away.

Wildlife

Take special care if walking in the bush, wetlands, or around lakes and rivers, near sand dunes and on Rottnest Island. Stay on paths, or where you have a clear view ahead. Snakes are the only dangerous animals you might encounter. They want to avoid you as much as you do them, and most snakes move away when they feel the vibrations of your footfall. But you should stay alert and avoid soft ground, long grass, etc.

D isabled Travellers

The starting point for disabled travellers should be the city's website: www.cityofperth.wa.gov.au.

Access maps show how to get around and feature accessible public transport and parking, toilets and easy access walking routes through the city.

Public transport

CAT buses provide a free, frequent and wheelchair-accessible bus service.

Railway staff are available to assist wheelchair users to access metro trains. The ferry from Barrack Street Jetty to Mends Street Jetty (South Perth and Perth Zoo) is accessible for wheelchairs and scooters. Wheelchair accessible Multi Purpose Taxis (MPT) are bookable through Black and White Taxis.

Wheelchairs and motorised scooters can be hired from Citiplace Community Centre (Perth Railway Station upper level; tel: 08-9325 3264; Mon–Fri 8.30am–3.45pm). A AUS$20 deposit and proof of identification are needed; bookings are advisable. Reciprocal ACROD parking rights apply to overseas visitors for up to three months.

EMERGENCIES

In life-threatening or time-critical emergencies, dial 000 and ask for fire, police or ambulance; if you are using a mobile phone you will need to dial 112 and say from which town and state you are calling.

For police attendance – in non-life-threatening situations – dial 131 444.

E lectricity

Current is rated at 230–50 volts, 50 hertz. Standard plugs have three flat pins, and you may need an adaptor for heavier-use appliances such as hairdryers. Universal outlets for 110 volts (for shavers, etc) are found in most accommodation.

Embassies and Consulates

In Perth

British Consulate General Level 26 Allendale Square,
77 St George's Terrace, Perth
Tel: 08-9224 4700
Canadian High Commission
267 St George's Terrace, Perth
Tel: 08-9322 7930
Irish Honorary Consul
PO Box 250, Floreat, 6014
Tel: 08-9385 8247
US Consulate General
16 St George's Terrace, Perth
Tel: 08-9202 1224

Abroad

High Commission, Ottawa
Suite 710, 50 O'Connor Street,
Ottawa, K1P 6L2, Canada
Tel: +1 613 236 0841
Australian Embassy, Washington
1601 Massachusetts Avenue, NW, Washington, DC, 20036
Tel: +1 202 797 3000
The UK and Ireland are served through:
Australian High Commission
Australia House, Strand, London
Tel: +44 (0) 20 7379 4334

G ay Travellers

Public attitude to gay and lesbian people is essentially neutral. The age of consent is 16, the same as for heterosexuals. A few prominent gay and lesbian politicians and other personalities have helped broaden Australian minds. Several entertainment and accommodation establishments cater to the gay scene *(see page 238)*, and in the club and nightlife sectors many more are totally accepting of gay and lesbian people.

Contact: Gay and Lesbian Community Services of WA, tel: 08-9486 9855.

H ealth and Medical Care

Visiting British citizens are covered by a reciprocal agreement with Australia which usually covers emergency health care only, not pre-existing medical conditions. Reciprocal agreements are also in place with Finland, Italy, Malta, the Netherlands, New Zealand and Sweden. Passport holders of these countries can reclaim the cost of medical treatment from Medicare in Australia. As most travellers will not qualify for free treatment, it's wise to carry health and accident insurance. The basic cost of consulting a doctor is AUS$35.

The main accident and emergency hospitals are Royal Perth (Wellington Street; tel: 08-9224 2244) and Sir Charles Gairdner (Hospital Avenue, Nedlands; tel: 08-9346 3333). Princess Margaret Hospital for Children is at Roberts Road, Subiaco; tel: 08-9340 8222.

If a medical problem arises while in Australia and you're unsure whether you need to see a doctor, or if you simply require

BELOW: Australia's distinctive coat of arms.

TRANSPORT

ACCOMMODATION

ACTIVITIES

A–Z

some minor medical advice, phone the Health Direct 24-hour advice line – (toll free) 1800 022 222.

Pharmacies

Pharmacies, also known as "chemists", are run by qualified professionals who dispense prescribed medication. They also sell non-prescription medication, plus toiletries, cosmetics, film, etc, and will advise on minor problems. Beaufort Street Pharmacy (647 Beaufort Street, Mt Lawley, tel: 08-9328 7775) opens 24 hours, seven days a week. Others open until 9pm or midnight: check Yellow Pages for the most convenient.

Visitors can bring up to three months' supply of prescription medication into Australia. To avoid problems at customs, carry a doctor's certificate and letter explaining your condition.

Dentists

Many dentists practise in the city centre or nearby. During business hours, find the most convenient surgery listed in Yellow Pages. Lifecare Forrest Chase Dental (1st floor, Upper Walkway Level, 419 Wellington Street; tel: 08-9221

2777; daily 8am–8pm) will take emergency cases. Otherwise, check the telephone directory again for dentists who may work late hours, or call any hospital accident and emergency department.

Mosquitoes

Use insect repellent, especially around still water, at dusk and in the early morning. Some mosquitoes carry viruses, and it's sensible to avoid their bite. Loose-fitting clothes, long sleeves and trousers are best in risky areas.

Water and food

Tap water is safe to drink in Australian cities. Bottled mineral water is also available everywhere. There are no particular problems with any foods in Australia. Many food premises display a FoodSafe sign that ensures staff have completed a food-handling course, and they follow safe practice. FoodSafe is a national standard that was first developed in Perth.

Sunburn

The Australian sun is very harsh. As a result the "suntanned Aussie" image is fading fast, as more people automati-

cally use sunblock every day.

Wide-brimmed hats or caps and sunglasses are essential for comfort and protection most of the year. If you are fair-skinned and/or unused to strong sunshine but do want to sunbathe, do so in the morning or late afternoon and take care not to burn.

Internet

There are numerous internet cafés in Perth, especially in Barrack Street/William Street area, and most backpacker hostels have access. Here are two:
Internet Station, 131 William Street; tel: 08-9226 5373; email: ncy311@hotmail.com.
Perth City YHA, 300 Wellington Street, Perth; tel: 08-9287 3333.

Left Luggage

Airport

Left-luggage lockers, provided by Smarte Carte, are located outside Terminal 1 at the international airport, and also at the domestic terminals.

There are no public luggage lockers in Perth, although temporary-use ones are installed at places such as the State Library, Art Gallery, etc. Some backpack-

BELOW: regional publications for sale in New Norcia.

ers provide left-luggage storage, for guests.

Lost Property

Airport

Telephone queries concerning property lost on the ground at the airport should be made to the relevant terminal. The numbers are:
Terminal 1 tel: 08-9478 8503
Terminal 2 tel: 08-9270 9504
Terminal 3 tel: 08-9478 8703

If you leave property on any Qantas domestic flight, tel: 08-9270 9504. If you leave property aboard any international flights – including Qantas – you should contact the airline.

(This does not apply to checked-in baggage misplaced by the airline.)

In Perth

Contact numbers are:
Trains: tel: 08-9326 2660
Ferries: tel: 13 62 13
Buses are more complicated, because routes are covered by different companies on behalf of Transperth. Contact the office of the route service provider, which is shown on the timetable. The right office can also be located online, by going to www.transperth.wa.gov.au/Default, and clicking on "passenger info", then on "lost property".

M aps

WA Tourist Centre *(see page 249)* stocks maps for all parts of WA. Local maps are also available at newsagents and bookshops.

Media

ABC (Australian Broadcasting Corporation) is best for up-to-the-minute news. National broadcast TV is Channel 2; national radio, FM 97.7, and AM 810 and AM 585; local radio AM 720. Tourist information radio is on FM 87.6.

Most commercial radio stations are music-oriented, with only brief news bulletins.

SBS national TV carries various

foreign-language news programmes in the morning and good world news coverage every evening at 6.30pm. Local community Channel 44 shows Aljazeera and is also strong on local events, tourist information, restaurant reviews, etc. Commercial TV stations are channels 7, 9 and 10, and they carry most of the high-profile sports events.

Press

The West Australian is Perth's only daily newspaper (Mon–Sat), and the *Sunday Times* is the only Sunday paper. *The Australian* is a national paper, printed in Perth and available Mon–Sat. Weekly news magazines include the *Bulletin* and *Time*. English-language weekly compilations from UK newspapers – *Telegraph, Express, Guardian* – are available at most newsagents.

Internet

Australia's media is more or less dominated by two powerful groups, News Ltd and Packer's PBL. Alternative views flourish only on the internet; www.crikey.com.au is one of the best for its take – generally scathing, often humorous – on politics, business, sport and other matters Australian.

Money

Currency

The Australian dollar is the local currency. Coin denominations are 5, 10, 20 and 50 cents, AUS$1 and AUS$2. Notes are AUS$5, AUS$10, AUS$50 and AUS$100. Rough exchange rates are as follows: £1 = AUS$1.61 and US$1 = AUS$1.01

Foreign exchange

Banks operate Mon–Thur 9.30am–4pm; Fri 9.30am–5pm. Some hotels will exchange major currencies for guests, and there's a 24-hour agency at the airport.

Travellers' cheques

International travellers' cheques

New Year's Day 1 January
Australia Day 26 January
Labor Day 1st Mon in March
Anzac Day 25 April
Good Friday March/April
Easter Monday March/April
Foundation Day 5 June
Queen's Birthday 2 October
Christmas Day 25 December
Boxing Day 26 December
New Year's Eve 31 December

can be cashed at airports, banks, hotels and motels. Thomas Cook/Travelex (tel: 08-9321 2896) has several city branches, the major one in Hay Street Mall (Mon–Fri 8am–6pm; Sat 8am–5.30pm). American Express is also in Hay Street Mall. Fees and rates of exchange vary between establishments. The WA Tourist Centre (Albert Facey House, Forrest Place) will exchange major travellers' cheques and currency.

It is advisable to change your money before heading out of Perth or Fremantle – banks are rare in country WA.

ATM's

These are common in the city but much less plentiful in rural areas. Remember that most banks charge a handling fee for ATM transactions abroad.

Credit cards

Best-known international cards are listed here, with numbers to call in case of problems.
American Express, tel: 1800 268 9824
Diners Club, tel: 1300 360 060
Visa International, tel: 1800 450 346
MasterCard, tel: 1300 135 538

O pening Hours

Central Perth business hours are usually 9am–5pm. Some companies, like stockbrokers which deal extensively with eastern Australian states, start earlier because of the 2–3-hour time difference. Retail shopping hours are: Mon–Sat 9am–9pm, Sun noon–4pm. Sunday opening is confined to central Perth, Fremantle and Rockingham.

Banking hours are Mon–Thur 9.30am–4pm, Fri 9.30am–5pm. Most banks close on Saturday, although branches in shopping centres may remain open.

P ostal Services

Post offices are open 8.30am–5pm, Mon–Fri, and the central post office on Murray Street also opens Saturday morning, 9am–12.30pm. Services include couriers, international and registered post. Some newsagents have a post office within them so you can buy stamps and envelopes from them. The postal system is very efficient, and, depending on how quickly you want your mail to arrive, will vary in cost. It is recommended to get insurance or send items certified mail if anything sent is worth more than AUS$50 so you can track its movements. Postboxes are fire-engine red. Poste Restante – known as general delivery – can be arranged at any post office. American Express's main branches also offer this service to their cardholders.

See www.auspost.com.au.

R eligious Services

Anglican
St George's Cathedral
38 St George's Terrace
Tel: 08-9325 5766
Sun 8am, 10am and 5pm; Mon–Fri 8am and 4pm; Sat 7.45am
Baptist
Perth Baptist Church
10 James Street
Tel: 08-9328 6507
Buddhist
Chua Chanh Giac Temple
45 Money Street
Tel: 08-9342 0609
Catholic
St Joachim's Church
Cnr Shepperton Rd/Harper St,
Victoria Park
Tel: 08-9361 1057
Sun 8am, 9.30am, 11am and 6pm; Mon 6.45am, Tue–Fri 6.45am and 12.10pm; Sat 7.30am and 6pm
Jewish
Temple of David
34 Clifton Cres, Mount Lawley
Tel: 08-9271 1485
Fri 6.30pm; Sat 10.30am

BELOW: public phones.

S moking

In 2006 WA banned smoking in all enclosed public places, with the one notable exception of the International Room at Burswood Casino. The Healthway Quit campaign has even resulted in open-air sports stadia such as the WACA and Subiaco Oval banning smoking. The WACA has special designated smoking areas behind the grandstands; Subiaco makes spectators leave the ground to smoke.

In pubs, smoking is only permitted in designated outdoor areas, and in restaurants it is not permitted at all, regardless of whether there is an alfresco area. Smoking is also not allowed between the flags at the beach, in cars with children under 17 years of age or near children's playgrounds.

Student Travellers

Students receive discounts to pretty much everything to do with travel and sightseeing. STA travel (www.statravel.com.au) is the most popular agency for students looking for discount fares and tours worldwide. The International Student Identity Card (ISIC) and International Youth Travel Card (IYTC) are the biggest internationally recognised student and youth ID cards. ISIC and IYTC card holders can take advantage of offers on travel, shopping, museums, food and much more.

T ax

A general sales tax (GST) of 10 percent applies to most purchases. Visitors spending AUS$300 or more can reclaim this tax upon presentation of a receipt on departure *(see page 243)*. Departure tax is included in ticket price.

Telephones

Local calls from public phones cost 50 cents. Long-distance calls to Australian and overseas num-

ABOVE: for letters home.

bers can be made from most phones. Some public phones operate by card, available from post offices, large newsagents, etc. For up-to-date rates and information, make a toll-free call to Telstra on 1800 011 433.

Overseas calls

Exit code from Australia is 0011, followed by the country code and number.

Overseas faxes: code is 0015. Country codes are all listed at the back of the telephone directory. Some commonly used ones are: **France** (33); **Germany** (49); **Indonesia** (62); **Italy** (39); **Japan** (81); **the Netherlands** (31); **Philippines** (63); **Spain** (34); **UK** (44); **USA and Canada** (1).

Mobile phones

The best course of action is to buy a "phonecard" (actually simply a receipt with a PIN that you insert in front of the number you wish to dial), which you can use with your own mobile phone (though it can also be used in public phone boxes). There are some very inexpensive deals around: simply ask the newsagent for his or her advice.

Time Zone

All of Western Australia, including Perth, is eight hours in advance of Greenwich Mean Time. Australia's eastern states are 1½ or 2 hours ahead of Perth. Because they operate a daylight-saving system, and WA does not, the eastern states are 2½–3 hours ahead between October and March.

Tipping

Tipping is not obligatory, and isn't expected in Perth restaurants (though a "service charge" is often added to the bill). That said, if you have had an especially good service and wish to tip, you will certainly not offend. Likewise, it is not necessary to tip taxi drivers, though it is customary to round up the fare to the nearest dollar or two.

Toilets

Department stores, Wellington Street train station, museums and other public buildings and places all have toilet facilities. In addition, automatic toilet booths are located at the west end of James Street, in Northbridge, and in the Cultural Centre. You will also find toilets in the changing rooms of the larger beaches.

Tourist Information

The WA Tourist Centre, Albert Facey House, Forrest Place (tel: 1300 361 351; www.westernaustralia. com) should be the first port of call for all tourism, accommodation and travel enquiries. It carries a wide range of information and offers currency-exchange services. Opening hours: Mon–Thur 8.30am–6pm; Fri 8.30am–7pm; Sat 9.30am–4.30pm; Sun noon–4.30pm.

Ⓥ isas and Passports

Passports are required by all nationalities. Visas are also necessary for all but New Zealanders.

Quarantine

All animals, including seeing-eye (guide) dogs, entering the country are subject to a minimum 30 days' quarantine. However, regular travellers with such dogs can make prior certification arrangements in their home countries.

Vaccinations

If you are arriving from areas affected by yellow fever or outbreaks of other infectious diseases it is advisable to have documentary proof of vaccination.

Ⓦ ebsites

www.westernaustralia.com Western Australian Tourism Commission. www.transperth.wa.gov.au Transperth transport information. http://perth.citysearch.com.au Entertainment guide. www.sensis.com.au Phone numbers, residential and business, plus addresses, websites, opening hours, etc. www.glcs.org.au Gay and Lesbian Community Services.

WEIGHTS AND MEASURES

Australia uses the metric system. Women's clothes are labelled in the UK way – sizes 8, 10, 12, etc, or simply as small, medium, large, etc. Shoes may be in UK or European sizes. In pubs some old-fashioned beer measures cling on: a pony is a very small glass; schooner is a bit bigger; midi is biggest, about half a pint. "Small" and "large" glasses (roughly half-pint and pint) are used in some establishments.

Easy-to-remember conversions:
1 metre is 3.28 feet
5 miles are 8 kilometres
1 kilogram is 2.2 pounds
1 litre is 2.1 pints (US)
1 litre is 1.8 pints (UK)
0°C is 32°F

Further Reading

General

Down Under, by Bill Bryson. If this is your first visit to Australia, this book provides some interesting insights and typically dry observations, though the section on Perth and Western Australia is relatively slight.

Cloud Street, by Tim Winton. Funny, roistering account of two rural families who flee to Perth and share Cloudstreet; it provides great insight into Perth life through to the 1970s.

Land's Edge, by Tim Winton. In this autobiography, Winton recounts his memories of growing up in Western Australia and the impact the beach had on his life.

The West Australian Good Food Guide 2011, by The West Australian. This is a definitive guide for restaurant and café goers in WA. Edited by The West's award winning restaurant critic and columnist Rob Broadfield.

Perth and Fremantle; Past and Present, by Simon J Nevill. A beautifully presented record of the lives of West Australians. A photographic journey, incorporating a brief history behind many of the photographs. Also includes a short history of the Nyoongar people and early settlement.

Perth, Fremantle and Rottnest, by Simon J Nevill. A photographic souvenir of Perth, Fremantle and Rottnest, covering the history, buildings, people, cultural activities, beaches, river and bush that make this area of the country unique.

Western Australia, by Steve Parish. The highlight of this book is the superb photography of Western Australia in all its wonderful diversity.

Perth's Best Bush, Coast and City Walks, by Paul Amyes. Introduces the best walks for visitors and residents alike, ranging from leisurely beach-side strolls to the more rugged tracks deep in the bush.

My Place, by Sally Morgan. An autobiography by artist Sally Morgan in 1987 about her quest for knowledge of her family's past and the fact that she has grown up under false pretences. The book is a milestone in Aboriginal literature.

History

The Fatal Shore, by Robert Hughes. Epic that follows and records the fate of 160,000 men, women and children transported to Australia.

A Short History of Australia, by Manning Clark. Considered the definitive work.

Land of Vision and Mirage – Western Australia Since 1826, by Geoffrey Bolton. A long-awaited short history of Western Australia from 1826 to the present. Vibrantly narrates the social, cultural, political and economic development of the most geographically isolated area in the world.

Spinifex and Sand, by David W. Carnegie. A narrative of five years' pioneering and exploration in Western Australia

Batavia's Graveyard, by Mike Dash. Tells the story of what is surely the strangest and bloodiest mutiny known to history.

A Fortunate Life, by A.B. Facey. A true classic of Australian literature, Facey's simple and beautifully written autobiography is an inspiration to the reader. It is the story of a life lived to the full – the extraordinary journey of an ordinary man.

Australian Language

G'Day! Teach Yourself Australian, by Colin Bowles. Light-hearted approach to everyday, and obscure, vernacular Australian; featuring a highly unlikely Oz family.

Macquarie Australian Slang Dictionary. Provides an opportunity to focus on the colloquial aspects of Australian English, encompassing everything from the mildly informal to the downright obscene.

Other Insight Guides

Insight Guides

Insight Guide: Australia is a top-selling title in the series, with superb photography and in-depth background reading on the history and culture of the Land Down Under. In addition, Insight's regional series includes Insight Guide: Queensland & Great Barrier Reef and Insight Guide: Tasmania to show you the larger picture of Australia's great states. Insight City Guide: Perth and Insight City Guide: Melbourne are both written by locally based writers, who show you how to make the most of these world-class cities.

Insight Smart Guides

Insight Smart Guides pack a huge amount of information into an easy-to-access A–Z format, with stylish photography and an atlas section.

PERTH STREET ATLAS

The key map shows the area of Perth covered by the atlas
section. An index of street names and places of interest
shown on the maps can be found on the following pages.
For each entry there is a page number and grid reference

Map Legend

Freeway with Junction	✈✈ Airport	Freeway	🚌 Bus Station
Freeway (under construction)	✝ ✝ Church (ruins)	Dual Carriageway	❶ Tourist Information
Dual Carriageway	✝ Monastery	Main Roads	✉ Post Office
Main Road	🏰 🏚 Castle (ruins)		✝ Cathedral/Church
Secondary Road	∴ Archeological Site	Minor Roads	☾ Mosque
Minor Road	∩ Cave		✡ Synagogue
Track	★ Place of Interest	Footpath	⸸ Statue/Monument
International Boundary	🏠 Mansion/Stately Home	Railway	⌷ Tower
State Boundary	※ Viewpoint	Pedestrian Area	🗼 Lighthouse
National Park/Reserve	⚐ Beach	Important Building	
Ferry Route		Park	

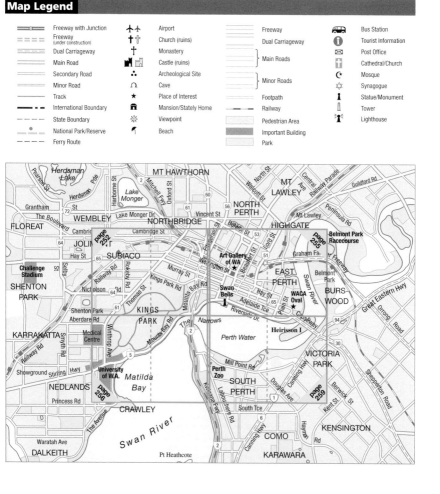

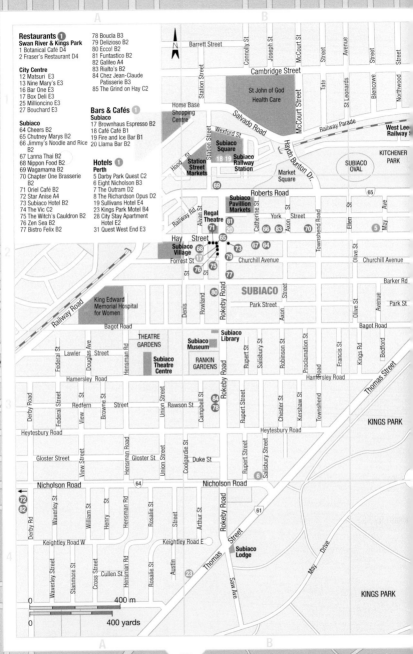

Restaurants ①
Swan River & Kings Park
1 Botanical Café D4
2 Fraser's Restaurant D4

City Centre
12 Matsuri E3
13 Nine Mary's E3
16 Bar One E3
17 Box Deli E3
25 Millioncino E3
27 Bouchard E3

Subiaco
64 Cheers B2
65 Chutney Marys B2
66 Jimmy's Noodle and Rice B2
67 Lanna Thai B2
68 Nippon Food B2
69 Wagamama B2
70 Chapter One Brasserie B2
71 Oriel Café B2
72 Star Anise A4
73 Subiaco Hotel B2
74 The Vic C2
75 The Witch's Cauldron B2
76 Zen Sea B2
77 Bistro Felix B2
78 Boucla B3
79 Delizioso B2
80 Ecco! B2
81 Funtastico B2
82 Galileo A4
83 Rialto's B2
84 Chez Jean-Claude Patisserie B3
85 The Grind on Hay C2

Bars & Cafés ①
Subiaco
17 Brownhaus Espresso B2
18 Café Café B1
19 Fire and Ice Bar B1
20 Llama Bar B2

Hotels ①
Perth
5 Darby Park Quest C2
6 Eight Nicholson B3
7 The Outram D2
8 The Richardson Opus D2
19 Sullivans Hotel E4
23 Kings Park Motel B4
28 City Stay Apartment Hotel E2
31 Quest West End E3

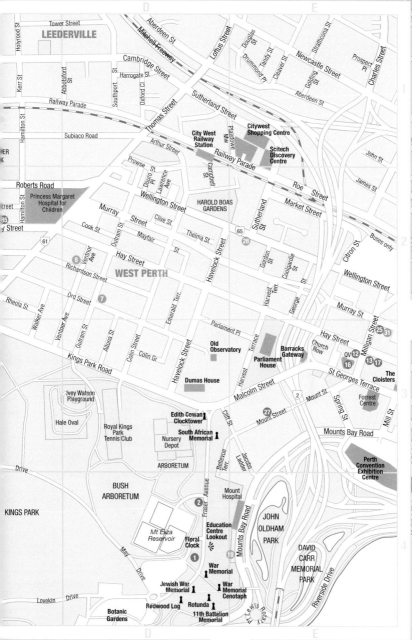

LEEDERVILLE

Tower Street
Holyrood St
Aberdeen St
Loftus Street
Douglas St
Tandy St
Strathcona St
Newcastle Street
Prospect Pl
Charles Street

Mitchell Freeway
Cambridge Street
Kerr St
Abbotsford St
Harrogate St
Drummond Pl
Cleaver St
Godrich St
Aberdeen St

Railway Parade
Hamilton St
Southport St
Oxford Cl
Thomas Street
Sutherland Street

Subiaco Road
Plaistowe Mw
City West Railway Station
Citywest Shopping Centre
John St
James St

Arthur Street
Railway Parade
Roe Street
Scitech Discovery Centre

Roberts Road
Prowse St
Dignam Pl
Lawrence Ave
Campbell St
Market Street
Buses only

Princess Margaret Hospital for Children
Wellington Street
HAROLD BOAS GARDENS
Sutherland St
Citron St

Murray Street
Clive St
Thelma St
65
28
Gordon St
Coghlan St
Wellington Street

Cook St
Outram St
Mayfair St
Harvest Terr.
George St
Murray St

8
Hay Street
WEST PERTH
25
31

Richardson Street
Ventnor Ave
Emerald Terr.
Milligan Street

Rheola St
Ord Street
7
Hay Street
QV
12

Walker Ave
Ventnor Ave
Outram St
Altona St
Parliament Pl
Church Row
16
13
17

Kings Park Road
Colin St
Colin Gr
Havelock Street
Old Observatory
Terrace
Parliament House
Barracks Gateway
St Georges Terrace
The Cloisters

Ivey Watson Playground
Dumas House
Malcolm Street
2
Mount St
Spring St
Forrest Centre

Hale Oval
Royal Kings Park Tennis Club
Edith Cowan Clocktower
27
Mount Street
Cliff St
Jacobs Ladder
Mill St

Drive
Nursery Depot
South African Memorial
ARBORETUM
Bellevue Terr.
Mounts Bay Road
Perth Convention Exhibition Centre

BUSH ARBORETUM
Fraser Avenue
Mount Hospital
JOHN OLDHAM PARK

KINGS PARK
Mt Eliza Reservoir
2
Education Centre Lookout
19
Mounts Bay Road

May Drive
Floral Clock
1
DAVID CARR MEMORIAL PARK

Lovekin Drive
Jewish War Memorial
War Memorial
War Memorial Cenotaph
Pt Lewis Road
Riverside Drive

Botanic Gardens
Redwood Log
Rotunda
11th Battalion Memorial

254

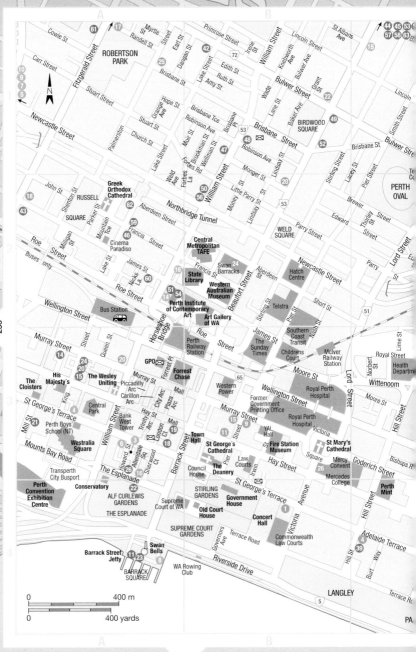

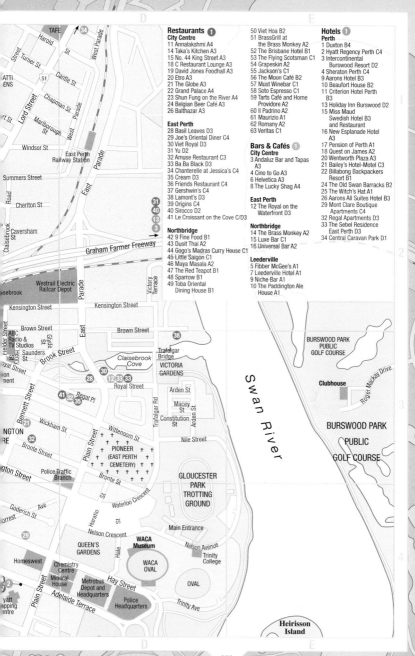

Restaurants ❶
City Centre
11 Annalakshmi A4
14 Taka's Kitchen A3
15 No. 44 King Street A3
18 C Restaurant Lounge A3
19 David Jones Foodhall A3
20 Etro A3
21 The Globe A3
22 Grand Palace A4
23 Shun Fung on the River A4
24 Belgian Beer Café A3
26 Balthazar A3

East Perth
28 Basil Leaves D3
29 Joe's Oriental Diner C4
30 Viet Royal D3
31 Yu D2
32 Amuse Restaurant C3
33 Ba Ba Black D3
34 Chanterelle at Jessica's C4
35 Cream D3
36 Friends Restaurant C4
37 Gerstwin's C4
38 Lamont's D3
39 Origins C4
40 Sirocco D2
41 Le Croissant on the Cove C/D3

Northbridge
42 9 Fine Food B1
43 Dusit Thai A2
44 Gogo's Madras Curry House C1
45 Little Saigon C1
46 Maya Masala A2
47 The Red Teapot B1
48 Sparrow B1
49 Toba Oriental
   Dining House B1

50 Viet Hoa B2
51 BrassGrill at
   the Brass Monkey A2
52 The Brisbane Hotel B1
53 The Flying Scotsman C1
54 Grapeskin A2
55 Jackson's C1
56 The Moon Café B2
57 Must Winebar C1
58 Soto Espresso C1
59 Tarts Café and Home
   Providore A2
60 Il Padrino A2
61 Maurizio A1
62 Romany A2
63 Veritas C1

Bars & Cafés ❶
City Centre
3 Andaluz Bar and Tapas
   A3
4 Cino to Go A3
6 Helvetica A3
8 The Lucky Shag A4

East Perth
12 The Royal on the
   Waterfront D3

Northbridge
14 The Brass Monkey A2
15 Luxe Bar C1
16 Universal Bar A2

Leederville
5 Fibber McGee's A1
7 Leederville Hotel A1
9 Niche Bar A1
10 The Paddington Ale
   House A1

Hotels ❶
Perth
1 Duxton B4
2 Hyatt Regency Perth C4
3 Intercontinental
   Burswood Resort D2
4 Sheraton Perth C4
9 Aarons Hotel B3
10 Beaufort House B2
11 Criterion Hotel Perth
   B3
13 Holiday Inn Burswood D2
15 Miss Maud
   Swedish Hotel B3
   and Restaurant
16 New Esplanade Hotel
   A3
17 Pension of Perth A1
18 Quest on James A2
20 Wentworth Plaza A3
21 Bailey's Hotel-Motel C3
22 Billabong Backpackers
   Resort B1
24 The Old Swan Barracks B2
25 The Witch's Hat A1
26 Aarons All Suites Hotel B3
29 Mont Clare Boutique
   Apartments C4
32 Regal Apartments D3
33 The Sebel Residence
   East Perth D3
34 Central Caravan Park D1

252

A | B

Tennis Courts

Derby Road

ROSALIE PARK

Thomas Street

May Drive

Tobruk Memorial

POW Memorial

Lovekin Drive

Aberdare Road

Bovell Kiosk

Broadwalk Vista

Broadwalk

Vietnam Memorial

Western Power Parkland

Queen Elizabeth II Medical Centre

Hospital Avenue

Winthrop Avenue

May Drive

Lovekin Drive

2nd/2nd Australian Commando Memorial

Sir Charles Gardiner Hospital

2nd/28th Battalion Memorial

Arras St

61

Forrest Drive

Monash Avenue

Park Avenue

Kings Park Ave

Hardy Road

Poole Avenue

Park Avenue

Wingfield Ave

Mounts Bay Road

Tareena Street

Kanimbla Road

Megalong Street

Crawley Lodge

Park Avenue

Crawley Drive

Park Road

Winthrop Avenue

University of Western Australia

St George's College

5

University of Western Australia

Mounts Bay Road

Whitfield Court

Hackett Hall

Cygnet Hall

Perth Dinghy Sailing Club

University Boat Club

Winthrop Hall

Hackett Drive

University of

Matilda Bay

Fairway

Reid Library

Western Australia

Broadway

Fairway

Myers St

Hackett

Drive

Jetties

Cook St

0 _____ 400 m

0 _____ 400 yards

11 3

4

A | B

258

DNA Observation Tower

Forrest Drive

Pioneer Women's Memorial

Lotterywest Federation Walkway (Tree-Top Walk)

Botanic Gardens

Bessie Rischbeith Memorial

Duyfken

WATER GARDENS

Old Swan Brewery

Point Lewis

The Narrows

Narrows Bridge

Point Belches

Mill Point

Mill Point Cl

Mill Point Road

South Perth Esplanade

Water Ski Area (Commercial)

Jetty

Melville Pl

Queen St.

Water Ski Area

Roe Memorial

Drummond Memorial

Drive

Mounts Bay Road

5

Stirling St.

Melville Parade

Kwinana Freeway

Scott St.

Stone Street

Frasers Lane

30

Ferry St.

Harper Terr

Mill Point Road

Mends St.

Mill Point Road

Judd Street

Bowman Street

WINDSOR PARK

Labouchere Road

Lyall Street

Melville Parade

Hardy Street

Charles Street

Richardson Street

RICHARDSON PARK

Amherst St.

ROYAL PERTH GOLF CLUB

2

Swan River

Melville Water

Point

Restaurants ❶
Swan River and Kings Park
3 Jo Jo's A4
4 Matilda Bay B4
5 Zafferano D1

Bars & Cafés ❶
Swan River and Kings Park
1 Old Swan Brewery D1
11 Steve's Nedlands Park Hotel A4

Hotels ❶
Perth
30 The Peninsula Riverside
Serviced Apartments E2

N

Restaurants ❶
Swan River and Kings Park
6 Ciao Italia C3
7 The Boatshed B3
8 Coco's A2
9 Mends Street Café A2
10 Incontro A2

Bars & Cafés ❶
Swan River and Kings Park
2 The Windsor A2
13 Broaken Hill Hotel Bar E2

Hotels ❶
Perth
12 Durham Lodge E3
14 Metro Hotel D3
27 Broadwater Resort Apartments A1

Swan River

Perth Water

257

Jetty

South Perth Esplanade
Mends Street
South Shore Piazza
Ray St
The Windsor
WINDSOR PARK
Mill Point Road
Gladey Estate
Parker St

SIR JAMES
MITCHELL PARK

CLYDESDALE PARK

Witcomb Place
Jubilee St
Thomas St
Pepper St

ZOOLOGICAL
GARDENS

Hopetoun St
King Edward Street
Hopetoun
Onslow Street
Clarence St
Forrest Street
Garden St
Street
Rose Ave
Swan Street
Olive Street
Coode Street
Mill Point Road
Leane St
Douglas Avenue
Lawler Street

Alexandra St
Edinburgh St
Swan Street
Wesley College
Swan St
Tate Street
Anthony St

York Street
Victoria Street

Amherst St
Angelo Street
Rose Ave
Albert Street
Angelo St

Riverview Street
Edward St
King Street
Angelo Street
⊠
Angelo Stre

Laboucheré Road
Onslow Street
Karoo Street
Ridge Street
Hill St
Strickland Street
Ansley Street
Coode Street
Waverley Street
Norfolk Street
Wattle Street
Sandgate Street
Hampden
High St

ROYAL PERTH
GOLF CLUB

0   400 m
0   400 yards

HENSMAN PARK
Hensman Street
Forrest Street
Carr Street
Hensman Street
Milson
Elizabeth
Addison St

27

PARKLAND
Lake Vasto

Riverside Drive

Point Fraser Wetlands Reserve

Causeway

Water Ski Area (WAWSA Members)

CHARLES PATERSON PARK

Heirisson Island

Causeway

Yagan

Water Ski Area (WAWSA Members)

McCALLUM PARK

Tennis Courts

Albany Hwy

Armagh Street
Hordern Street
Street

Oswald

Street

Colombo

Washington

Geddes Street

Cargill St

Taylor St
Gartland St

Fisheries Depot and Swan River Managment Authority

SIR JAMES MITCHELL PARK

Ellam Street

McCallum Lane

Canning Highway

RAPHAEL PARK

Street

Hurlingham Road
Manning
Terr.
Brookside Ave
Swanview Terrace

Lamb St

Scenic Crescent

Henbingstone

Mill Point Rd

Armagh Street

Gloucester St

Colombo St

Berwick Street

Geddes Street

Gloucester St

Mackie Street

McMaster Street

Daglet Crescent

Banelagh Crescent

Delamere Avenue

Way Road

Westbury Rd

Lansdowne

Gwenyfred

Avenue

Road

Cargill Street

Street

HAWTHORNE PARK

Meadowvale Ave

wvale pping entre

Mill Point Road

Hovia Terrace

6

First Avenue

Second

Mackie

Courthope St

St

King George

Berwick

Rosebery
Street
Brandon

Banksia Terrace

14

7

Hovia Terrace

Third Avenue

Fourth Avenue

Fifth Ave

Eighth Ave

Susan St

George Street

Gladstone Avenue

Dyson

Darling Street

Salisbury Avenue

Street

Vista Street

Brandon

Banksia Terrace

Street

Sixth Avenue

Seventh Avenue

Kennard Street

Gwenyfred Road

Jameson

Avenue

Shaftesbury St

Broome

Canning Highway

Pennington St

Collins

King St

Vista Street

Market St

View Street

Bright Street

Anketell St

Pitt St.

Ambon

Lansdowne Road

Lawler Street

Douglas Avenue

King St

Market St

Street

MORRIS MUNDY RESERVOIR

Dyson

Oxford Street

George Street

Anketell St

Kennard Street

Arundel St

Carey St

Street

STREET INDEX

ART AND PHOTO CREDITS

Map Production: Stephen Ramsay and APA Cartography department

©2011 Apa Publications GmbH & Co. Verlag KG, Singapore Branch

Production: Tynan Dean, Linton Donaldson, Rebeka Ellam

GENERAL INDEX

Restaurants

BARS, BREWERIES, DISTILLERIES AND CAFÉS

INSIGHT GUIDE

PERTH
& SURROUNDINGS

Project Editor
Astrid deRidder
Art Director
Steven Lawrence
Picture Manager
Tom Smyth
Series Manager
Rachel Fox
Series Editor
Rachel Lawrence

Distribution

UK & Ireland
GeoCenter International Ltd
Meridian House, Churchill Way West
Basingstoke, Hampshire RG21 6YR
sales@geocenter.co.uk

United States
Ingram Publisher Services
1 Ingram Boulevard, PO Box 3006,
La Vergne, TN 37086-1986
customer.service@ingrampublisher
services.com

Australia
Universal Publishers
PO Box 307
St. Leonards NSW 1590
sales@universalpublishers.com.au

Worldwide
Apa Publications GmbH & Co.
Verlag KG (Singapore branch)
7030 Ang Mo Kio Ave 5
08-65 Northstar @ AMK
Singapore 569880
apasin@singnet.com.sg

Printing
CTPS-China

©2011 Apa Publications GmbH & Co.
Verlag KG (Singapore branch)
All Rights Reserved

First Edition 2006
Second Edition 2011

www.insightguides.com

ABOUT THIS BOOK

What makes an Insight Guide different? Since our first book pioneered the use of creative full-colour photography in travel guides in 1970, we have aimed to provide not only reliable information but also the key to a real understanding of a destination and its people.

Now, when the world wide web can supply inexhaustible (but not always reliable) facts and figures, our books marry text and pictures to provide that more elusive quality: knowledge. To achieve this, they rely on the authority of locally based writers and photographers.

This new edition of *City Guide Perth* is carefully structured to convey an understanding of Perth and its citizens as well as to guide readers through its many attractions, from Kings Park and the Swan River to Rottnest Island and the beaches of Western Australia. The book was commissioned by **Rachel Lawrence**, and edited by **Astrid deRidder**. This new edition of the guide was com-prehensively updated by Perth local **Hermione Stott**, who has been a jour-nalist and editor in Perth since 2003 and has written for many Western Australian publications. These include News Limited's *The Sunday Times* as a news reporter and feature writer, as well as community news-papers throughout the metropoli-tan region.

Earlier editions of the guide were the work of managing editor **Dorothy Stannard**. Assisting her in this task was lifestyle writer **Vic Waters**, a British-born journalist who has lived and worked in Perth for some 20 years.

Former contributors include **Jes-sica Dawe, Emma Green, Bron Sibree, Sian Briggs, Laura Richardson** and **Christine Waters**. Most of the striking images that bring the city of Perth to life were taken by **Glyn Genin**, a long-standing Insight photographer and regular visitor to Western Australia. The captions were written by Insight's **Catherine Dreghorn**. Finally, the book was proofread by **Janet McCann** and indexed by **Helen Peters**.

SEND US YOUR THOUGHTS

We do our best to ensure the information in our books is as accurate and up-to-date as possible. The books are updated on a regular basis using local contacts, who painstakingly add, amend, and correct as required. However, some details (such as telephone numbers and opening times) are liable to change, and we are ultimately reliant on our readers to put us in the picture.

We welcome your feedback, especially your experience of using the book "on the road". Maybe we recommended a hotel that you liked (or another that you didn't), or you came across a great bar or new attraction that we missed.

We will acknowledge all contributions, and we'll offer an Insight Guide to the best letters received.

Please write to us at:
Insight Guides
PO Box 7910, London SE1 1WE
Or email us at:
insight@apaguide.co.uk

Houtman Abrolhos Islands